The Thing Is

SELECTED WRITINGS
BY
Patsy Garlan

FICTION, MEMOIR, PERSONAL ESSAYS,
MISCELLANEOUS SCRIBBLES, POEMS,
VERSES, LIMERICKS, AND THE LIKE

DRAWINGS BY CHRISTIAN McCARTHY JOHANSEN

SAN RAFAEL, CALIFORNIA

SUMMERLAND
PUBLISHING

ISBN: 978-0-9963736-1-6

Printed in the United States of America

Library of Congress Control Number: 2015915160

Cover art by Michael Morshuk
Cover design by Judy Garlan White
Drawings by Christian McCarthy Johansen

Dedication

To my four offspring, with deepest love and respect,
without whom this book would never have been written,
just for being and being who they are.

OXFORD, ENGLAND

David Garlan, Ph.D.
Professor, Computer Science
Carnegie Mellon University

Judy Garlan White
Artist, Art Director, and
Graphic Designer

Robert Wallace Garlan, Ph.D.
Clinical Psychologist

Sarah Garlan Johansen, M.D.
Emergency Medicine and Faculty,
Dartmouth-Hitchcock
Medical Center

SANTA BARBARA, CALIFORNIA

Acknowledgements

Putting this book together has been fun mostly, but no picnic, especially for Dana Cook Grossman, who did both editing and design. I am deeply grateful for her working with my havering and pickiness — on the whole cheerfully — and especially for her rare sensitivity to the nuances of both writings and writer.

My grandson Christian, though up to his ears in his college courses and travels and acting gigs and sports and mountain climbing, somehow found time to do the charming drawings that adorn *The Thing Is*. It is a special pleasure for me to have family a part of this book, and that includes my daughter Judy Garlan White, an award-winning art director, who designed the cover.

The cover art is the work of Michael Morshuk, who created it as the illustration for my story "Doggone," which originally appeared in *The Atlantic Monthly* in December 1997. Michael is best known for his dog portraits, and I thank him for this tiny representative of the canine kingdom revealed here.

For the actual launch in finished form of *The Thing Is,* I am deeply grateful to my always-supportive and infinitely patient publisher, Anya Petersen-Frey of Summerland Publications.

So many family members and friends and lovers and colleagues have provided inspiration for these writings along the way — with or without their knowledge — how can I name them all? It would require another book. I must, however, mention Annika Van Wambeke Black, who came into my life to help with filing and now continues to clear away my clutter as a treasured friend.

And then, there is, and has been for close to 30 years, my dear friend and loving partner, Nancy Gillis, who, like food and drink and other necessities of a good life, has sustained me and laughed with me and prodded me to keep a healthy perspective on a life full of challenges and delights.

To you, my readers, whether many or few, you are out there in the future and you, too, have drawn me forward. My philosophy has always been that any contribution a person can make, however small, is worthwhile. And here's mine.

‡ ‡ ‡

An Invitation

TO MY GRANDCHILDREN
AND MY CHILDREN, NIECES,
AND SYMPATICO FRIENDS,
AS WELL AS THOSE
WHO COME AFTER, UNTO THE
SIXTH DEGREE OF SEPARATION

These stories are gathered here especially for you. And whether they are personal essays or fiction or verses or whatever, they are all, in their way, stories.

What do I mean by that? It's all stories, isn't it? I mean, even history books are stories, because they are selective accounts of what happened and what it all means, and that's why we are wise to speak of "*a* history of" and not "*the* history of." And like a history book, this book is written by a person who is trying to convey what seems to be the truth of it: the Thing.

This book is titled *The Thing Is* because each story has something to impart, discovered during the process of writing it. And also, gathered here for you in this particular way, the stories take on a broader meaning. As you will see. I hope.

So it's not a party you are being invited to. But I hope you won't find it dull. So, well, what's it about, I hear you cry. Sex? Not so much. Love? Oh, yes. And birth and death and heartache and joy and the mysteries and surprises lavished on us by nature, and the universe on high and all the vast ethereal sky. And a lot in between. Of course, it is the merest twinkle of these things, so vast are they all, really.

:: :: ::

The Thing Is has several parts, and each part has a different "Thing." However, all the stories in a particular part have, I think, the same Thing. For instance, Part I is titled "When Worlds Collide: Connections and Ambiguities." The stories in Part I are about persons struggling to reconcile disturbing ambiguities in their experience of another person or circumstance or thing. The *struggle* allows them to *transcend* the clash and arrive at what the Thing really is — a connection, an aha moment — including the recognition that ambiguities within oneself are a part of being and growing as a person.

Puzzle: When is a thing not a thing? *When it is a symbol or metaphor*. Literally, a "thing" is an object; it has mass. But sometimes it has far greater weight when we mean a particular thing to stand for something else. For example, an hourglass is a thing. But it also is often thought of as a metaphor, standing for *time — and the passage of time*.

:: :: ::

And speaking of the passage of time, I've lived almost 90 years so far. This book is my attempt to give you a tiny piece of your family's history, as well as glimpses of living in the world as your grandmother experienced it over the years. I hope it will resonate with you. Perhaps one or another of you will be emboldened to tell it as you see it? I hope for that, too. Writing is such fun. So is reading. Enjoy, and think of me.

Your Grandmother, Gratsy,
Gramma, Friend
Patsy

RSVP

A Rough Chronology

Some people may want to know when a particular piece — a story, a poem, an essay, or whatever — was written. I'm a little vague about some of that, but here's a rough chronology of my literary career for those intrigued about a writer's circumstances and changes over time.

:: :: ::

The writings in each of the six parts of *The Thing Is* are united by that part's central theme. But within a part, the time frames may be wildly divergent and quite a jumble, ranging over seven decades — from the 1950s through the 1990s and on to the 20-teens. It's all somewhat arbitrary, anyway. One piece or another might fit as well under that theme as this one, and my dates are also a bit fuzzy.

The thing is, I've done it this way because with the thematic juxtaposition of the stories and poems, they help each other "pop," as we say. Their meanings shift and shine in each other's light. (I've used italics for the titles of the poems in this volume, to distinguish them from the prose pieces, because poetry seems to sound a different note, more like music.)

Still, it might be helpful to have a notion of the kind of things I was writing in each decade, and, to me at least, it is interesting to note that these themes did seem to endure in their various forms through those decades.

Actually, my poetry varied quite a bit in form and subject as my interests, readings, and life experiences changed, and it became less dominant in my writing as my prose undertakings grew. Early on, stung by the offhand remark of a guy I met, who taught college literature courses, to the effect that women's only poetic subject is love, I was inspired to demonstrate that he was an arrogant, ignorant asshole.

My interests and therefore my poetic frames of reference included, over the decades, religious mythology laced with Jungian psychology, with a dab of Zen Buddhism, Platonic philosophy, metaphysical and spiritual reflection, social commentary, war, children, the ups and downs of everyday life, nature's metaphors, and . . . well, yes, and love. My poems are short. Formal verse. Free verse. Satire. Limericks. There's a sampling of them all here. My first poem after the literature teacher's nasty sting was about the birth of a child. It is a poem only a woman can write. It is called "Delivery."

The Fifties. During the 1950s, which were the heart and soul of my marriage years, I was writing mostly poetry, the occasional prose piece, and extensive letters home to Mamba (my mother) during our family's year in England (in 1954). Much of this decade was focused on the fascinating, mind-blowing, all-absorbing wonderment of living with children, of which there came to be four. During the at-home years, entangled in our life of the mind at Reed College, I wrote, too, about the counter-balancing glories and mysteries of the natural world, so beautiful in Oregon, in the '50s.

The Sixties. On June 1, 1961, the whole family took off for Japan, the first stop in our extraordinary 10-month sojourn abroad, on a Fulbright grant. We had short stays in Kyoto, Hong Kong, and Rangoon before settling down in Mandalay — the basic purpose of our going. We lived in Mandalay for nine months, from mid-June 1961 to mid-March 1962, topping it off with a two-week sojourn in India and almost four months in Greece, Spain, and Rome. The whole experience, copious and vast, provided food for the writer's mind, as can be imagined.

Sadly, it all fell apart in the 1960s; the family, and my writings during this period and on to the present day, are shadowed by and sometimes engulfed by that personal catastrophe. Nevertheless, it was a time of growth and change and renewal in exciting ways (as it was for the nation and California in particular). These were the Maryjane years. I met her in Burma, and back in California we became partners and writing collaborators. I wrote love poems like mad. Together, we wrote children's books set in Burma and two college readers, projections into possible futures now unfolding before our eyes. Everyone was crazy about the future. Miraculous advances in technology made anything and everything seem possible, and we wanted to help everyone take a hand in guiding our precious Spaceship Earth's choices.

Through most of this decade, I worked for a repertory theater in Marin County, administering a federal grant to bring live theater into the schools. I found this highly stimulating. It also offered an opportunity to edit and write critical articles for the Festival Theatre Study Syllabus, an 11-part series, and progress reports to the grantparent, the federal government.

At the same time, and into the '70s, I was working for psychology researcher Paul Ekman, helping him develop his writing skills and write his professional papers and eventually his groundbreaking books. In his lab, for the study of human interaction and conflict at the Langley-Porter Institute at UC-San Francisco, he wrote about how our face reveals our emotions, our lies, and our truths. And he, most generously, credited me with teaching him how to write.

The Seventies. Early in the 1970s, I went to work for public broadcasting station KQED in San Francisco. It was a full menu. I wrote lots of grant proposals to foundations and government agencies, raising millions for KQED and, as a side dish, other struggling nonprofits. This went on for 21 years or so, till my "retirement" in 1996. Did that take the place of my own writing? Heck, no. Just slowed it down a bit. In these years it was mostly poetry and, with Maryjane, the completion of the second book about the future.

These became the Julie years, with the creation of Dovey's Old Place, our cottage at Anchor Bay, and then the Devie years, filled with friends, parties, the ballet, the theater, tennis, and lots of travel — Mexico, England, France. Most important of all were the times when one or another of my four children lived with us and — later, during their college years and the beginning of their marriage years — when there were holiday and summertime visits. And on into the '80s . . .

The Eighties. For the first time in my life, I was living on my own. The aloneness was not for long as terrifying as I had expected, largely because I was so busy. Still working for KQED, I launched myself into the creating of a musical. Based on Bernard Shaw's *Saint Joan,* with the approval of the Society of Authors in London, and in collaboration with New York composer Nick Scarim, I wrote the book and lyrics for *Wings of Fire*. Funding support, a brave director, and stunning stage settings brought it to audiences in Marin County, where it created a bit of a stir. But all these years later, it still awaits realization by a producer in a larger venue. In this decade, Nancy came into my life. It was and is such a good thing.

The Nineties. A two-week artists' and writers' workshop in Assisi, Italy, was an invigorating renewal. We were expected to write a short piece overnight and read it to our writers' group next day. I think it was here that I began to embrace the short story, personal essay, and memoir genres. I'd had it with poetry. I must admit that I could never drop it completely, and occasionally the urge overcomes me. My personal essay "Doggone" appeared in *The Atlantic*. Later on, so did a second piece. Both were republished in five collections of readings intended to provide models for students in composition classes. "A Link to the Living" and a second essay, "Rounded With a Sleep," were also published in a medical journal. This was fun.

Meanwhile, at age 70, I retired from KQED. I settled down with Nancy, though each in our own abode. We traveled in Europe, vacationed at Anchor Bay, cultivated our gardens, fretted over the state of the world, played golf and tennis, and attended live theater, dance, and musical performances and constant movies. She worked and I wrote.

The Twenty-First Century. Though I found that I was really happy in the genres of the personal essay, and the always-popping-up poetry, I was itching to write true fiction. So I began with a novella, *The Sixth Charm*, which wasn't really fiction; the plot line was, but the characters were based on people I knew. So I took a deep breath and tackled a genuine novel, which became *Sea Change: The Uncertain Realm of the Married*. I loved writing dialogue, as it turned out. The novel has gone on to see the light of day, published in 2012; the novella has not, which is probably just as well.

So here we are. And the thing is . . .

‡ ‡ ‡

Table of Contents

Dedication i

Acknowledgements...ii

An Invitation iv

A Rough Chronology...viii

PART I: When Worlds Collide: Connections and Ambiguities 1

Horrors: The Ominous Audit..2
Meeting the Mishpocha 12
As the Twig Is Bent 17
Computers: This Is the Dawning of 34
Lament for Violin...40
Naptime at the Hotel Giotto 42

PART II: Embracing Life — Anyway 45

A Tale of Two Lives 46
A Link to the Living 52
All Things Bright 56
Dovey's Old Place 58
A New Day 60
Riggs 63
Through Thick and Thin 64
An Open Letter to Mary Oliver 70

PART III: Love and Loss 73

Doggone 74
Old Friends 77
Scattered Filings 82
Rounded with a Sleep 84
When I Was Small 94
A Song of Us 96
Prayer 97
The Wind Stirs 98
Eros and Agape 99
Yes 100
Love Woes 101
To the Sun 102
Moth and Flame 103
The Logic of the Web 104
When You Speak 105
My Friend 106

PART IV: Being and Belonging: Out of Joint? 109

Hail to Thee, Once Blithe Spirit 110
Heavens to Betsy 117
Midnight Reflections 119

A Paradoxical Conversation 121
Winning 125
Chronicle 126
Door to Door 127
The New God 129
Punditry 130
The Great Society 132
And God Said 133
Fireworks 134
Through a Glass, Darkly 135

PART V: Nature: Food for Thought 155

Bamboo 156
Barrier 157
Bee Worlds: Introduction 158
Bee Worlds: I and II 159
Changing Seasons 161
Destiny 162
Mystery: I, Sea and Rocks 163
Mystery: II and III 164
Mystery: IV 165
Ninth Month 166
Projection 168
Resurrection 169
Rock Paintings 171
Salmon River Wilderness 172
Teatime with Children 173

PART VI: Comings and Goings 175

Sermon Off the Mount 176
Of Saints 178
Absurd 180
Family Tree: I 182

Family Tree: II 183
Delivery 184
Child of the Future 186
Coming Alive 187
Mamba 188
The All 190

APPENDIX: The Thing Was: Living With the World 193

About the Appendix 194
FOUR AMERICANS INVADE EUROPE
A Memoir (England) 196
Letters to My Mother, a.k.a. Mamba (Italy and France) 210
The Memoir Resumes: The Unforgiving Minute
(England Again) 235
(France and Italy Again) 236
(Another Season of Returnings, Lovings, Leavings) 242
SIX AMERICANS AT HOME ABROAD
Mostly Burma, With Smatterings of Several Other Countries
(Letters to Mamba) 245
(Patsy's Letters and the Kids' Say-So) 298
(Independence Day: A Children's Story for Grown-Ups) 304
CAPTURING CHINA
In Eight Little Poems 309
THE GREAT GETAWAY
A Grown-Ups' Holiday at the Florida Keys 317

PART I

When Worlds Collide: Connections and Ambiguities

Horrors: The Ominous Audit 2
Meeting the Mishpocha 12
As the Twig Is Bent 17
Computers: This Is the Dawning of 34
Lament for Violin 40
Naptime at the Hotel Giotto 42

IDLE THOUGHTS

The mind that is not baffled is not employed.

—Anonymous

Horrors: The Ominous Audit

A PERSONAL ESSAY
CIRCA 2005

Ten minutes to two in the afternoon, and the fateful moment loomed. Staggering under the weight of my two unwieldy boxes of "evidence," I lurched indelicately up an endless flight of stairs to the second-floor offices of the Internal Revenue Service.

An open doorway beckoned me into a small lobby that was graced with a few chairs, lined up in a row like schoolchildren, but not a single living soul. I gratefully perched my burden on a chair and looked around as I recalled the instructions I had received over the phone from the receptionist, when I had asked the name of the auditor who would be receiving me.

"I can't tell you that," she had said, cheerily. "When you come in, just push the green button on one of the phones and someone will come and get you." *Oh. Okay,* I thought and, figuring it could be helpful to show an interest, inquired, "Then who are you?"

"My name is Elaine," she'd responded. *Oh.*

So here I was. On the wall to my right was a floor-to-ceiling bank of dense, newsprint-type documents, explaining everything you need to know about the IRS. On the wall facing the entry was a door with a sign that read sternly, "Do not knock on this door for any reason." And on the wall to my left was a bank of phones, each with various colored buttons. *Ah-ha.*

I lifted the receiver of one of the tacky-looking, much-pawed phones and punched the green button. A recorded voice said, "If you know the three-digit extension of the party you are seeking, dial it now." Well, I didn't even know the party I was seeking. Then the voice said, "To use the directory, press star and the first three letters of the party's name." *Well, but . . .*

I decided to try the first three letters of Elaine's name, to which the disembodied voice replied, "This is not a valid number." Quite at sea, I ran through the routine several times — perhaps I had misunderstood? — with the same non-result.

I had been feeling anxious about this encounter for weeks, not because I felt guilty about my tax return, but because I feared I would not remain calm enough to present my case persuasively. Sort of a vicious circle, really. I intended to say, charmingly, to the auditor, "My conscience is clear. But so is my memory." But now, this inability to get through to anyone at all threatened to unnerve me completely. Was I really stupid or what? What if I was late? Would that be interpreted as a sign of disrespect for the federal government? Or of sloppiness? Or of carelessness? Or, heavens, of guilt?

I looked helplessly around once more and noticed a small sign near the uninviting door at the back, a sign I could have sworn had not been there a few moments before. I began to feel like Alice in Wonderland, as I approached closely to read: "If no one responds to the green button, use the phone in the hallway." *Thank God*. Moving from the lobby to the also-deserted hall, I was much relieved to discover a phone fastened to the wall. Eagerly lifting the receiver, I heard, "Please press star and the extension of the party you are seeking. To use the directory, press star and the first three letters of the name of the party you are seeking." *Arrgh*! Now feeling a little annoyed, I punched star yet again and, lo, a live male voice said, "Yes? How may we help you?"

Urgency flooded my response, as I poured out the details of my plight. "You see, I don't know the name or the number of the person I am seeking, and the machine keeps asking me that, but I don't know the answer, I just know I have an appointment at 2:00 with someone, and I don't know what to do, and I'm afraid I will be late, and . . ." The voice interrupted this babble with "Just a moment. Someone will come out to get you."

Back into the lobby I dashed, just as the uninviting door opened and a dumpy woman — could it be Elaine? — popped out, took an appraising look at me, and promptly scurried back through the door. Had she, perhaps, been the White Rabbit? *Oh, please,* I said to myself, *get a grip. Progress is being made.*

Next, a large man with a small mustache appeared, grabbed up one of my boxes, and turned to the door with a beckoning nod. "Hi," I called in a friendly voice to the retreating form, hoisting my other bulging box under my left arm. He turned, with a little impatient flick of his head, as I thrust out my hand, told him my name, and inquired, "What's yours?"

"My name is Jim Frank," he replied, holding open the door and again trying to lead me forward.

"How confusing," I called to his imposing back, as we moved rapidly down a long corridor. "Two first names."

"Not really," was his unappreciative response.

In my anticipation of this encounter, I had pictured a nice conference room, rather like a boardroom, with a capacious table on which to spread out my various exhibits. I had anticipated taking charge from the start by beguiling the auditor with some background — about me and my "business," my writing business, which was the subject at hand. Schedule C. My Schedule C had indicated that my expenses so far exceeded my income that eyebrows had been raised at the IRS, I took it, and they wanted me to come in and explain it all. They wanted me to know my rights, to know that they were not persecuting me. That they might even discover that the government owed *me* money, their communiqué had assured me, and if I was not fully happy with the results of the audit I could bring the matter up with the auditor's supervisor. My privacy would be strictly preserved.

Well, good. I, too, would take a nonadversarial position. Hence, I had determined to bedazzle my auditor with my boxful of manuscripts and books published (quite a while ago, admittedly); of magazine articles (more recently published); and of the book, video, visuals, and press coverage of my musical. I would explain to him that we were on the same side, the two of us. We both wanted me to make more money and both would be pleased if I could do so, and then send some more to the government.

Jim Frank led me into a small cubicle dominated by a crowded desk, which he circled in two strides, and gestured me toward a chair facing the desk. There was no semblance of privacy. My two boxes now occupied most of the open space on the desk, and as I sank into the indicated chair, I found that my chin barely cleared the edge of the desk.

There was I, again like Alice, grown oddly small in this outsized world.

Jim Frank's computer was flanked by many documents and by a telephone bedecked with little pastel-colored stickers. I looked up to his open face, his sandy-haired head sporting an earring in his left ear, and said brightly, "Oh, look at your phone! So frivolous! I mean, for an IRS auditor."

"Or perhaps you have a misconception about IRS auditors," he replied without a smile. Or much of one, anyway. I could not be sure.

I rose from my chair with the intent of delving into my box of writings and opened my mouth to begin my spiel about background, when he cut me off with, "Yes, we'll get to that eventually. I would like, however, to follow my own system, if you don't mind. Otherwise I will become confused."

Confused! Jim Frank had foibles! Suddenly he was human!

And he wanted me to know that he cared about my attitude toward the proceedings.

Obediently, if reluctantly, I lugged the box off his desk, dropped it on the floor with a thump, and bumped up the other box, the one containing various account books, bank statements, receipts for my new laptop and printer, and especially (because they had made such a big deal of it in their summons), a rundown of my car expenses. Regrettably, in my preparations for the audit, I had discovered that my estimate — or, rather, my accountant's estimate — of 5,000 miles traveled for business purposes was a gross exaggeration, and I knew I would have some explaining to do on that point.

He began by informing me of all the precautions and niceties the IRS observes to assure fairness. I already knew this. However, it was as if he needed to read me my Miranda rights. I knew he wasn't trying to make me feel like a criminal, of course. He didn't say I had the right to remain silent — although, as I continued in my nervousness to interject chirpy asides, it was clear he wished that I would.

He was calm. He was focused. I told him the bit about our being on the same side. How we both wished I had more money to give to the government. He agreed. He was glad I felt that way. Could we proceed now?

He came right to the point. I needed to show a profit in order to demonstrate a serious business intent. The government wants me to show a profit at least every five years, in fact. Do I have a serious business intent? Well, of course I do, I said. Naturally, I want my musical to make a great deal of money from large, enthusiastic audiences all over the world. And I want my novella to receive critical acclaim, though it would probably acquire only a select readership . . . Well, but . . . take a look at my magazine articles; they garner $1,000 or so a page. Admittedly, they are short and this is not a lot of money, but you have to understand that for a writer motives other than money are, must be, paramount.

"That's all well and good," Jim Frank said, "but if you wish to consider your writing a *business*, financial viability is a critical part of the equation. Have you *ever* made a profit from your writing?" His tone was not really hopeful.

"Of course! Not recently," I felt compelled to add. But at last, here was the chance to do my "show and tell." I hauled out the materials I customarily use to seek a new production opportunity for my musical. There were drop-dead-gorgeous pictures of the set it had in its maiden production. He leapt on these. "Oh, I love sets and costumes," he cried. "Let me see them." He studied them avidly. *I wonder if he's gay*, I mused, enjoying his enthusiasm.

Then I showed him my one-page bio. "Oh, you worked for public broadcasting." His face lit up. "I have a bone to pick with them; the programming is horribly boring these days, and I hate those pledge nights!" Sighing, I replied that everybody hates pledge nights but that they *do* make money. I thought that observation should be up his alley. "Fortunately," I added, "after 22 years, I don't have to make apologies for public broadcasting any more because I'm retired now." I then steered him back to my musical. "Did you know that it took Lerner and Loewe 10 years to develop *My Fair Lady*? Did you know they threw out 30 songs? These things take time, Jim. And publishing fiction in today's market? It's a tough sell."

He had heard this kind of thing before, I think. He explained that I should reserve my expenses until I had income to offset them. He wanted to move on to those very expenses. Expenses must be ordinary and necessary. "Ordinary and necessary," he repeated. It was clearly a mantra.

We moved through my maze of claims. "Let's look at all these 'Other Expenses.' Books and magazines? Okay, but you have not listed their titles, when you bought them, and how they relate to your business." He'd allow me half of what I'd claimed, presuming personal use of the other half. In future, I should keep receipts *with titles*. Theater tickets? Same thing: half. Postage and copying? Fine.

Mailings? Fine. And so forth. As we wended our way along, I did begin to feel he was being generous.

Then we came to the car expenses. "Yes, I have something to tell you about that," I interposed quickly. "That figure of 5,000 miles was an estimate . . ."

"I know it was an estimate," he cut in. "Do you know how I know? Because nobody drives exactly 5,000 miles. Don't ever, ever use even numbers. That's why this was flagged."

"Well, I've figured out the exact mileage," I began, waving my sheaf of notes at him.

"Never mind. I believe you. I'll give you half." Lo and behold, as I stared at my notes, he was surprisingly close, and it didn't seem wise to quibble. "I've been doing this for quite a while," he purred.

"You are sloppy all through this return, as a matter of fact. I really hope this will be an education for you. Look — a proper return is mostly presentation. Look here. You have nothing under 'Office Expenses'! What do you think postage and supplies and copying and so forth are? Think *presentation*!

"Now, what about this trip to Portugal? How is that a business expense?"

"Well, you see, I like to go abroad for an unpressured place to write and for inspiration, a change of scene, a change of pace . . ."

"If you could show me that you went to Portugal to do research on Manueline church architecture for an article you have sold — do you see what I mean?"

"But that's not the kind of writing I do. I am preparing a piece, for instance, on Marguerida, this wonderful cook and housekeeper who took care of us . . ."

"When you publish your piece on Marguerida would be a better time to claim expenses for your Portugal trip. Remember, ordinary and necessary." The mantra. "Otherwise, you'll be back here every year. And you won't necessarily get me, I may add, and other auditors might view your return . . . differently. Ordinary and necessary. I audited an artist once who said that as an artist, everything he did in his life was ordinary and necessary to feed his art."

"Exactly!" I broke in. "Yes. That's exactly right."

He looked at me, resignedly.

I said, rueful, "I wish my CPA had explained this stuff to me. At his big-bucks stipend, don't you think he should have?"

At this, Jim Frank rose abruptly, went out, returned with a phone book, and, lowering his voice as he paged through it to the section labeled "Tax Preparers," muttered, "My boss would fire me if he knew I was doing this." His voice was a whisper, as we both leaned across his desk to look where he was pointing. "Do you see that name in caps? She is what is called an 'enrolled agent.' She is very, very good. When she brings me a client's revised return, I accept it without question. *Without question*. Her clients include a number of writers and artists. And you won't be paying big bucks. You might give her a try."

Oh, thank you, thank you . . . I will, I will, I wanted to cry.

The reckoning came quickly on the heels of this advice, but, to my surprise, in spite of the healthy bite the proffered number would take from my bank account, I felt quite good about it at this point. I wrote out a check for hundreds and hundreds of dollars without a sniffle.

Then, suddenly, Jim Frank was saying, "Now, I can tell you that I used to be in the entertainment business myself, designing sets and costumes in Los Angeles for movies and theater productions."

"Really? You're kidding!" It seemed so unlikely. This sensible, serious man, creative? In show biz? He went on to elaborate on his various activities as a designer, and we chewed the fat for a while about the theaters in our neck of the woods. He said I should take my musical to the Ashland Shakespeare Festival, which struck me as a very good idea.

"How did you ever decide to give up all that for — well, for this?" I glanced disparagingly around his cubicle. But it began to dawn on me: left brain, right brain; yin and yang; a balance in the soul.

"I'm four years from retirement myself. I wanted something steady. With benefits. With a retirement plan. Without the hassle of southern California. It was a great ride, but," he shrugged and smiled, "enough was enough."

:: :: ::

As I descended the stairs to re-enter the real world, my burden of boxes now tucked neatly under my arms by a solicitous Jim Frank, I felt buoyant — a feeling that seemed to me to be totally inappropriate under the circumstances.

What had I wanted from this man? Not to be let off scot-free, no. There had always been the niggling knowledge that I had been pushing my luck by remaining ignorant of what would and what would not pass muster. And, appropriately, the phones with their green buttons and the computers with their uncanny manipulations and the not-quite-real Elaine, despite minor malfunctions, had done their job, had secured a just accounting. I had forked over the many hundreds of dollars the rules demanded. Give unto Mammon that which is Mammon's.

What had I wanted from this man? What had I received from this man that had evoked such a feeling of, well, of elation?

Emerging from the IRS building into the sunlight, I was struck with the truth of it. It was, it must have been, a sort of validation. Authentication. I was a businessperson. And still a writer. He had given me that.

‡ ‡ ‡

DOGGONE
ORANGE ROBED BOY
WINGS OF FIRE
SEA CHANGE
CMJ
The Boy WHO Played
PATSY GARLAN
THE THING IS...
THE THING IS... SELECTED WRITINGS
BILL
EXPENDITURES
RECEIPT
TAXES ETC.

Meeting the Mishpocha

A PERSONAL ESSAY
CIRCA 1985

I used to think that my in-laws did these things on purpose to unsettle me — these outpourings of excess generosity. Because they *did* unsettle me. Lavish meals set forth. Extravagant presents conferred with great ceremony. Glowing faces eager to let me know — no, insistent on my knowing and acknowledging — that they had gone way, way out of their way for me.

Nothing could have been more contrary to my stiff-upper-lip, understated, never-invite-emotion, Anglo upbringing. To attempt to elicit feelings of gratitude or approbation was so rude, so crude as to constitute a crime against Nature and Society. You just didn't do it.

But on that first occasion in 1948 when, as a young bride, I was taken to meet the *mishpocha* — my husband's extended family, to use their Yiddish term, or clan, taking my Scottish father's perspective — I was enchanted. They all crowded around, noisy, hearty, welcoming, singing my praises. I was enormously flattered. "Mazel tov," they cried. "Mazel tov." They like me, I thought. They really *like* me. And they did, it turned out, all except my mother-in-law.

My husband, 14 years my senior at age 34, had attempted to prepare me for the encounter. I was familiar with such terms as *shiksa* and *goy* and *oy veh* and thought them a little exotic and charming. Of course, this was because I, fresh from college, was so crazy in love with my philosophy professor husband that I could not see straight. I had just graduated amid the excitement of a campus romance — he, grinning, in cap, gown, and blue-and-white satin Columbia hood as he sat on the platform with his distinguished, similarly plumed colleagues; I, stalking stiffly across the stage in unaccustomed high heels, in cap and gown, to receive my diploma. All to profuse, in-the-know applause from the assembled multitude.

After our marriage a month or so later, we traveled from Oregon to Boulder, Colorado, to present ourselves at the appointed hour for the introductory dinner party at my mother-in-law's house. She had not attended the wedding, nor had the other now-gathered relatives. It was, after all, the 1940s, and normal people did not journey great distances readily — especially not European immigrants who, once settled, stayed put. So this was to be the momentous occasion of the introduction.

I was looking pretty spiffy, I thought, and my tinge of apprehension was somewhat offset by that invincible feeling which deliciously encircles two people in love.

We entered a room brimming with overstuffed furniture — dark, puffy, maroon things. With heavy drapes. With garishly patterned carpets. (My own taste ran to light, airy spaces, clean lines, and natural fabrics and colors — the "contemporary look.") Incongruously, a huge refrigerator also stood in the living room; it took center stage, having apparently shouldered everything else into a strange jumble. This, I was told proudly, had been a family present to my mother-in-law, who had, it seemed, no space to put it in her tiny kitchen. Also, I sensed, it was deemed too grand to be hidden away.

We were, as a group, also a strange jumble of ages, I being the youngest by far. Even my husband's nephew was older than I. His mother was 14 years older than her little brother, my husband, who had come as rather a surprise (or, worse, as a mishap), his mother having thought herself well beyond childbearing age when he was born.

She, my mother-in-law, was by now probably in her eighties, people said. No one knew exactly, nor did she, they said.

Most of the *mishpocha* were small-business folk who, having not ventured out of their provincial hometown, hid, under jocular banter and good-natured jibes, the fact that they were much impressed with those who had — my husband, the professor, as well as his much-older brother, the faraway New York society doctor who had broken his mother's heart by anglicizing his name.

The joyous cries that had greeted our arrival soon drew my mother-in-law from her kitchen, and there she stood stolidly in front of me, her eyes taking me all in. With not even a smile to soften them, her first words were: "My son never did go for *pretty* girls."

The lesson had begun. Of *course* she would not think me pretty. My hair was short and curly, not flowing and luxurious. Wrong. My nose tilted up. Wrong. My smile, though big, was crisp, not full and curvy. Wrong. My body was too slim, my legs too long. Wrong. Wrong. Wrong.

And above all, as I came to realize much, much later, I was too cheerful, too content. I had not a look of suffering. *I was not an old soul.*

:: :: ::

In subsequent encounters with my mother-in-law, I always felt somehow off-center, disoriented. The mismatch of our mores cut deep. She cheated at cards. I was incensed when, during three-handed bridge, she would slyly (but all too obviously) sneak peeks at everyone else's hands. When I confided my outrage to my husband, he shrugged and told me I was the most honest person he had ever met. And he told me that in the olden days, when his Orthodox father was alive, she only pretended to keep strict kosher, but, actually, unbeknownst to him, used the same dishes for everything. Well, no wonder he thought me abnormally honest!

When at last she visited us, she tried to teach me how to cook. I thought of myself as a pretty good cook, actually. But I learned to put cinnamon in the pot roast. And I learned to make gefilte fish and chopped liver and matzoh ball soup. But her matzoh balls were like little round marbles that sat on the bottom of the soup plate, while mine were light and fluffy and floated on top of the soup. Hers were authentic, mine were not.

There were foods she would not eat together. My husband had explained, of course, about not mixing meat and dairy, but she never admitted that this was a religious taboo. No, it was rather that she didn't *like* the combination; it made her ill.

Just when I thought I had mastered her tastes and, more importantly, distastes, I served up some dish involving tomatoes, and she suddenly spat a mouthful of it onto the tablecloth and shrieked in disgust. *What was the matter, what had I done?* Then came the story.

When she was a young girl and had just gotten off the boat from the Old Country, she was walking along the docks when someone handed her a "piece fruit," which she thought was an apple. Well! On taking a bite, she was revolted and repulsed by the soft, slimy flesh of a tomato. And forevermore she could not bear the taste of them. *Well, I mean! How could I have anticipated that such profound personal idiosyncrasies would arise to confound me?* The focus of my efforts had been on differing religious customs. It wasn't fair.

She was also prejudiced against "Negroes." I was shocked to learn that a people who had themselves been subjected to oppression could so scorn another such group. But her views were unequivocal. There were Jews. And there were Negroes. And there were Americans. The last category did not contain either of the other two. And I think that is why she never could take me to her bosom. I was, when all was said and done, an American. A *shiksa*.

I will not say that my mother-in-law taught me how to be miserable. But being around her made me stretch. She initiated in me a way of being that became indispensable, as the years brought experiences — as the years bring to all of us experiences that strain to the limit our capacity for empathy, for sorrow, for joy.

Eventually, when time dissolved the bond of love that had held our family safe and close, when our shared world shattered — through my needy, intolerable transgressions, and through my husband's — was it because the bred-in-the-bone difference between us was too unyielding? Could my mother-in-law have been right all along? That you must not mix that which it is forbidden to mix? It could be so. It could at last explain why he divorced me, claimed our children, and pronounced me dead.

Yet I cannot believe that is the sum of it. As children, we are the center of *our* world. Not only that, but we tend to grow up with the assumption that we are the center of *the* world. Yet somewhere along the way, when we are obliged to take in others' reality, we begin really to grow up. Subtly we begin, deep within our psyches, to move over, to make room for the "other." We suffer it to come unto us.

We do not, any longer, like the refrigerator, dominate all the living room but soften our contours to accommodate the alien within ourselves. Our souls begin to age.

‡ ‡ ‡

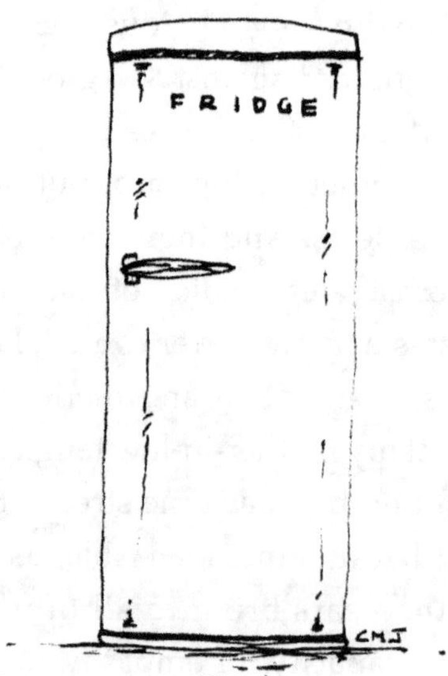

As the Twig Is Bent

A VIGNETTE
JULY 2003

There he stands, a bit behind and to the side of the somewhat disheveled, bespectacled man at the podium. There he stands, just outside the limelight, at graceful ease in his finely tailored suit, as tall and composed as a birch tree beside a stream. There he stands, poised like a dancer in the wings, in quiet equilibrium, awaiting his cue.

Across the back of the stage, a huge screen proclaims:

The 26th International Conference on
SOFTWARE ENGINEERING
Edinburgh International Conference Centre
Scotland, UK

"And now!" announces the speaker, with a little academic smile, "it is my very great pleasure to introduce to you the winner of the ICSE's most prestigious award, given — as all of you know — to the software engineering author of the most influential paper in his field — as judged 10 years after its publication. Please welcome a distinguished scholar from a distinguished university, Professor . . ."

Can this *be*? My mind is skittering from this present reality back across the waters of time, like skipping stones, to images of my infant son, howling with colic; to memories of his boyhood innocence, challenged time after time by life's cruel intrusions into his childhood's ever-expanding world; to the vulnerabilities of his adolescent years — and, wrenchingly, to the terrible dissonance that has increasingly threatened to destroy our mother-son bond. The ripples of my reflections become intermixed in a crazy swirl with the scene before me now. His height, his gravitas, his self-possession — all these features of the man he has become contrast poignantly with my mind's-eye images of his skinny little childhood self.

I glance backward, from my front-row seat, to the rear of the huge, tiered auditorium, packed with academics. I steal a sideways look at the excited crowd around me — at his students, his siblings, their children, his children — all congregated from their far-flung homes to do him honor, all applauding, grinning, proud, as he moves to the podium and the center of the stage.

:: :: ::

There he stands, poor little guy, at four years old, pale from the fright of confronting his mother, defiant (a stance he never took with his father, though — he didn't dare), looking up at me from about knee level, all impotent fury. And I melt. I say, "Just you wait. Some day you'll be taller than I am. And you'll be able to pick me up and swing me around your shoulders." He likes that idea a lot, I can tell. "But for now," I conclude, "like it or not, I'm the boss."

:: :: ::

He opens his laptop at the podium, switches it on and begins, in that soft, pleasant, sure voice of his: "When my colleagues and I were first trying to get our heads around a way for software components to talk to one another, for software designers to share a common architecture, we were stymied more than once. But gradually, some solutions seemed to emerge. We were pretty excited about it," he says, with a grin. "So, hoping we were on the right track, we put out the paper."

Now he looks directly at us, his eagerly listening family, his gangling six-foot-four son, his stunning six-foot daughter, his nephews, his nieces, and says, "You know, it's like raising kids. You do what you can, you send them out into the world, with hope in your heart." He pauses, smiling. "And sometimes they succeed." Again he pauses, continuing to look at our little group.

Of course. He had told us, I now recall, that there would be messages in his speech especially for his family. Yes, I think, for his daughter — wildly, flamboyantly punk, but boldly pursuing her bizarre wardrobe creations in a prestigious design school. And for his son — a painfully shy, budding concert pianist and computer whiz who was just admitted to the computer school of his dreams. Yes, my son can be justifiably proud.

:: :: ::

There he stands. His worried little face is looking, beseechingly, up into mine. His skimpy little shoulders are slumped in misery.

"What's the *matter*?" I bend to hug him. He ducks and drops his school books in a heap on a chair. I know it's that damned bully again. That kid in second grade, that Neanderthal who has been making him feel like two cents.

So I say, "Honey, just you wait. That kid has probably gone as far as he can go. He'll probably burn out at 11, he'll probably reach the height of his powers by sixth grade. But you! You have just begun! To grow! To learn!" I'm thinking to myself, as I say these words, *To strive, to seek, to find, and not to yield!* "To be more and more the person you are," I continue. "And, darling, you are a gentle person. And you will be a gentle man. Look, honey, you have more potential packed in that small body of yours than he has in his whole big loathsome frame."

Does he feel better? I try to decide. Hmm.

"You'll be big and tall, too," I add. He seems to brighten.

"And strong!" I throw in for good measure.

We talked in those days. He heard me, I think. But I'm not sure he believed me.

:: :: ::

He glances at the huge screen behind him and brings up a title: "A Ten-Year Perspective on Formalizing Architectural Connection." *Well! I have a longer perspective than that*, I'm thinking. There are charts now on the screen and phrases like "using rich abstractions for component interaction (or system 'glue')." And he's saying, "At times, our concept threatened to run away from us . . ."

:: :: ::

He's still pretty young when he decides to run away from home. I make him a sandwich and tie it up in a bandana. He trudges off as I wave good-bye. He camps all day in a little forested area at the end of the street. I go to peek at him once, but I'm not really worried. He knows he has to be home before dark.

:: :: ::

More charts. And now I notice that in the lower right-hand corner of the screen there are short, basically unintelligible phrases. Are they in Gaelic? No, in Scots! What is all this? Not only do I not understand what he is saying and what the charts are showing, but I don't understand these phrases that I suspect are meant, again, for the family. "*It's just a ween o'blethers.*" What in the world does that mean?

:: :: ::

He comes in one day from playing in the neighborhood. We chat until he says something bold and shocking. Was it bad language? Or, even more appalling to me, bad grammar? I now can't remember, but I say, "We do NOT talk that way in here!" He says, "Well, we do out there!" I concede the point. He does, after all, have to get along in the world. "Okay. You may talk that way out there. But not in here. Okay?"

Is this the beginning? I am propelled further back, to when he has just turned five. We are at Oxford, where his father is a visiting scholar. He and his four-year-old sister are on that steep learning curve, when new words come rushing into their vocabularies, all with proper English-boarding-school pronunciation. They attend a small preschool that is officially called St. Michael's but is known to everyone as Miss Skerry's. Miss Skerry — wearing a black cape over her bent form and with her gray hair tied up in a bun — appears to me to be scary indeed. The children tell me that she has a broom, a witchy sort of broom, standing in a corner of the schoolroom. They say at first that they are terrified of her. But they get over that feeling soon, start speaking of her as Miss Skeddy, and are not at all afraid of her. "Well, at least they are learning how to speak properly," she tells me.

Each morning, my little four-year-old and five-year-old set off up the lane from our cottage on Old Boar's Hill outside of Oxford to meet the bus that will take them down the road a mile or two to Miss Skerry's. They are model English children, in their school uniforms of navy blazer, long gray stockings, short gray flannel pants for him and gray pleated skirt for her, "St. Michael's" blazoned in magenta on their lapels and navy caps. He holds her hand in one of his and their two huge English pennies for the bus in the other. Sometimes she insists on carrying her own penny. But he is five, and he is in charge. She looks up at him with total trust. I just dissolve with love for them.

He tells me one time of a strange and distressing dream, induced, no doubt, by his exposure to history at Miss Skerry's. He dreams that he is looking up at a huge, frightening Saxon, with shimmering sword and glistening shield. He says to the Saxon, "Are you going to kill my daddy?" And the Saxon replies, "I might. And I mightn't."

I think he must always have been grappling with ambiguity.

:: :: ::

There he stands, one hand resting casually in his pants pocket, as he glances again at the screen and says, "Let's move on to 'Gross decomposition of a system into interacting components.'" *This ought to be good,* I'm thinking. "Let us note, first," he goes on, "that this process is typically hierarchical." *Typically* hierarchical? Well, yes. I now remember how I thought, *If we get this one right, he'll be an incredible role model for his siblings*. And we did. And he was. From the time he was three years old and his little sister was a toddler, through the years as a younger brother and sister swelled the family, he was all that I wanted him to be. His sister adored him, and all the children looked up to him, following his gentle, always-well-behaved lead. Was that so wrong?

:: :: ::

His audience is rapt, as he moves us all along from point to point. It turns out his central proposition is all about connectors. "Connectors are where the action is. Get this right, and the rest is gravy." That's what I think, too! Something about specifying connector behavior and about pipes. Pipes? Connector pipes. Connector pipes? Bagpipes? "We can check," he says, "whether a filter's interface is compatible with a pipe role." Oh. We can?

:: :: ::

Of course, there are minor transgressions, occasions when his interface is not really compatible with his role. I only learn of this much later, when we are *all* adults. They confess to the time when he and his sister transport in a sand pail my special jars of Spice Island spices out to the sandbox at the bottom of the garden and proceed to make concoctions of what must seem to them delectable crypto-edibles.

And then there is the time at an elegant restaurant in Italy, when he and his sister somehow slip beneath the dinner table and, under cover of a sea of gleaming white tablecloths, whisk along unseen on hands and knees through the dining room. I have no idea, in retrospect, how they avoided the intervening legs and feet they must have encountered along their journey. Indeed, I am not fully aware of their departure until a flustered waiter points it out. "*Scusi, Signora, Signore, vostro bambini . . .*"

:: :: ::

There he stands, really in his element now. His clear, user-friendly tones belie the mind-boggling (at least to me) complexities of what he is saying. I wonder whether in this erudite audience — professors, students, scholars all — there is anyone else like me. Even the youngest family members seem to be getting it, for God's sake! Ooh, there's now another Scots encryption in the corner of the screen: *Let the tow gang wi' the bucket*. I'd love to, but what does it mean?

It seems as if I was always egging him on. And look at him now! But, alas, he doesn't see it that way. The way he sees it, he was being molded into my creature, into the person *I* wanted him to be. And, well, yes. I guess. Maybe. Up to a point. But isn't that what parents do? Attempt to civilize the little heathens?

:: :: ::

There he stands with his little sister, the two of them meeting other children, reaching out. "Do you have any songs?" they'd inquire, for openers. Later on, when the two younger ones come aboard, we'd all of us belt out rounds on car trips: "Ah, poor bird, take your flight; far above the sorrows of this sad night" and "White sands and gray sands, who'll buy my white sands, who'll buy my gray sands" and "A boat, a boat, haste to the ferry, for we'll go over to be merry" and "Go to Joan Glover and tell 'er I love 'er . . . "

:: :: ::

There is a new chart on the screen, and he is talking about performance, throughput, latencies, reliability, security, fault tolerance. Fault tolerance! Now, there's a concept.

:: :: ::

Images fly fast now. I try to bury the ugly ones, the anguished moments. I try to cover them quickly, like a cat in its litter box. I am trying to talk to him about the upheaval that tore our family apart. But he — overwhelmed? — says, "Don't tell me your troubles! They are not my troubles. I have troubles of my own!" Reliability? Security? Gone.

He is in high school, the computer revolution is in its infancy, and he gets the bug, so to speak. He pursues his passion in the computer lab at the college where his father teaches philosophy. These are the critical, crisis-ridden adolescent years. There is a divorce, and I am gone. When he comes to visit, we tiptoe very carefully around the deep subjects, the ones that matter, for these are the years that wound. Is it my fault? Is it his father's fault? Does it really matter? The bottom line is the same: I wasn't there. Gross decomposition of a system into its component parts.

And now he is off to Amherst. He falls in love a few times, but, as he tells me with sorrow in his voice, "I thought that when I went away to college I would at last be able to be myself." But, try as he might, he cannot get away from his father and me; he carries us within him and seems to experience life as through a hazy screen, a film, a fog. He feels he is like his father — head ruling the heart, getting in the way of direct experience. But he keeps falling in love with women who, he discovers with dismay, are like me: heart ruling the head, making them unpredictable, unreliable.

I think again of the time when, as a child, he ran away from home. I thought I was being clever, sending him off with a kiss, attempting to deflate his anger, or whatever it was that prompted his need for escape. But even then, I must now admit, I had a vague sense that I was robbing him of something — his dignity? his personhood? — that even a child has a claim to. Was it always, always a battle, a deeply submerged battle, a conflict both within himself over his need to break away, to be a person, and with me, over my need to mold him, to continue to create him?

"As the twig is bent, so is the tree inclined." I think this is true — though whether for good or ill, who can say?

:: :: ::

He leans on the lectern, very relaxed. Is he beginning to wind down? We seem to be coming to the end of the charts — or maybe not. We are up to "How can we establish intellectual control over this new world?" How, indeed!

:: :: ::

I am spinning off again, and he is at Oxford. He and his fellow students subsist on chewy, treacly "Mahs Bahs" and with respectful envy try not to watch the tutors feasting at the High Table. His love of dance picks up, and he dances with a traveling troop of Morris dancers whenever they perform in the vicinity of Oxford. In the summers, he travels to the Balkans, where he wanders through villages, knocking unannounced on cottage doors in search of traditional dances and unusual musical instruments. He is heartily welcomed and tells me that the first thing the villagers say to him is the traditional greeting: "How is your mother? Is she well?" He thinks I will like this. He is right. He buys — and plays — a Macedonian bagpipe, of all things. He cooks exotic dishes with exotic spices that he collects on his travels.

While he is at Oxford, his father dies. He flies home to his father's bedside. At the moment of death, he later confides, my son experiences the flowing of his father's spirit into his own. He inherits with it an unexpected release from bondage, a joyful, yet pregnant freedom — as if qualities he had shared with his father have now been bestowed exclusively upon him.

Now, where I am is where his home is. He sets up in a tiny cottage and takes a teaching gig at a private high school. He marries a woman who seems his complete opposite, except for their mutual love of dance and music. She is an accountant — a down-to-earth, no-nonsense woman. She is also quite lovely, joyful, and spirited. She plays the fiddle with gusto in small combos, he his bagpipe; she performs ethnic dances in costume, as does he. She is fiercely independent, her own person — and he likes that a lot. She is not particularly intellectually curious. That's *his* long suit.

Still, she balances him well, and opposites attract, so people say. Yet I am a bit uneasy, aware that when we come, over time, to apprehend and to *appropriate* the qualities that underlie the attraction, the attraction itself lessens — or vanishes.

He and his wife and, now, daughter move to an eastern university, where he acquires a Ph.D. in computer science, then on to the Pacific Northwest, where he does computer research for a large electronic technology firm. A son is born, they move back to the university, he takes a teaching position in the College of Computer Science, and the long climb up the academic ladder begins.

He tells me "the anecdote of the mayonnaise jar," which, he says, is a metaphor for his marriage. It seems that when his family is seated at the lunch table, he likes to leave the mayo lid ajar — in case anyone wants more. His wife, however, wants the mayo lid tightly screwed on — in case anyone inadvertently picks up the jar by its top.

During these years, when he comes to visit, or when I go to visit, we talk about everything and anything, sharing confidences in perfect candor.

:: :: ::

He is drawing me into his world. I am visiting him and his family in their huge, old-fashioned house. He is eager for me to share his enthusiasms. He takes me into his study, an impeccably clean, serene, tidy haven so unlike the heavily, richly furnished rest of the house, which is more a reflection of his wife's taste. He sits me down at one of his computers and introduces me to my first Mac, my first mouse. I am afraid of the mouse, awed by the Mac.

He says, "Come on, sit here. Try moving the mouse around."

"Oh, but," I whisper, "but I might mess everything up!"

"No, no, don't worry. The mouse is tame."

"Ooh! The little arrow is shooting all over the screen!"

:: :: ::

I think we are good friends. We take long walks together in fields, in parks, and we talk about his interest in dance, his career vicissitudes, his curiosity about the supernatural, his travels, his marriage, his children — he raising a family, me still hollow from the loss of mine. We talk about his brother and sisters, now grown, preoccupied with raising their families, buying houses, pursuing professional careers, scattered between the East Coast and the West. I confide the joys and strains of my varied career, my varied love life. We talk about our mutual enthusiasm for food and cooking, for gardens and gardening, for books and writing. He tells me he has been making beer and wants to know how to grow garlic.

:: :: ::

We are strolling in his garden. We stop to inspect his bamboo, his climbing rose, his collection of mosses under an arbor. With modest paternal pride, he eyes the tiny green carpets, each in its own little flat. Tenderly, he bends to inspect each one, cool in the sheltering quiet of the arbor.

:: :: ::

We are walking through an autumn day, full of massive trees in reds and auburns and gold, among leaves falling on vast, green lawns. We are talking of the books we are currently reading. I am reading Carl Jung and the Jungians; Buckminster Fuller and the Buckies; and a book about bringing up kids called *The Trauma of the Gifted Child,* which my daughter has given me, for some disturbing reason. He is reading *The Continuum Concept,* by a British doctor named Jean Liedloff.

"What's it about?" I ask.

"It's about Stone Age mothers she lived with in the jungles of Venezuela who carry their infants 'in arms' at all times for the first few months of their infancy."

"Ye, gods! How do they get anything done?"

"Why do they need to?" responds he.

This is the thing about him, the thing that makes him such a good teacher. He doesn't tell you anything until you are dying to know it. He just trusts in a person's innate curiosity.

"Well, I mean," I sputter, "what about the cooking, the cleaning, the washing, the diapers . . ."

He laughs. "What diapers?"

"Oh."

"Actually, she's very active, fetching water from the river, making brooms from twigs, sweeping the dirt floor, stirring the cooking pot . . ."

"I suppose it can be done," I acknowledge, with some skepticism. "And what does this do for the infant?"

"Oh, the infant goes along for the ride — as he did in the womb, by the way: it's part of the continuum. When he's hungry, he nurses; when he's sleepy, he sleeps; when he's awake, he takes in all the bustle and sounds and sights and smells of the life of the village. He has, in fact, no unmet needs. He bounces around on his mother's hip, or in a sling on her front or back, and just enjoys."

"Sounds like a pretty good deal," I concede. "But, then what? I mean, when does this all come to a screeching halt?"

"When he's ready. When he's had his fill of everything he needs, to prepare him for an active role in the life of the village. He's not *required* to do anything, to become anyone. It just comes naturally. His in-arms experience furthers his inborn drive to fit in and readies him for independence, confidence, and expanding selfhood."

"Then that's the continuum?"

"That, and the fact that for countless millennia nature has been developing and refining him, through generations of ancestors — human and otherwise."

"It sounds, somehow, so much more sensible than all the child-raising theories that we mothers today are crammed with," I say, suddenly resentful. "But what happens when she has other kids to deal with — I mean, what about sibling rivalry?"

Again, he laughs. "What sibling rivalry?"

"I was always so afraid someone would be jealous if I paid attention to someone else . . ."

"Well, the older siblings have already had everything they need from the mother. They've moved on to other things. And, of course, everyone loves babies. Everyone welcomes the help of the children as they grow into active participation in the business of the village — hunting, fishing, making canoes, making arrows . . ."

"So the adults are not competitive, either?"

"Of course not. They are comrades."

"It sounds like heaven," I say, wistfully. "Unattainable."

:: :: ::

As I watch him, through the years, I admire his way with his students, his children. As with his garden, his way is to nurture but not constrict.

I remember the sad account he shared with me, back when he was in college, of the hazy screen that he perceived between himself and real, unmediated experience. I recall the exhausting, 20-hour labor that heralded his birth. My bond with him must have begun then, in the knowledge that he must have been exhausted, too. I think of the fearful colic that wracked him as a tiny infant, how he screamed endlessly with pain, how his father and I, unable to quiet or comfort him, unable to bear his misery, would rush from the house to be for a few moments released from the burden of his cries.

I look at him now, in all his individuality — his exquisite taste, his passions, his keen and questioning mind, his hobbies, his loves. He is a caring, conflicted, profound, decent, deeply human man. I think of the many ways, the many times, he has tried to get me to understand. I just didn't make the connection.

:: :: ::

He is leaning on the lectern. The charts have changed again. He is saying, "In real architectural descriptions, connectors often represent complex multiway interactions." You can say *that* again! "And," he goes on, "understanding whether a set of components can correctly interact only makes sense if you know what the interactions are." This sounds ominous. *Is* this ominous?

:: :: ::

When was it, then, that it all turned sour? When did the bitterness set in? When did the gross decomposition start? When did the wine turn to vinegar?

The years fly by. He travels throughout the world, explaining to computer people in corporations how to get their software designers to talk to one another, how to bridge the gap of misunderstanding and ambiguity. His children are grown, about to leave the family nest. His marriage is falling apart. He is wracked. He desperately wants to save it. He is seeing a shrink. He is beset by "gremlins." He is seething with an anguished anger. His bitterness breaks out: he cannot trust *any* woman. It is because of me.

I try to explain. To free him from this trap of his own making. "Are you mad at me because you are afraid of falling into a pattern? But, you see, you do not *have* to be like your father in that, in his possessiveness . . . and she is *certainly* not like me." He is trying to get a word in. I rush on. "Perhaps she is not unfaithful to you. Perhaps she just needs a bit of slack. I did, honey . . ." He blurts, "You are just trying to . . ." I break in. "I had my reasons. Perhaps so does she." He is towering over me. And, now, his scornful rebuttal, "You are just trying to justify your own self!"

And then comes the time when he and his siblings, leaving spouses and offspring to fend for themselves, take me to the Florida Keys for an unprecedented, just-us, family celebration. I think we are celebrating their dawning awareness that I am growing old —

well, older. And — oh, damn — now comes a memory of the evening when the five of us are merrily wining and dining. I begin to reminisce about the adventurous car trips of their youth, everyone singing in lusty harmony . . . so great. I stop to sip my wine and beam tipsily at my four grown children, the fruit of my womb. Unexpectedly, in the candlelit quiet, he stuns the group with an announcement: "I hated it! I hated every minute of it! I hated *having* to sing!" I flee the dinner table, the restaurant, the sparkling illusions shattered like broken glass.

Oh, god, must I dredge up this whole thing again — oh, please, not here, not now. Oh, god, is it all about betrayals of trust and self-deceits and unbridgeable gaps in understanding, then? No!

I snap back into the present moment, to the caress of sudden, enthusiastic applause.

Oh, god — it *is* all about connectors! There he stands, smiling, nodding to the audience, waiting for the first question. On the screen is a last Scots phrase: *Bide awee*. This one I do understand. It means: "Stay a bit." *Bide awee*. It is somehow so comforting, the sound, the sense of it. *Dinna worrit*. Don't worry. All will be well. Just you wait . . .

Behind me, a small figure rises. His 11-year-old nephew speaks in a comradely voice, as one colleague to another. "I'm just wondering. When computer components use their own symbols to talk to each other, how do other computers, or even *people*, understand what they are saying? I'm just wondering."

How, indeed. How can the human thinking / feeling apparatus bridge the chasm to the wildly different information-processing apparatus of the computer? What are the pipes? Where does the interface take place?

And what of the chasm between mother and son? The life experiences so different, the mental processes so increasingly different. Some species don't bother to maintain the connection, of course. Do we?

His nephew's question — so simple, so profound — startles me back to the beginning of the speech. "You send them out into the world . . . and sometimes they succeed . . ." And suddenly I have a brainwave. He was, of course, speaking modestly of his team's innovation leading to the award as being akin to the hoped-for success of one's kids or siblings or nieces and nephews. With the personal subtext of himself as a father. But not only that! Could it be he was thinking also of his success *as my son*? "We do what we can." Yes, we do!

Could it be? Might he really be reaching out, making a connection, making peace, acknowledging my efforts, however inadequate, making me a part of his success? He might and he mightn't. I don't know, I don't really know. So I, too, must live with ambiguity.

He is preparing to grapple with his nephew's probing question.

And there he stands. His own man. My son.

‡ ‡ ‡

Computers: This is the Dawning of...

A PERSONAL ESSAY
CIRCA 1965

The swallow-flight tongue of the instructor in Computer Language does dip once to my pedestrian level, just once during our eight-session survey of the field. I understand when Mr. Swallow (yes, his real name!) says there is a heady elation in being able to prove that the Computer is not the master. "You are the master," he says, meaning me, I surmise. Apparently, he can tell that I think of the Computer-with-a-capital-C as an animate entity. The machine can only do what I tell it to do, I remind myself.

The utter appropriateness for our times of this new form of humanity's metaphysical thrust — that is, of mastery over machines — strikes me hard. Here are the new gods with whom we must come to terms, but terms much more favorable than those we struck with the old gods, to whom we must relate, but certainly not in the old ways, ways dictated by ignorance, fear, and superstition. The dominant intellectual mode is now quite a different proposition. Knowledge, confidence, and power have put an end to propitiation. We do not beg, bribe, or praise in pursuit of what we want from one of these gods, these room-sized monsters. No, we do not pray. We program.

But perhaps it would be more telling to suggest not that the machine is a god, but rather that the man-machine partnership, working in perfect unity, is a new creature under the sun, omniscient and omnipotent. I write coded instructions on punch cards, a single word on each card, and the pile of cards is then fed into the maw of the machine by the unseen hand of a trained professional. My Program runs without a hitch, if fortune shines, and the Computer delivers its bounty.

Yet what of omnibenevolence? Along with the profound spiritual satisfaction we may now experience as we scan a perfectly executed Program, perfect in word and deed, perhaps will come in time a lessening of our need — that old, old need, programmed in and left in storage by some careless, long-extinct God — to dominate our own kind. Then we will be free of passionate impulses toward men as toward gods. But for the moment, we move along in the ancient track, battling for mastery over the minds of men through control of language.

Wanting to put two eggs, at the very least, in one basket, I undertake to write a Program in Computer Language that will permit the machine to construct, in principle, any healthy English sentence. To give, in short, the God its voice — or, rather, a cultivated English voice.

The Computer, though apparently eager to learn, does make a production of it. None of the hit-or-miss, learn-by-doing of the two-year-old child suits its intellectual apparatus at all. Therefore, while it is much harder to teach, I think we can be more sure that the results will not be unexpected, that we can count on no new structure emerging from its slat-like lips to pitch us, headlong, into a new key.

Vocabulary is no problem; its oral-aural perceptions and productions are flawless and its memory capacity prodigious. But there is a wooden inflexibility in its approach to varying structural forms. Once launched on a certain pattern of Z = A + B, for instance, it proceeds compulsively to produce every version of this particular form until its vocabulary is exhausted. Only then will it accept a variation. And if it seems that this should be, when it comes, a welcome relief, bear in mind that the Computer now proceeds to sound its *new* note without variation in form or style, by so much as a burp.

I think we are unaware how elliptical we are in our communications with each other. To communicate with the Computer, we must realize that it has not the wit to be elliptical, nor to understand an elliptical command. It compensates by being methodical; it would be the "grind" in any classroom. Thus, we cannot ask the Computer simply to perform a certain operation, such as "Brush your teeth after every meal." We must instruct it to gather toothbrush and paste, apply paste, turn on the water, etc. Before instructing it in this way, we must ask it to start: viz, first to start registering the instructions, then to start performing the operation. ("First listen to me. Then do as I say.") And at the end, we must first ask it to stop and then announce that this is the end.

Thus it is evident that words are extremely cumbersome as a medium of communication with machines. And, as a matter of fact, the Computer does not think in English. No, it converts our English instructions to its own native language: numbers (another indication, perhaps, of its essential godliness, if we bear in mind that mystic communion with God has been felt, even traditionally, to be furthered by the divination and incantation of magic numerical symbols).

Two distinct approaches to Computer Language may be isolated. One, SPS (Symbolic Programming System), is for the use of the expert programmer, requiring him to present his Program in language that is easily, quickly, directly convertible to the Computer's native language; this is comparable, I suppose, to pidgin. The other, FORTRAN (*for*mula *tran*slation), is a transitional language, designed for use by the semitrained as well as the expert programmer; this language is closer to English but requires much more converting on the part of the Computer. One may compare FORTRAN, perhaps, to the Basic Patterns approach to the teaching of language.

My Program is in FORTRAN, for the admittedly extraneous

reason that the only authority I could buttonhole was a FORTRAN expert, by which I do not mean to imply that the SPS expert speaks only to God. Consequently, it may be noted, however, that the Computer's version of my Program (on IBM cards) is much longer than the programmer's version.

The key to producing any acceptable English sentence in FORTRAN is an operation quite charmingly referred to as "the nested do-loop," an expression that would, I should think, delight Mr. Swallow if he were not, alas, an SPS man.

Let us at this point refer to the Program itself. The first set of cards is the FORTRAN Program as designed by the programmer; the second set is the Computer's translation of it. Even the first version is represented in numbers by the Computer, but this is, on the whole, gibberish to the machine, I expect, until it has made the further conversion. The Program that finally emerges generates only the very simplest form of an English sentence: viz, Article (A) plus Noun (B) plus Verb (C). The Program can be run on the 1040 or the 1620 Computer, with the addition of vocabulary cards. After the set of instruction cards one must add, first of all, the A words, one to a card; next, the B words; and next, the C words. The resulting "output" will be a printed list of every possible sentence following the A + B + C pattern, limited only by the number of words in the vocabulary.

A second Program, based on the first, could add the structural forms A + B + C′ + A + B and A + B + C + D + A + B, where C′ is an intransitive verb and D a preposition. Comparing this Program to the first, one may observe at once that it is much longer. The question now arises, peskily, as to whether each additional form requires an additional nested do-loop. If so, we will have an expensive and extensive aviary to maintain. And this is my horizon; I have penetrated no further and must leave to subsequent researchers the task of determining if there is a shortcut.

One last personal note, on my own metaphysical experience

with Mr. Swallow's insight, leads me to observe that while I may be the Computer's master in the sense that it can do only what I tell it to, I am not — any more than my nonmechanically oriented forebears — able to make a silk purse out of a sow's ear. I cannot prevail upon the Computer to risk being original, creative, or even a little odd. I cannot induce it to indulge the tiniest whim or caprice. And, somehow, I feel that if we were to turn our language over to the Computer for safekeeping, we might come to regret the loss of the poet from our language, just as the primitives among us may pine nostalgically for the vanished, unpredictable, and exciting universe once inspirited by the capricious gods.

‡ ‡ ‡

ENIAC
MUSIC TO MY EARS
GRATEFUL DEAD
CMJ.

Lament for Violin

A WHIMSY
OCTOBER 1959

I'm a violin. And, God, there are *such* things I could tell. If I had a chance, that is.

I play in the symphony with Adam — forgive me, with *Mister* Leonard — and I'm so sick of this job. I sometimes wonder if I'll get through a concert without splitting a gut.

Let's face it, there's no love lost between Adam and me. You know, he's referred to me as "this lousy fiddle." Charming, isn't it? So, he's unhappy. So, he's got issues. Who isn't? Who hasn't?

There are things in me . . . if I could only . . . if someone would just give me a chance to speak. There is so much I want to say. I know there is more to me than this, because — well, because I have such a longing . . . But he makes me feel like a cheap hunk of wood with a hole in the middle. I feel raped every time he touches me.

My nerves are all a-jangle. I'm all strung out, so to speak. I don't know. Maybe I need a psychiatrist.

I must admit, when we play with the quartet, it's not nearly so bad. The one thing Adam and I see eye to eye about is Mozart. And, really, that is not a negligible point. But you can't *always* be playing Mozart. Anyway, with the quartet I actually feel sometimes as if I'm coming alive. And — it's odd, really — it seems very familiar. It's as if I'm seeking a repetition of something I already knew, as if there were vibrations in me still as vital and as strong as when I was first formed. But somehow they don't come out. God, I'm boxed.

Maybe I'm too dependent. Well, yes, I *am* dependent. I can't help that. It's my nature. *And* my condition. If I don't have someone who can bring out what's in me, I might as well *be* a hunk of wood.

Sometimes I wish I did own my own voice. That I didn't need someone to draw me out. I could converse with myself, I could be my own audience.

But then I realize that, for me at least, expression involves harmony. I have insights, with the Mozart. I dream, then, of the kind of partner whose own subtlety matches mine, whose own depths fathom my depths, who releases like a mirror the images hidden in my darkness, whose sympathetic touch sends quivers to my core, whose sensitive ear can follow my reverberations to infinity.

Oh, but God, who am I kidding? Well, intermission is over. Wake up, here he comes. Oh, how he grates on my nerves! If he says "Come on, Eve, back to the grind" *once* more, I know I'll scream.

‡ ‡ ‡

Naptime at the Hotel Giotto

JUNE 1997

As if the exuberance of the cloud-filled sky
were not enough, the air above Assisi
must continuously resound, and
all must play their part.

The cheerily gossiping birds. A signora's sudden,
shouted, joyous chit-chat, flung from a stone doorway,
across tiled rooftops, to a friend a mile away —
and all between.

The in-your-face bells, with their *Come now, come now,*
come now, come now, come now, and their
This means you . . . and you . . . and you.
No rest for the weary. Get up and pray.

Somewhere, a tenor runs through his scales and offers
an aria from *La Bohème*, with full-throated largesse
from his balcony, to the thirsting ears
of a presumed music-parched world.
Banging doors and solid thuds drum an
obscure accompanying beat.

In overly generous response, an amplifier down the way
blares "JESUS CHRIST SUPERSTAR" . . . Would
Saint Francis be pleased on this, his very own turf?
Of course he would.

Capping it all, there's that relentlessly barking
dog. *Yap-yap. Yap-yap-yap.* One-two.
One-two-three. Like a snappish dance master
commanding his class-full of oafish, clumping boys
and tentative girls to cut loose. *Yap-yap.
Yap-yap-yap.* I may go mad.

Yet, miracle of miracles, naptime a distant dream,
this canticle of canticles invades
the listening heart and bids it arise
and be glad.

‡ ‡ ‡

PART II

Embracing Life — Anyway

A Tale of Two Lives 46
A Link to the Living 52
All Things Bright 56
Dovey's Old Place 58
A New Day 60
Riggs 63
Through Thick and Thin 64
An Open Letter to Mary Oliver 70

IDLE THOUGHTS

The essay is an enactment of the creation of the self.

—Philip Lopate

A Tale of Two Lives

A REFLECTION ON COURAGE
CIRCA 2014

What a marvelous thing, the arc of a life. Hmm. Is that the right image, I wonder. Perhaps, if you take a long, long view? But eyed a little closer, a life is not a smooth progression, is it, but more like an ever-changing landscape bristling with hurdles and jumps, hills and vales, rocks and rills, treacherous slides, watery depths.

And living a life is like flying a kite in and over this landscape. Coaxing it up till the air begins to take it; guiding as best one can its unplanned swoops, its abrupt turns; enduring its sudden twirls into a doom-laden, earth-seeking plunge — will it, can it, rise again? — until, with a swelling change of heart, it truly flies and at last you can thrill to its thrust up and up against the blue, blue sky. And that's just for starters! Hardly a gentle, predictable arc, no.

This is a very personal tale of two lives, about two persons who are very dear to this teller, but it is only one tale among many, because, of course, there are as many tales as there are tellers. In this tale, then, the two persons are characters in this teller's story, as we are all characters in each other's stories.

:: :: ::

Is there anything on earth more heart-rending or more lovely than the raw trust a child bestows on a mother? At first, the infant's need may be, with nature's blessing, easy to meet. The tiny suckling mouth, the bursting breast, eager to merge — these are the heart's universe. And the trust continues, matched by mutual total love, once given, never lost, through a lifetime. But along with that bred-in-the-bone trust, a shadow of doubt may arise, if the crippling action or inaction of the mother somehow fractures it . . .

She was born with a hemangioma — probably caused by a misapplied forceps — a round, red lump about the size of a quarter on her chubby baby cheek. Her father and I found, in consultations with a gaggle of doctors, that it could be removed through one technique or another without a lasting scar of any significance. After agonized weighing of the options, we chose surgery as the least disruptive of her infant life and the most predictably successful. And, as her small face grew, in later years she could have the scar reduced to practically nothing, if need be. So the operation was a success, and later on there was little lasting scar — *to be seen*. However . . .

I think she was about two when we took her, all trusting, to the hospital. We handed her over to a nurse, who installed her on a bed in a small room with a huge plate-glass window, there to await the upcoming surgery. But here's the thing. The nurse told us we were not to go to her, not to be with her at all until it was over, because it would upset her when we left and she would cry! Yes, but this was wrong, this seemed so wrong, she needed us *now*. We could watch her through the one-way glass window, said the nurse, and take her home in the morning.

And in those insular days of medical practice, you simply did not question the judgment or authority of the doctor, the hospital, the nurse. Today, that seems like the middle ages. Today, we would challenge such barbaric nonsense. Wouldn't we? But on that day, we stationed our dutiful, dubious selves outside the one-way window and helplessly watched our bewildered little daughter coping with her abandonment.

She was sitting up on the bed, her back straight, her chubby legs a balancing arc in front of her, her sweet face sad but composed. This image is burned in my heart to this day. I ached to put my arms around her. But there she sat, and we watched, until at long last the nurse came and held out her arms, and our child lifted up her arms to the nurse in automatic compliance.

How little we know, really, the heart of another person. How ignorant I remained for many years, until she told me of the scar left by that desolation, an inner scar that accompanied her to adulthood.

Thinking of her now, I take solace in the knowledge that I am the mother of a daughter who grew into a gentle, lovely woman with the mettle to forge a career as an award-winning artistic director of prestigious magazines; who married a comparably talented music journalist and editor-in-chief of *Billboard* magazine; who became, with him, the mother of twin sons. On her sons and all who are close to her, she bestows the gift of her inner strength, her beauty, and her unconditional love.

:: :: ::

I marvel at how life's lessons, wittingly or unwittingly, shape who we are. Because of those particular hurdles and jumps along the way, the hills we climb, the valleys we cross, the roads we follow — because they are these and none others — we become not who we might have been but who we are. Perhaps this is why, sometimes despite common genes, each one of us is unique? Perhaps . . .

A few years after our little daughter's surgery, her younger brother was born. She already had an older brother, whom she revered and followed around like a vassal to a lord. And after that more years passed, and a little sister was born, and after that, for reasons that had nothing and everything to do with the four siblings, the family dissolved, their known world fell apart, and the flying pieces were carried here and there by the relentless winds of change.

Her younger brother, who was about six when our family returned in tatters from a year's trip abroad, was tossed hither and yon in the turbulence that ended in separation and divorce. And when it was over, he remained at home in Oregon with his father, stepmother, and two older siblings. Their little sister stayed in California with me.

There was a great weeping willow tree in the garden at the Oregon home. He was six years old when the willow was brutally struck down by hurricane winds, in what came to be known as "The 1962 Columbus Day Storm." I think he linked this deeply affecting loss with the dissolution of our family. As he told me much later, and it was clear that this explained everything, "It was my best friend." The two dread-filled events became intertwined. Both threatened to break his heart.

Several years passed, and when he was 14 years old it was my turn to be overturned with weeping and fresh grief. I was living with *my* best friend and my daughter in a homemade A-frame house on a little canal in northern California when he called me — and this is what he said: "It is not right," he said, "for a boy to be this unhappy." It was a sentiment that had been building for years. His; mine.

And so he came to live with us, in our A-frame house on a boardwalk on a little canal. His heart was deep and vulnerable, and though I loved him with an extraordinary passion, I felt that he was alone in his soul.

Over the years, during college and after, he formed deep friendships that connected him with life, though he still and always was subject to harrowing depressions. These were countered by his wit, humor, and Rabelaisian appetite for fun. He became an enthusiastic cook. He became a psychotherapist. He had a loving life-partner, with whom they cared for a threesome of cats. My son's reality was a great involvement with life, and, as T.S. Eliot has pointed out, "Humankind cannot bear too much reality." But my supremely human son can, and bravely does.

:: :: ::

So, I've been thinking. About courage. And it seems to me that courage starts at the moment of birth — instinctively. We scream, we yell, for what we want. Regardless. This act of self-assertion, refined as it becomes over time, broader as it becomes through empathetic joining with the world, is at its roots the courage to live.

After all that bopping about in the womb, building stamina, building commitment to life, all cozy-warm and constantly fed, we are being prepared for a rude awakening. There must have been a moment, though I admit I don't recall it, when we thought, "Whew! I made it!" — only to realize, "But I don't like it!" We're hungry. We don't understand *air*, this is weird, breath is coming, skin is crispy, we are heavy, that's the worst, really weird, weighted down by something, something is wrong — and we are definitely hungry!

Perhaps in the womb we hummed a bit, little tunes, but now, with air in our lungs — we have lungs! — we can really give voice to our feelings. And courage is born. The courage to live, to be.

Well, maybe not exactly like that.

So, we all have it, because we were born with it. Some become heroes, celebrated for their willingness to put their very lives on the line in service to the lives of others. A hero rescues a child from a burning building, abandons a too-small life raft that others may live, marches into battle in concert with his comrades. And whatever his innermost, private need — for self-approval, public praise, atonement, escape from parental judgment — his bravery is an homage to life, and it feels wonderful.

And then there are the unsung heroes. For each of us human beings, the motivation for our actions, the arena, the goal may be different. The challenges for some of us are far, far greater than those for others, and yet the smallest hurdles must be met with courage. The thing is, if you let yourself dwell even on some ordinary little act or action of yours with all this in mind, don't you feel that, by golly, deep within you there is courage? Getting up in the morning — we know it as "facing the day"? Making coffee — an act of awakening? And doesn't the heart rise, then, with affection for oneself and the rest of us mortals? And don't you feel that, actually, just embracing life anyway is courage enough for starters? It is the courage to live with it all and, sooner or later, when all is lost, the courage to die.

And as I think about it, is it too huge a step to suggest that, after all, the arc of a life is not the thing? *What elevates the spirit is to see the luminosity in all of living, to experience the eternal in the now.* I think that's the thing.

‡ ‡ ‡

A Link to the Living

A PERSONAL ESSAY
SPRING 2000

You can imagine how startling it was when my daughter the medical student inquired, "Would you like to see my cadaver?" A glance at her eager young face, filled with cheerful expectancy, made me soften the fervor of my denial to "Oh, no, darling, no; I don't think so. No. No."

Ye gods.

But then I thought, *How often does a person, a layperson, have an opportunity like this — to look inside the body of another human being? You'll be forever sorry if you pass up this chance.* I glanced at my daughter again. She was waiting for me to come round. As she always did. As kids always do. "Well," I said, "what would it be like?"

So off we went, into the warm dusk of the New Hampshire evening. In such a situation, you fight your apprehension, your worry that you might not be able to control your queasiness.

:: :: ::

As we descended the stairs — deep, deep into the cavernous basement of the medical school building where the anatomy lab was housed — she began to prepare me. It will be cold, she explained, because . . . you know. And there will be a smell of formaldehyde; don't mind it — you get used to it.

We entered the dimly lit lab. I want to say we crossed the threshold, like Dante following his guide and mentor Virgil into the Underworld — though no sign warned "Abandon all hope, ye who enter here." And though my daughter never took my hand, I felt as if she had.

We wound our way among the sleek gurneys, with their sheet-shrouded gray burdens. Not another soul breathed in that vast space. The smell of formaldehyde was an assault. The silence was thick, as if the bodies had absorbed all the sound, like flannel. Like blankets. Like snow.

She showed me first the trays of parts, stainless-steel basins of raw things — one full of kidneys, another of livers — like offerings in a meat market. She spoke in hushed tones, as if we were in an intensive care room or a nursery. Then we approached the gurney that bore the cadaver she had been dissecting for many weeks. Slowly, gently, she turned back the cover from the thin, white feet and legs. "We'll start here," she said. "The head is so very personal." I knew she was allowing me time to prepare for the intimacy of that encounter.

She pointed to a clipboard hanging on a nearby low wall, where the history of her cadaver was detailed. He was an old man — and an old cadaver, it seemed, having been in storage for many months. I don't remember what he had died of. She told me that in some medical schools' anatomy labs, the students make dark jokes and horse around, probably in an effort to handle their feelings. She, however, was grateful that the attitude here at Dartmouth was one of respect for this, a human presence.

She raised the sheet from the lower torso, which was laid open like a display package. I was astonished to see that our bodies' essential parts are all neatly organized, many in their own little membranes, like plastic-wrapped leftovers in a well-maintained refrigerator. I had always assumed, I guess, that the stomach, the liver, the spleen, and the coils of the intestines would be all jumbled up together, resembling more the inner workings of a radio. The tidiness of the reality before me was strangely satisfying.

She had been working on a section of colon, I think it was. And by now my curiosity and, yes, my awed fascination with everything in that room had fully taken hold. "It is so important to us as students to have this experience of dissecting an actual body," she said. "And if people are willing to donate their bodies so that we can do this, we must . . . must give them due respect." I felt very strong as she carefully removed the covering from the head.

I gazed upon the small face of an old man, an old man who somehow linked my daughter and me and all human flesh together, in the semidarkness, in this moment out of time. He was nothing and yet everything to me.

:: :: ::

Outside, green, growing leaves were gleaming softly under a star-studded sky. Up into the freshness of evening we came, full of a sense of the enduring connectedness of all beings, and of the child who becomes the parent and the parent the child.

This essay first appeared in the May 2000 issue of *The Atlantic Monthly* and was also published in the Winter 2000 issue of *Dartmouth Medicine* magazine and in several subsequent collations.

‡ ‡ ‡

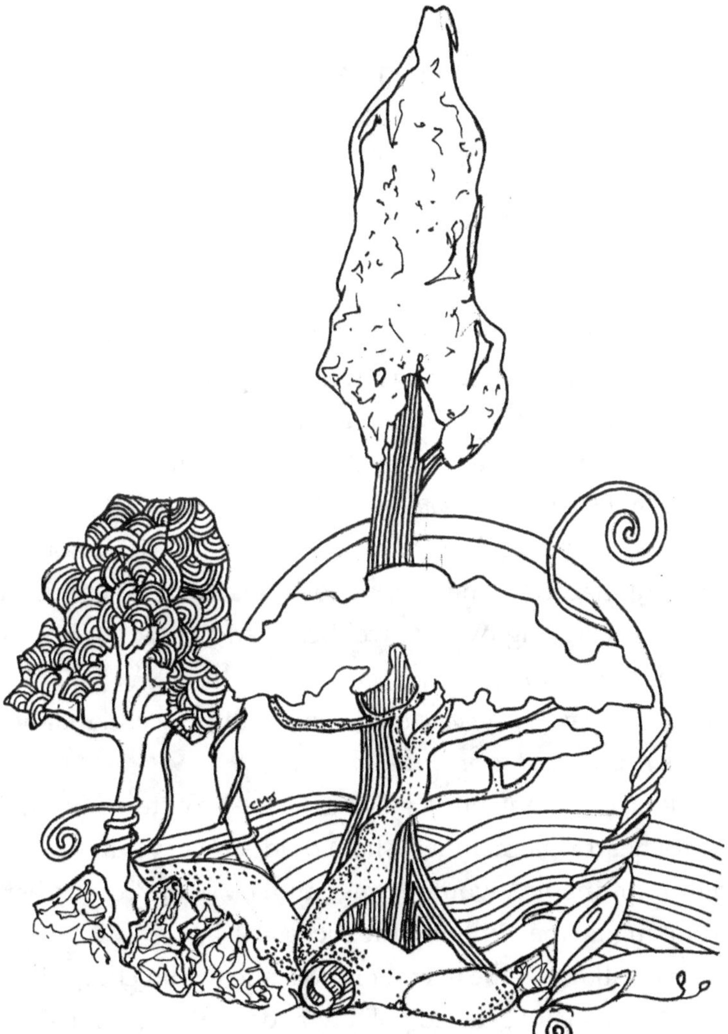

All Things Bright

A VIGNETTE
SEPTEMBER 2012

I knew an old lady who talked to things. It started with the roses in her garden. *Oh, how beautiful you are, and so, so fragrant*, she would say to one of them. And, sniffing another, *You too, dear, but not so much. Yes, and you, you sweet thing*. During pruning, she would tell the rosebush, *Don't worry, you'll feel like a new woman afterwards*.

She was particularly fond of a delicate fern in a pot on her patio, a plant that was in need of frequent watering. She tried not to let it see her worrying over its wellbeing and talked to it reassuringly about the weather.

I'm so glad you're happy here, she said to the graceful red maples, *you bring such panache to my little garden*.

She joined the tiny birds in song, as they twittered in the towering oaks nearby. Sometimes, she would sit very still, so that the visiting hummingbird would come quite close and check her out before sinking its long bill into the fuchsia.

When walking in the neighborhood, she would chat with passing dogs, who usually listened politely, and would tell a meandering cat how very fit it looked today. It would wave its extravagant tail at her, roll ridiculously on its back at her feet, get up, shake a little, and saunter off.

Inside her house, she chastised an urgent spider scurrying

along a wall. *You'd better skedaddle! And stay out of my sight, you little devil.*

But she never, ever said to any of them, *I'm talking to you because I'm deeply lonely — my children grown and gone, so many friends dead or dying, my dearest living miles away — and I'm aching with pent-up love.* No, it was always about the here and the now, about the comfortable, casual, living-together relationship she enjoyed with the creatures and the plant life around her. Sometimes, however, she would murmur, to no one in particular, *Whew, I'm stiff this morning.*

Lately, she'd taken to talking to inanimate objects. To the kettle on the stove she'd say, *Just let me know when you're about to boil over, please.* And to the Cuisinart food-processor, *You really are sharp, ha ha, aren't you.* And to the scalding-hot water streaming from the kitchen faucet, *Wow, I didn't see that coming. So cool it, okay*? And to her small le Creuset pots and cooking spoons and razor-sharp knives — she loved to cook — assembled on the countertop, *Well, well, suppertime. Let's see what we can concoct.*

At night, settled under her downy quilt, she would read until the book slipped from her hand. Reaching to douse the lamp, she would call softly, *'Night, House.*

:: :: ::

One morning, when she woke, she felt too tired to rise. So she slept and woke and slept again and woke. And in the late afternoon, she lifted her bedside phone and called her dearest friend.

Please . . . care for my roses, she whispered, as the gathering dusk took her away.

‡ ‡ ‡

Dovey's Old Place

A PAEAN
SEPTEMBER 2013

From the very beginning — till now, this special time of belonging for our family — Dovey's Old Place has always beckoned. And it has always fulfilled.

At first, we wondered if the incessant rumble and splash of sea on rocks would become maddeningly insistent at times. Yet if you were intent on pulling out a clump of weeds in the meadow above the cliff's edge, say, to reveal an uninterrupted view of the rocks and the waves and the sandy beach below, you could hear or *not* hear the sea at will.

The same would be true when, having trudged up the wooden steps to the cottage perched like a treehouse on the wooded hillside above the meadow — after a day's labor stacking firewood and trimming the over-determined trees and encouraging the more reluctant azaleas and the vulnerable, sweet lilac — and having at last tumbled into a welcoming bed, with a happy sigh, the weary worker would tune in the softly breaking waves. For a short while, the sea sound would inhabit your mind — and be gone.

The always-present firmament, in one form or another, might also bewitch the time. The early sun's call to action, with its threat of too much heat if you lolled about for long. Or at night, the brow of the rising moon making insignificant the candle on the dining room table and drawing the diner's suddenly enchanted gaze across the bay to the hills suddenly serving up the full-faced moon. Or, later, the creeping stars, the promise of which had beguiled both bed and groaning body out onto the deck, to be both watcher and watched over.

Or, again, stepping into the cottage after a hectic game of tennis or a long round of golf, achy and thirsty, you and your friends would invariably be brought up short by the panorama of pine trees and seas and skies crowding through the expanse of windows framing the scene. And if the day was becoming a blustery one, the sea now churning, the pungent scent of salt thickening the air, the wind whipping up the wild pines, your grateful group would turn to the cottage's offer of a fire, a Bloody Mary, a steaming bowl of minestrone, and a quiet read.

In such a place, contentment, and even joy, can come to fill the person whose rhythms pulse with its rhythms, the person whose senses are both follower and leader in life's dance.

Good things happen here. Actually, *unpredictable* things happen here.

And that's the fun of it.

‡ ‡ ‡

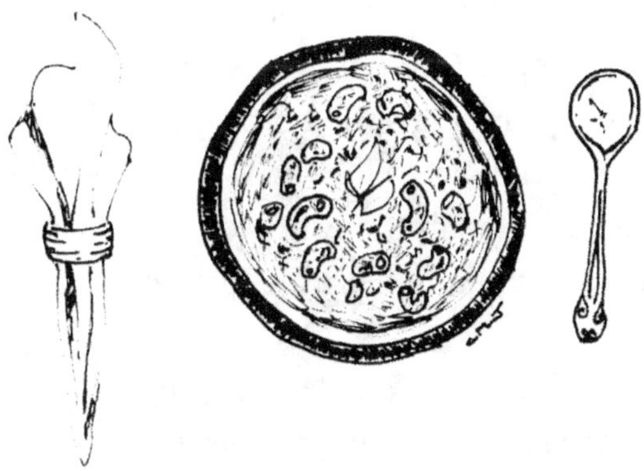

A New Day

A SHORT STORY
2003

Not exactly springing out of her old desk chair, wondering whether her body or the chair was the more decrepit, Maggie grabbed a saggy sweatshirt and staggered out the door for her mid-morning walk. The vulnerable spring leaves were newly hatched and gleaming greenly in the morning sun, fluttering like tiny ballerinas *en pointe,* so unsteady were they on the stately, ancient trees nodding to her as she passed.

Loosening up now, she swung along — quite smartly, she thought — then immediately wondered, as she so often did, why her energetic mother had always chastised her for lagging. Even in her adult years, evening "constitutionals" with her mother had been somehow challenging. "Don't dawdle. Pick up your feet. Come along." So, in her head, echoed her mother to this day.

But on this gently smiling spring morning, as her senses sharpened to the fragrance of lilac, to the mad, musical chattering of the nest-minded birds, a different thought arose and an image loomed in her mind's eye, summoning her little-girl self.

She is trudging along the two-mile route from school to home. In . . . what, maybe second grade? It is spring, and she is in the rhythm of her walking.

Maggie held the image in place, aware that she was slackening her pace as the old experience began to swell within her.

For a few blocks, she kicks a small stone in front of her, while trying to maintain her rhythm. It is a long way home. The gardens along the route are very pretty, and she runs her fingers along the slatted fences as she goes. And, oh, here is a puppy! It is a wiggling, happy-to-see-her, happy-to-see-anybody, fluffy, white creature, now scrabbling at a little gate to come out.

Maggie found herself now trying to head off what she knew came next, as she crossed the street in an effort to pull her mind away from a dreaded scene.

The puppy wants so much to be hugged, to be touched, to be held. She shrugs aside the twinge that says she shouldn't . . . and unlatches the gate. In one great rush, the puppy bounces out, past her, and into the street. A car . . . And after that, it is all a blur. The puppy, lying panting on the grassy strip next to the sidewalk, she, Maggie, running up the path to knock frantically at the front door, people coming out, confusion, voices, grown-up activity.

Did they take the puppy away? Maggie wondered. Did an ambulance or something come? And how did she get home? Slowing almost to a standstill, she was flooded again with overwhelming regret, wanting it all undone, knowing that she and she alone had brought about the misery. Her mother had suggested that she write a note, a condolence note, to the lady whose puppy it was and send it with flowers. Somewhat relieved by the idea of flowers, she had labored over that note. And it did help.

And yet, and yet . . . had the shock that clung to her unwitting, her *unsanctioned,* act squelched forever the unfettered impulse? Had this one act banished her from the child's Garden of Eden? Did she now always drag a little, just to be on the safe side?

Again, she picked up her pace. *Accept it,* she thought. Childhood disasters, with their consequences to the psyche, are a part of life. This is how we grow up. This is the beginning, not the end, of being a responsible human being.

And yet, and yet . . . other, more recent memories rustled like dry leaves in the corners of her mind. Faint, brief snatches, still carrying their freight of guilt, of regret, of remorse. "For all sad words of tongue or pen, the saddest are 'it might have been.'" *Who wrote that*? she wondered. *Whittier, maybe*? The years had brought a world of painful, pointless emotions like these. Her broken marriage. The family dissolved. Three of her four children lost to her in that storm of dissolution — though later restored, but not unscarred.

Had her old childhood experience taught her nothing, after all? Was this her *inevitable* pattern? The unthinking act, the heart-rending regret? She had let her heart lead her around by the nose! How's *that* for an image. She had followed her passions. She had followed her passions again and again, until, finally, she could bear no greater burden of guilt. But no more. Now she was settled and had vowed never to hurt anyone, ever again. She had encaged her heart; it was not to be trusted. Was that possible? She hoped, oh, how she hoped . . .

But look, here, now — in this tree-lined street, fresh spring leaves dancing on the ancient limbs were covering with their promise the gnarls and furrows shaped by countless changing seasons — here, now, the dreaded memories dispersed in the quickening breeze and Maggie turned the corner for home, wondering what lay ahead, even now, in this new day.

‡ ‡ ‡

Riggs

(A Portuguese Waterdog)

CIRCA 1980

There he goes
and when he goes he goes lickety-split,
so eager is he to be going,
so eager is he to be there,
there
where the ball is,
and back he comes with his trophy,
lickety-split, only to be gone again,
and joy jumps
from this dog, a *joie de vivre*
such as we all
have occasionally
burst upon
and lost
and again found
and again lost —

and ever after
sought.

‡ ‡ ‡

Through Thick and Thin

(Surviving the Crash)

A PERSONAL ESSAY

MAY 2013

Cats. We had so many of them, over the years. Probably at least 40, counting kittens. Boots alone (well, not exactly alone) produced 28 of that number. We named every single one and found homes for most of them. Yes, for most of them. The others? Oh, dear, that was . . . well, that was so very long ago, how can one remember exactly?

I do recall that cats can be infuriating. But, then, the same behavior may be . . . well, entrancing. Literally. That is, a cat can go into a trance.

If you have had cats, you know what I mean. It's that *je ne sais quoi*. It's that heavy, unseeing stare the little beast assumes at times, when you can't tell, can you, if it's reflecting on the wisdom of the ages, reviewing its nine lives — previous and yet to come, or meditating on a Zen koan ("What is the sound of one paw clapping?"). Or has nodded off. Or, just as likely, is simply being stubborn.

When you pick one up, you can never be sure if it will scramble to get down or sink gratefully into your arms, a fluffy deadweight.

When I was a little girl, Boots, our cat of longest standing, had one of her litters under my covers, way at the bottom of my bed. It was such a surprise when my toes found them in the morning, as you can imagine.

We also had a dog — Bimbo — who was a huge, bejowled brindle bulldog, much bigger than we were. Bimbo established excellent rapport with the cats. We'd all be sitting around in the living room, my parents sipping their Cutty Sark, my little sister and I on the rug (Persian, which Boots wasn't) in front of the stone fireplace, playing at something — jacks or cards or whatever. And Bimbo would lumber in, all the way from the kitchen, where Boots's babies were nested under the stove — through the butler's pantry and the dining room and the front hall and across the living room — with most of a kitten delicately held in his massive jaws. Carefully, he'd set the drooping, acquiescent kitten down in front of my mother, so it could be part of the cocktail-hour gathering. And off he'd go to fetch another. Boots just trotted alongside, keeping a close eye on the transfers. But I think she was his teacher, his guru — how else could he know? Dear Bimbo. He was a giant among dogs. Anyway, somehow, it was a perfect collaboration.

Boots was the comfortable kind of cat, not easily ruffled. Your basic homemaking cat, you'd think. A good provider, a great mouser. But sometimes she'd catch and chew up a lizard, and her coat would get all scraggly. My mother would be quite cross with her when this happened, and Boots would lay her ears back and *defy* my mother. My mother, too, like Boots, was a small person — small in size, but not in stature. And on occasion they'd resort to the martial arts, in thought if not in deed.

Sometimes we would scream, "Boots has caught a *bird*!" This always made my mother fly out the door into the garden, to the rescue. But what could we expect, really? Webster's dictionary says "cat: *noun*, a carnivorous mammal."

But the days when Boots would lead her kittens into the garden for their first look at the out-of-doors? We would watch through the window, nudging each other and laughing to see them exploring, moving across the lawn — one of them, tentatively, jumping at a straw; another plowing recklessly ahead, wee paws stepping high through the funny-feeling grass. We'd debate which one would be the pick of the litter, which one the runt. I liked the explorer; my little sister liked the runt — and would coo about it: "Oh, the sweet little *thing*!"

Boots had a great many gentleman callers. Over the course of her nine lives, she produced her 28 kittens in seven litters.

At some point, she became careless. Or forgetful? Or perhaps just exhausted? She deposited one litter in the soft ashes in the fireplace.

Finally, my father — who had grown tired of the family sport of naming every one of her too-frequent offerings (though he was very good at it) and of the challenge of finding a home for each of them — took the latest batch of tiny, blind, squealing creatures away in a bag. This was a terrible thing for my father to have done, and uncharacteristic, too, for he was at heart a kind, loving man. We wanted to ask our mother exactly what happened, but in our heart of hearts we knew. And did Boots know, too? Was she broken-hearted? Or did she perhaps feel it was for the best, under the circumstances?

But how could he *do* such a thing, I wondered. My mother said he was under stress. Because this was at the beginning of the Great Depression. (I knew *she* was under stress: she had to keep the family going on the single $10 bill my father gave her each week — for food and drink and soap and even *toilet paper*.) Nevertheless, I was finding it very hard to forgive him.

My mother sat us down and explained that we had lost all our money when the bank it was in had "failed." It was called The Crash. And she said we must be frugal, so as not to lose the house, too — a possibility that to us was unimaginable. She did try not to worry us. It would be a shame to spoil our childhood, she told our father.

One day, a strange man came up the walk to the back door. Bimbo and Boots went with my mother to investigate. It was not the milkman or the iceman. It was a man unlike anyone any of us had seen in our lives. (I think the animals found the look, the scent of him depressing; Bimbo sniffed, and Boots just wandered off. No threat there.) He appeared stooped and tattered and tired, as if he'd given up on life. Knocking tentatively, holding a wilted cap in his hands, he asked my mother most politely if he could do any kind of work for us, in the garden, perhaps, in the orchard, or splitting wood, in exchange for a meal, for "just something to eat." My mother of course found a task for him. He could not bear to ask for "a handout," she said. He needed, almost as much as food, his self-respect, his dignity. He sat on the back steps and ate the sandwich she made for him. He saved the other things she put in a box for later.

He was the first of many. "Hobos." "Tramps." So many new words. So much misery. They tried so hard, and they were so forlorn. When one would appear, Boots would absent herself and Bimbo would just lie on the back steps beside the wayfarer, a hopeful lump, not in the least worried about accepting a handout. The misery of our visitors seemed to be our misery, and it made us children want to cry. We were too young to understand this new reality. At our age, everything happened for the first time.

Old Mrs. Childs opened her estate near the beach to them. My mother thought this was a lovely thing for her to do, so that they could set up their hobo camp not too far from the train tracks and have a place to be — to make little fires and cook and sleep.

We children were mostly dealing with our day-to-day goings-on. What to wear to school today? You mean it's *my* turn to feed the animals? Because always there were the animals to be fed. And, always, *What's for dinner?* we wanted to know. My mother made a casserole she called Depression Lamb. There was no meat in it, just hard-boiled eggs. But sometimes dessert was cherry pie, or chocolate cake, so that helped.

And we would beg and bargain. "*If* we straighten up our rooms *now, then* can we go to the *beach*? *Please*?"

And off we'd go to the beach, piling into our mother's old Packard convertible, Bimbo sedate in the backseat.

Not our father, however. Our father, who used to run laughing into the waves, with one or another of us perched on his shoulders, clinging to him and shrieking with joy, never came with us to the beach any more. Our mother, coping, doled out among us at the lunch table a single can of Campbell's tomato soup, which we ate with small spoons. Our mother, keeping us all on track, was stern but seldom cross. Our father, dour as only a Scot can be, had no time for us now, but we could hear him loudly in the kitchen, going on and on, with our mother seeking to assuage his worry and his fear.

Our mother, like Boots, doing the needful. Boots and our mother. They were two of a kind. Sometimes our mother would have us wean the kittens, when she felt they'd gotten old enough and a bit much for Boots. I can almost feel a kitten now, a furry blob cupped in the palm of my hand, on its back, on my small, receptive lap, my fingers supporting its tiny head, its pink mouth open wide to receive the eye-dropper of milk.

Well, a family is a living organism. During those days, ours was pretty much a female-run household. My father was out scrounging a living any way he could. The Great Depression ended with the advent of the World War, which galvanized the country. And eventually, when for our father the worst was over, and he was able to invest again, over the years came the revival of our fortunes, came enormous satisfaction — his profound and simple satisfaction that he could leave his life, his family in good stead.

There came other animals, of course, into our lives. Gushy Fat Cat — a favorite. And Penny, who was such a pain, in my view, so demanding and grumpy, but my grandmother said she had character. And there was another dearly beloved dog, Anzac, an Australian sheepdog, named by my father for the Australian and New Zealand Army Corps — I don't know why, because Anzac was rather timid, just a ball of fluff when freshly bathed. And I could tell you stories about each of them. Just as, I'm sure, *you've* got stories on stories to tell.

But talk about character! Boots was like women of yore, like the ones who crossed the country in covered wagons; like the stalwart, resigned countrywomen who turned out a baby every year to work the farm; like the suffragettes, defying all authority, demanding their right to be who they were, to have a say in things.

I find it sad, now, to think of the families — throughout the world, really — that do not include these unfathomable members. I realize what a hub Boots was, what a significant hand . . . well, paw . . . she had in maintaining the coherence of the household. In a cat-enhanced family, these enigmatic beings command our attention, require us to rise above our petty differences, our communal worries, even our fear-filled trials and tribulations, and give ourselves over to the fullness of family life.

‡ ‡ ‡

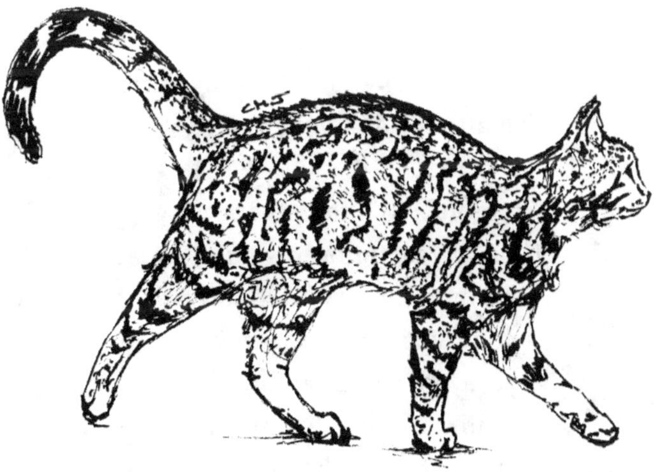

An Open Letter to Mary Oliver

(On Reading "Dog Songs")

CIRCA 2014

What would we do without dogs, you ask.
And very young children, too, Mary. Yes,
and all of nature's yet unmolded lives —
the pup, the bud, the babe . . .

Why do we love them? Why
are they so beautiful to us?
Inquiring minds want to know.

Oh. Yes, yes, I see, it is because
nature needs us — to encourage life.
Nature is in love with life.

But more's to it than that, Mary.
These sweet innocents recall us
to our own unmolded innocence,
don't you agree, Mary, yes,
your poems call upon this,
call us to this, too, when
a dog so heartbreakingly,
heartwarmingly burrows in the woods,
burrows in the depths of our nature, of
our own sweet innocence

before the molding
begins.

And, Mary, the thing is mainly,
isn't it, to incline us to recall —
as we will need this later,
much much later, so we hope —
our oneness, which is the All.

‡ ‡ ‡

PART III

Love and Loss

Doggone 74
Old Friends 77
Scattered Filings 82
Rounded with a Sleep 84
When I Was Small 94
A Song of Us 96
Prayer 97
The Wind Stirs 98
Eros and Agape 99
Yes 100
Love Woes 101
To the Sun 102
Moth and Flame 103
The Logic of the Web 104
When You Speak 105
My Friend 106

IDLE THOUGHTS

Loss and possession, death and life are one,
There falls no shadow where there shines no sun.
—Hilaire Belloc

Doggone

A SHORT SHORT STORY
JUNE 1992

You never knew which one of you would get it next. Or which one it would come from. You just knew that, out of the blue, the little creature would show up — secreted in your top drawer among your socks, or tucked in the toe of your sneaker, or nestled in your lunch pail under your sandwich. Your probing fingers would discover the (by now familiar, but always unexpected) painted white-ceramic toy dog — a small handful, sitting on its fat haunches, with a ridiculous grin on its doggy face.

One time it was even found smuggled into someone's mashed potatoes. How everyone would laugh at the unwary recipient's surprise. And the butt of the joke would laugh hardest, feeling loved.

Later on, when you had gone off to camp, or, even later, to college, there it would be, falling into your hand as you unpacked your lonely suitcase. *Gotcha*! it seemed to say, bringing family and home close.

It came into our lives first, I suppose, as a present to one of us, who thought it so silly that it had to be pawned off at once on an unsuspecting sibling — or parent. Probably every family has such an object — an object that becomes a talisman, taking on a significance related not in the least to what it is, but to its entanglements in webs of relationship.

At Christmastime and on birthdays, in the first few years, we were all very careful about largish, beautifully wrapped packages of unknown origin — large, to conceal the actual size of the contents. And we tried to be as sneaky and deceptive as we could in passing it along. Not knowing who it came from would be a problem, of course, because that person would be on the lookout, and the surprise might be aborted. But what fun it was to anticipate the pleasure given and received, just to be in touch.

As the years passed, it got to be years sometimes between "sightings." Then it got to be many years since the last sighting. And in those years, the fabric of the family loosened, lost its holding power. There were marriages and breakups and partings and misunderstandings and hostilities and bitternesses. There were deaths and resentments and heartaches and not-speakings. I think every family has these, too.

And then one day . . . well, you know what should come next in a satisfying story. But, alas, no. Vivid as that dippy dog's smile in my mind's eye, tangible as its smooth-skinned, lumpy body is to my mind's touch, I cannot quite visualize it in a *place*. I have searched and searched the recesses of my knowledge, turning memories over like piles of discarded garments. *Who* could have had it last?

And then one day came the staggering thought: could it have been *I* who let it fall, who let us all fall, from grace?

This story first appeared in the December 1997 issue of *The Atlantic Monthly*.

‡ ‡ ‡

Old Friends

A REMEMBRANCE
OCTOBER 2005

Riggs greeted Maggie with a broad grin and a wild tail. Then he rushed to the den to grab one of his tattered tennis balls. Ever hopeful.

Dee came with a ready greeting: Hi, sport. Maggie clutched her. Warmth was exchanged. Tall Maggie said, over small Dee's snuggling shoulder, Just a sec, Riggs. Dee said, Down, Riggs, though Riggs *was* down, just urgent in his prancing. And very tall, being a Portuguese water dog. He's okay, Dee. Let's go outside.

They sprawled in Dee's old Brown and Jordan chairs on her spacious deck. In front of them, a crisp, fragrant lawn led down to a dark pool that rippled invitingly in its woodsy setting. Maggie tossed the ball high, and Riggs galloped pell-mell across the lawn to intercept it in midair. He would leave Dee's side these days only for something really important, like a flying tennis ball. And only if he could keep her in view.

How's it going, Dee? What have you been up to?

Dee was easy, relaxed. Let's see, what have I been up to? They're all here, you know.

Who all?

Oh, you know. They can't wait for me to die.

Oh, puh-lease! Maggie felt that scoffing was the right response. Or maybe not? You know everybody loves you. Everybody wants just to help.

I *am* dying you know. Matter of fact.

Aren't we all! No, no, that wasn't right. Respect. Acknowledgment. You don't die from it, Dee. I don't think. Pause. Well, anyway, what did you do yesterday? Did Angela come over? Her daughter, the person-in-charge.

Oh, Angela! Contemptuous dismissal. She's so bossy!

Maggie laughed. Acknowledgment. It's true. Yes, but, you know, what would you do without her, Dee. And she's doing it all for your own good. How prissy does that sound. Dee, I was so touched, she told me it was a privilege.

Dee was watching Riggs, who was taking a time-out under the maple. What would I do without *him*?

Riggs now came loping — this time snatching the ball up on the run, like an outfielder — and crouched on the deck in front of Maggie. He kept nudging the ball with his nose, ever closer to her feet, while trying to catch her eye.

So what *did* you do yesterday?

Yesterday? She draws a blank. Then, Riggs has a problem. I need to take him to the vet.

Again? What is it now? He looks fine to me.

Well, look at his teeth! His bottom teeth? They've pulled all of them out, except those two on the sides that are sticking up. The others are just stumps!

Dee! That's the way dogs' mouths are supposed to be, you know?

Really?

Well, yeah. Those are called canine teeth, or something. Maggie pulled Riggs close to her chest and began to scrub his furry black back, just above his tail. Riggs smiled a closed-mouth smile and stood there, waggling his rear end, lifting one foot and then the other, like a Sioux Indian doing a war dance. I think he's perfect, Dee. And he's so smart. And he loves you so much.

It's mutual, Mag. Dee laughed. You heard about the night I went down the dirt road below the house? They captured the house, not this house, the other house . . . She trailed off. You heard?

Um-hum. Maggie stared at Dee. That was two weeks ago, when she ran away, but what other house? Where did that come from?

How did you hear? Suspicious.

You told me. You called me, Dee. You were very frightened. That's why you ran away, before I could get there. It wasn't a very good idea, Dee. Scared us all to death.

It was fun.

It wasn't fun at the time, if you recall. Which, of course, she didn't.

There were those dreadful men in the kitchen . . .

No, Dee, there were no men in the kitchen.

No men?

No, Dee. You were having one of your, your — what I call "your spells."

I had the dog with me. And the other dog.

What other dog?

I don't think I had the cat . . .

You mean Ophelia? Ophelia had been dead for years.

I never can remember names.

Do you remember how you got home?

That really nice lady down in that big house, down in the canyon? You know, what's-her-face? She got a policeman to take us home. He was really nice, too. The road was so full of rocks and holes. It was dark.

And you were barefoot, Dee. So you couldn't go back that way. Please, please, don't do that again?

Why? It was fun.

It makes us worry, Dee. Don't you love us?

I'll always love you.

They sat in silence for a while. Riggs had ambled through the sunshine down to the pool, to sit on its top step and soak his paws and other underpinnings in the cool water, which glistened like Schweppes around his half-submerged body.

I *am* dying, you know.

This time Maggie nodded and took one of Dee's hands in both of hers. It's the pits, isn't it?

Maggie couldn't stand it when Dee's face would crumple and her eyes moisten. Just couldn't stand it. Let's talk about the Good Old Days, Dee. Do you remember . . .

Dee laughed. Of course, I always remember the old times. It's just the new ones . . .

Remember the time the poodles got away from us? When we were up at the coast? I don't know if my Eliot or your Emily was the ringleader, but I'll never forget the image of those two jet-black dogs, way off in the distance, etched against the skyline, merrily chasing that little herd of cows — chasing them along the cliff's edge, remember? — toward that huge drop-off to the sea below. Egad, Dee, and we screamed and shouted, but the wind carried our voices away, and we ran and ran toward them . . .

Dee was laughing with delight.

. . . and our frantic shouts — Eliot, Emily, come! — reached them just in time to call them off!

Why did we call them that, I wonder?

Don't you remember? I named Eliot after T.S. Eliot — instead of Hopkins, after the poet Gerard Manley Hopkins — because you said Hopkins sounded like a butler. And when I named him Eliot, you said, "Now he sounds like a chauffeur!" Sheesh. And your Emily, of course, was Emily Dickinson.

I never could remember names.

Tell me! And remember the time . . . And on Maggie went, calling up image after image from bygone years. Maggie looked at Dee, who was nodding and smiling and chuckling and laughing. *Did* she remember? Or was she pretending? In any case, those times were gone, gone, bygone. Looking at Dee, so dear, so near, and yet so far, Maggie felt her heart drop in her chest, and for a moment she found it hard to breathe.

And then Dee and Riggs sat, a sweet twosome, looking out, over the lawn, down to the dark pool in its woodsy setting. And Maggie sat beside them. There was no future. Very little present. And a diminishing past. What was there left?

What was there left — but to laugh?

Maggie reached into her own mind's literary store. And there was Christopher Fry's *The Lady's Not for Burning*. And there was the rebel Thomas Mendip and the Lady, alone together in the year 1400, seeing no future for themselves at all — he about to be hanged, she about to be burned at the stake.

And Thomas said, and Maggie now echoed, "For God's sake, shall we laugh? . . . Since laughter is surely the surest touch of genius in all creation."

‡ ‡ ‡

Scattered Filings

A MEMOIR
2007

"Will you miss him very much?" Her voice was soft, tender. It tore the heart right out of my chest.

Thus it was that my 14-year-old daughter murmured into the phone, from miles and miles away, with an empathy that invaded my whole being. I was off in the countryside for the weekend; she and her brother were holding the fort at our home.

They had received a phone call bearing the news that my ex-husband, her father, had succumbed at last to brain cancer. It was ironic, as he was a philosophy professor, that he should be struck in the mind.

"Will you miss him very much?" Her innocence reached out and touched the buried part of me that was *my* innocence. That someone was there to share this feeling astonished me into the knowledge of it. And that moment has hung on in memory through the many passing decades.

Though we had been divorced some 10 years earlier, with enough bitterness and anguish to scar hard, she knew, from the time she was three, only that we were not together any more. She had a large, framed photograph of him on her desk, which over the years kept him alive and current for her. I was glad of this, because why should she totally lose her father?

But to know why this particular moment was one that affected me so, afflicted me so, you need to know that it brought up, like an inrushing tide, a freight of chaotic debris.

Such a moment is beyond difficult to think about, as any divorced person with children would know. There is debilitating guilt, there is simmering regret, there is self-justification and self-condemnation, and, more than all of these, there is a sense of betrayal — not only by one's one-time mate but also by one's own dreams.

So a moment like this is a magnet for all the scattered filings, buried deep. It pulls them from wherever they lurk and assembles them in one overwhelming mass of meaning.

Will I miss him very much? "Yes, oh, yes." I did and I do. I miss the only other person in the world to have lived what the two of us lived — the tiny triumphs, the huge hurdles, the vivid trifles of the day-to-day — the glory years of building a life and raising a family together.

I had forgotten. But, yes, my darling daughter. He died more than 30 years ago. And, yes. I miss him very much.

It is somehow liberating, exhilarating even, to realize this now. My daughter opened my heart to me, and the truth that flowed in with her question has . . . well, has set me free.

Epilogue: Edwin died in 1973. This story was written in 2007. It is still true today.

‡ ‡ ‡

Rounded with a Sleep

A PERSONAL ESSAY
SEPTEMBER 2001

Introduction

At the time of these events, nearly half a lifetime ago, I was beset to distraction by the fear that with the passing of each generation, we are becoming less — as individuals and as a people. *Why*, I wanted to know, does our world change as it does? I mean, why in this *particular* way? That's what I wanted to know then and still want to know now. How is it possible — strive though we might, with all our will and our science, with all our technological prowess and our penchant for art and our thirst for survival and our passion for power — that our potential as fully formed human beings is ever more diminished, generation after generation?

And I wonder, too, whether others experience as I do the dreadful sense that we *personally* are less than our parents were. Are we handing our future over to brilliant machines? And if so, what will become of our children, and their children, and so on *ad infinitum*? What will they *be*?

Or is it just me? Perhaps my understanding of this new age is just plain deficient, and each new generation is brimming with wisdom and heart and soul in ways I can't grasp, being a product of a previous time? Well. I do hope so.

This is a story of two deaths and of changing times and of doctors . . .

:: :: ::

My father lay dying in a hospital bed, succumbing at last to the multitude of ills the aging Scot was heir to. As a young man, he had survived the long sea voyage from Scotland to Canada, whence he had enlisted to fight in the Great War. He had survived the journey back across the ocean to the battlefield horrors of that "war to end war." He had survived mustard gas in the trenches of France. He had survived the return trip to the new world. He had survived a subsequent trek to Santa Barbara, California, while still young, to make his living. He had survived losing his savings in the Great Depression — and then afterwards built for his family a small fortune.

And now here he lay quietly, half-dozing, in the early evening. My mother sat in a chair at his bedside, reading by the light of a small lamp in the dimmed-down hospital room. The strident, intrusive cacophony of the day was muted now to an almost subliminal purr, a distant rumble from the vast machinery that kept afloat the busy hospital and its inhabitants.

Or so I imagined it when I called.

"How's Daddy?"

"Resting. Would you like to talk to him? Here he is."

"Ah, hello, daughter." That warm, burred, Scottish voice of his came with incredible intimacy into my ear, across phone lines stretching for hundreds of miles. Its timbre was somewhat rough, somewhat breathless from his emphysema, which had finally caught up with him — that and his ulcers and a dozen other ailments that his warring medicines were unsuccessfully addressing. How was I doing, he wanted to know, how were the kids. We chatted briefly, but his fatigue was patent, so I forced a cheery goodbye.

My father died later that night. In the evening, shortly after my call, his doctor, checking on his patients one last time for the day, found him responsive, apparently lucid, grateful for the doctor's attentiveness.

But by then, my mother later related, my father had entered that realm where free-ranging thoughts rearrange themselves to frame a lifetime. The heartbeat and thrum of the hospital became transformed for my father into a numinous vision, more real than a metaphor, as he confided to my mother his deep appreciation for that busy man's courtesy to his passengers, for his graciousness in pursuit of his many duties — as the captain of the ship that was carrying my father back to his homeland, to Scotland.

:: :: ::

The memorial service for my father was held at our small but elegant Episcopal church, which my father thought of as Anglican. "You can't go far wrong with the Church of England," he would say — not that he ever attended a service.

There was heather on his coffin. A piper in full Scottish regalia piped him off with a rendering of the stirring, majestic "Scotland, the Brave," which echoed beautifully in the jewel-like "wee kirk."

Friends and family and business associates filled the church. At the very back sat a woman alone, in a heavy black veil. Nobody knew who she was, it seemed, though I have a strong suspicion that my mother knew.

Afterward, at home, everyone gone after the long day, my sister, our very tired mother, and I sat around the kitchen table, sipping nightcaps, reminiscing, swapping stories about my father. Laughing. Crying.

:: :: ::

He used to tell us bedtime stories, bloody and violent, as befitted his heritage — such as a story we thought he had made up, about a great but not good nobleman named Macbeth and a wonderful hero named Macduff. Oh, we shivered to hear about how the great Birnam Wood came to Dunsinane and destroyed the wretched Macbeth.

He would sometimes pick out show tunes on the piano, and he played romantic pieces like "The Barcarolle" on the violin, but he eschewed any song he considered a "dirge" — of which there were many.

He had a wee, Scottish sadistic streak, sad to say. At one time we had ducks, who paddled about in the fish pond in our back garden. My father would feed them little squares of bread soaked in his evening Cutty Sark, inviting us to laugh with him at the sight of their staggering. Those ducks learned to recognize the sound of his red Buick coupe coming up the gravel drive. They would scramble out of the pond and come tearing around the side of the house and down the garden path at a fast waddle to greet him. My mother was amused by these shenanigans, in spite of her disapproval.

In the early days of their marriage, toward the end of the Roaring Twenties, our large, rambling adobe house, perfect for parties, would fill with doctors and attorneys and businessfolk, who danced furious tangos till dawn and foxtrots to tunes like "Bye, Bye, Blackbird." I, in my party dress, was allowed to pass platters of hors d'oeuvres and be made much of, before being sent off to bed at the far end of the house.

There were also beach parties and barbecues, my father carrying me on his back into and over the enormous waves, and mad races home afterward with friends in their Chevys and Buicks and Fords, carrying us hollering children in rumble seats, largely evading the occasional police officer on patrol.

But then came the Crash of '29, and the glory days were over. My father lost everything, everything except the house, and the long climb back was propelled by his fear of losing that as well. By the time the next World War came and went, my father had become a serious investor. His fear was gone. But so was his youth.

It turned out, as my mother discovered on arranging his papers, that he had deceived her about his age all those years, having shaved off an extra 10 years beyond the five-year discrepancy in their ages that he'd admitted to.

"Your father was quite a guy," my mother said, shaking her head in a sort of wonderment. It seemed a conclusion many years in the making.

And so we closed the evening and, for the time being, the sorrow.

:: :: ::

When it came my mother's turn to die, some 11 years later, she chose to do so at home, in her own bed. The process lasted about a month. Our fond recollection of the role the medical profession had played in our father's dying — supportive, attentive, caring — did not prepare us for the very different climate that prevailed a decade-plus later; it did, in fact, cruelly belie the new reality.

In recent years, every bone in my slender mother's spine had been crushed from osteoporosis, some more than once, and both hips had given way. Oddly, when her second hip snapped and she fell down the stairs, the surgeon who came out to talk with us after pinning it back up had cheerfully remarked, "Your mother doesn't have osteoporosis; her bones are very strong. I should know, I've just drilled through them!" The surge of hope this extraordinary pronouncement engendered, against all reason, was quickly dispelled by the continued deterioration of her spine. She had probably crushed more bones in her spine when she fell, but, recuperating in the hospital from the hip fracture, she was required to sit in the hall for long periods, by nurses under various doctors' orders, none of whom seemed to understand that sitting was impossible for her without excruciating pain. The medicines she was given resulted in a complete change in her personality; in her powerlessness, my well-mannered mother actually stuck out her tongue at a therapist who tried to get her to stand.

I think it was then that she made her decision. This is a guess, because she didn't ever discuss "it." However, on learning that her family doctor — for whom she felt great fondness, in whom she had placed her faith and her trust when my father lay dying — would be away on vacation for a month, her cryptic remark was, "Ah, he'll miss it, then."

Lying in her bed at home, her small, trim form grew more skeletal by the day. Yes, her broad, trademark smile was still at the ready for anyone who came into the room, and her wit was as quick as always. But she soon became unable to hold a book. For a person of her erudition, this, one might have thought, would have been a disaster. But her rich mental life had sustained her through her many confinements. Her knowledge of languages included French, German, Latin, and a little Greek, and she had been recently studying Russian, at age 80. English history was a passion for her, and she could rattle off the succession of British monarchs with a flick of her mind. I think she must have had a photographic memory. Propped up on pillows, recuperating from one or another of her frequent spinal breaks, she would play Trivial Pursuit with her grandchildren and would always beat everyone, popping up with facts like who played shortstop for the Red Sox in 1954.

Now, she confided, she could read her favorite books in her head, scanning the pages as she mentally turned them. These were often long and intricate turn-of-the-century novels that she had loved in her youth and had then read aloud to us when we were young and off enjoying a family picnic somewhere.

And now we watched her cope, as she had always coped, as mothers everywhere cope, with the task at hand.

My mother was a strong-minded woman. Men throughout her life found her intriguing, if also somewhat intimidating. She had once inspired in my husband a deeply unsettling dream, in which she had — to describe it as he did — put clothespins in his balls.

She had a particular fondness for certain kinds of men, men she could respect. These were men, of whatever calling, who were good at what they did. Like doctors. (She herself, as she would tell us, would have been a doctor if she had been a man.) Like auto mechanics. And like gardeners. I was never quite sure whether this special category included my father. She did, it is true, often recount for us children the Hans Christian Andersen fable about the old woman who, no matter what folly her husband might be engaged in, would say, "The old man is always right." And of course in the story that turned out to be the case.

My children loved to visit her. She was quite strict with them. About meals. And bedtime. And manners. I think they found this a refreshing challenge. She also made good things happen, when they were earned.

And now, helplessly, we watched. She took very little sustenance. Her tummy sat on her small, reclining frame like a beach ball. Nurses came from the hospital to deal with this, and one evening a doctor, one we did not know, came. He asked if she would like to be in the hospital. For what purpose, she wanted to know. Upon learning that she could be fed intravenously there, she politely declined. I saw the doctor out and down the garden path to his car.

"When will Dr. Haskell be back from vacation?" I asked.

"Oh, he came back a week ago," was the jaunty reply.

But, but . . . but why had he not come to see her? It would have meant so very much to her. Surely he knew? Was it possible he didn't care? Was it possible he cared too much? It seemed a profound betrayal.

Friends came. Her grandchildren came. A minister who was also a dear family friend came. For everyone, she had her bright smile.

She began slipping in and out of consciousness, but her mind never wandered.

The night before the day she died, she woke at 2:00 in the morning, wanting to dictate a note. Here is what the note said:

> "To all of you who have been so good to me and kind in these last few days, I thank you one and all."

:: :: ::

Now, my many years surpass those of my mother at the time of her death. I think about my mother, who had wanted to be a doctor. I think about my daughter, who is a doctor. My daughter became a doctor because, even in her teens, she could see that life is not complete without death and that doctors, as dedicated as they are to preserving life, as certain as they are that death is the enemy, need to be equally certain in the knowledge that their presence at the time of death is . . . vital. And I think about that inspired line in *The Tempest*: "We are such stuff as dreams are made on, and our little life is rounded with a sleep."

Now, as my daughter's youthful idealism has ripened to the wisdom of a seasoned doctor, I struggle still with the loss, not just the personal one, but the loss to the world at large of the grace, the nobility, the courage that stamped the lives of my parents' generation. And yet, the outrage I felt at her beloved doctor's long-ago perceived betrayal has continued to press for a revisiting, a reconsidering. In particular, I feel a nagging guilt about ignoring one small incident that occurred during my mother's last sojourn in the hospital, an incident that, I have come to realize, changes everything. It was an occurrence so tender, so poignant, and so intimate that I feel an intruder even now in recounting it. Yet my mother's eyes glistened, and her smile was fringed with delight, when she told me of it shortly before her death.

One evening, her doctor had entered the dimly lit hospital room, much as he had on the evening of my father's death, making one last visit to her bedside before his departure on vacation. It was warm, and the covers had slipped from her slender legs. Noticing that her toenails had grown long and untended, he proceeded — with great care, but with the casualness afforded an everyday event — to trim her nails himself. My mother took this compassionate gesture as an expression of his abiding affection for her. And I have come to understand that whether she was right or wrong, she was right. She had the truth of it.

:: :: ::

This is the thing about doctors today, as I have learned from my own daughter. This is what she told me. When they come, all starry-eyed, most of them, into the profession, they do so because they care so much about people that they want to dedicate their lives to making a difference.

But as the reality of medical practice in these times strikes home, the demands, the distractions, the chronic fatigue, the mountain of details attending each day's activities, become almost overwhelming. Choices must be made. The impulse to visit a dying patient one more time must be suppressed. They know that their visit means much to the patient and the family, that this dying, for these people, comes only once; but they also know that they, as doctors, experience dyings again and again and yet again. Because of these wildly differing perspectives, perhaps they are not aware that just five minutes of their time can make an eternal difference to the patient. Or perhaps they are aware and must somehow juggle that knowledge with a judgment call: can I, should I, make the effort to fulfill one more need? There are so many patients, so many critical moments, so many things to do, some of them mundane, some meaningful, it is hard to weigh the impact of making even one extra phone call — of sympathy, of support — hard to feel that making that small gesture of humanity is worth it.

So said my daughter, and I do understand that though there are doctors who easily write off the dying patient, there are those who, like my daughter, wish to make their grandmothers proud. They are not to blame. They are a mirror of our times. And, after all is said and done, the good that they do far outweighs the good that they simply can't embrace — and in our imperfect world, this is much.

‡ ‡ ‡

When I Was Small

When I was small, I thought
love happened in bathrooms,
being concerned with that portion
of the anatomy.

It seems to me I gave
no thought at all
to some day being grown
and married and
having a family.

And when a mystifying
wound left scars,
I thought about my place
among the stars.

What occupied me then
was the quick ring of seeing
with the heart
that time and space are
intimately close.

Was I inspirited, do you suppose?
And did you think these things, then, too?

And did it happen, then, to you
that the fierce brilliance of the stars at night,
the radiance of birds in flight,
and glistening seas, climactic clouds,
all promised in time's fullness, peace?

‡ ‡ ‡

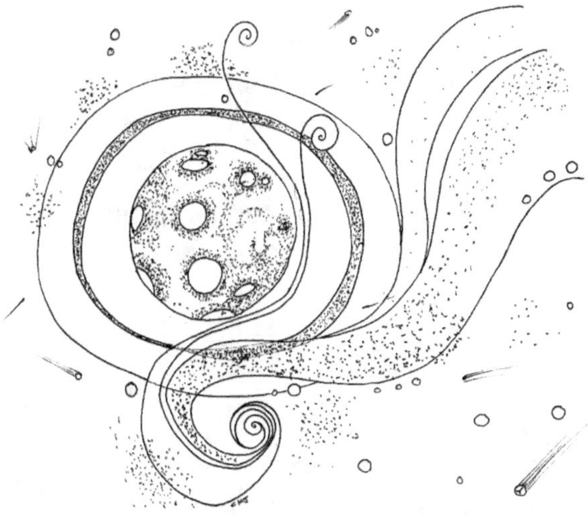

A Song of Us

You coming toward me,
the leap in the heart,
the loin.
You coming to me,
and the fine, grateful tears.
Ours.

You, going from me.
The careful closing of doors,
the unsung years.
You, gone.
And the final echoing tears.
Mine. Yours.

‡ ‡ ‡

Prayer

My only god, my analyst, my own
True love, to whom all desires are known,
From whom no secrets are hid,
Bone of my bone, o, id of my id:
Take each in their time the song and the sob.
Keep in your time tap of toe and the heart's throb.

‡ ‡ ‡

The Wind Stirs

The wind stirs in the arms
Of the tree and whispers:
There is nothing
I would not say to you.

‡ ‡ ‡

Eros and Agape
CIRCA 1959

Love forms like clouds,
Vast, white, turbulent,
Scattered overnight
By a cold wind.

And love is knit
In the warp of the black soil,
Grows in the root of the pine,
Flows to the tip of the tender needle,
Traces its joy in a peaceful sky.

‡ ‡ ‡

Yes

It was there at the moment of meeting,
The muted form of the coming moon,
Cupped in trust in the new moon's hands,
Our souls' whole embrace in shadow dwelling,
Nascent love tendering
Hushed tribute to an old god.

Let us let, my darling, without fear,
The god assume her, and her dark fullness disappear
In the brilliance of the crescent's swelling.
For if Apollo grant that consummating grace,
Would she presume to hinder the sun's gliding,
Biding his time, across her face?

‡ ‡ ‡

Love Woes

I have laughed in the sun
and burned,
cackled and crackled.

Loved I was,
and spurned,
hugged and shrugged.

And when I learned
that joy was only
love and laughter joined,
they both were gone.

Purloined. Sirloined.

‡ ‡ ‡

To the Sun

In the passing of a minute
I have learned there is no hell.
The human soul could not endure
This, through eternity.
Leave me, and leave me no span to spell
In horrible-peopled aloneness
Where ghosts of our almost-selves
Loom and mock. We have lived too long
This time, gone too far into nights
Not meant to be lit.

Oh, Sun, set! Let another doomed day die.
Day, unclock it. Or I am undone.

‡ ‡ ‡

Moth and Flame

Then must we end this brutal game
And feel its fury just the same?
And must I take the total blame?
Who is the moth and who the flame?

‡ ‡ ‡

The Logic of the Web

Rare in recklessness, the fleshed creature
Appears, wholly exposed. In air, expanding
Circles emanate, as from a dropped-in-water
Rock, defining her limits. She floats,
Nearly free in time, suspended by a few
Uncertain threads from solid points
Beyond her own invented realm.
Angled ladders of her personality
Convey the creature's heart.

Here, at the core,
Shiny clear, darkly obscure,
The void itself lingers and
Shimmers in the sun, awaiting consummation
With whatever eager sacrifice Eros,
Who unites, too, the moth and the flame,
Shall fling into the meshes of her dreams.

‡ ‡ ‡

When You Speak

When you speak
Let it be all.
Your hard pain,
Your hate hiss, or
Your whispered prayer
To bless your love,
Your fair, your bliss-mate.
Whichever breaks —
Your instant yes, your no —
Let it be all.

So brief the spring,
So dear the loan,
So dead on the winter bough
The bud unblown,
This bubble world
So pressed in its pall
Our only own.
Nor guard, nor hide, nor save,
Nor qualify:
Let it be all.

‡ ‡ ‡

My Friend

Why, not how, do I love her? She
continues to amaze.
Her moods of night, her buoyant days,
to name a few. The way she plays.
She dotes on cats
and that's a clue.

She bolts from spats —
three strikes and she's Out.
Her will is such that there's no doubt
what she's about.
She'll share her zest.
And when in jest
she's at her best.

She frightens fast — a bee, a bat,
a hint of doom, will send her
scampering from the room.
As thick as tar, her gloom.
Her smile, the welcome of a daisy's bloom.

She walks on paws, at once is here
and there. Her sorrows are
her own; she doesn't bare.
And yet she lets you know
that she does care.

She's very vain. And squeaky clean
beyond belief. She'll claim she doesn't preen.
She'll scrub and wash and fluff
her hair and mousse it to enhance the sheen.

Sleek, not flabby; chic, not shabby —
she's no tabby, she's too fancy.
Loving her is ever chancy.
She's entrancing. My friend Nancy.

‡ ‡ ‡

PART IV

Being and Belonging: Out of Joint?

Hail to Thee, Once Blithe Spirit 110
Heavens to Betsy 117
Midnight Reflections 119
A Paradoxical Conversation 121
Winning 125
Chronicle 126
Door to Door 127
The New God 129
Punditry 130
The Great Society 132
And God Said 133
Fireworks 134
Through a Glass, Darkly 135

IDLE THOUGHTS

Life is a battle and a sojourning.

—Marcus Aurelius

Hail to Thee, Once Blithe Spirit

A PERSONAL ESSAY
1998

It is embarrassing to admit it now, but I could not, at the beginning, take Tom Kelly seriously — because he did not wear socks. Even with dress shoes, when he took me out for a steak dinner on Sunday evenings, his slim ankles shone white and bare. He was mild-mannered, soft-spoken, and usually gently smiling. He was lanky, fair, and graceful in his body. He was, everyone said, "a nutcase."

He had come back from the war — not the Great War or the Vietnam War or the Korean War or the Gulf War, but World War II — sooner than the other vets to this small liberal arts college in the Pacific Northwest. He had been left alone too long in the frozen wastes of the Aleutian Islands; the Army had forgotten he was there. By the time he came out, something had snapped.

Like other students, Tom Kelly took courses. But unlike them, he elected to take certain courses, like Humanities, again and again. He enjoyed them, he said. He read a lot, but when he wrote papers he made up his own references — footnotes, dates, titles, authors, publishers, and all. He knew the professors expected a bibliography, so he gave them one — though his writings were his own, so what was the point? One would think this shook up the professors a good deal.

The students loved him. He was a breath of fresh air amid the mustiness of their thinking. He came as a delicious shock, like the shock of poetry, with the incongruity of his take on everything.

Tom, however, was one among many idiosyncratic, shall we say, Reed College students. Perhaps some enlightened soul in the Admissions Office picked them for that very reason — as long as they also evidenced a flash of brilliance.

Student contempt for authority in those days — even in this small school as generous-spirited as a favorite uncle — occasionally took the form of physical pranks, such as "liberating" a dead and desiccated cat from the biology lab and leaving the stiff, flat body concealed in the library stacks to develop its putrid potential. Standard student fare in many colleges, I suppose.

More often, the gauntlet flung was a verbal one, and pretty mild at that. The Registrar was a frequent butt of such antics. It was college policy not to divulge student grades, in order to encourage the pursuit of learning for its own sake. Nevertheless, because most students went on to graduate school, grades were maintained in the Office of the Registrar. The Registrar herself was an austere, full-chested, forbidding sort of a woman, who, unaccountably, blushed easily. She would send out admonitory notes on small memo sheets inscribed at the top "From the Desk of Margaret Scott." This habit of hers prompted the circulation of a bit of campus doggerel that ran:

My name is Margaret Scott.
I'm a keeper of records and rot.
If you're making an issue
I'll give you Scott's tissue
That's not worth a tittle or jot.

Most of this was pretty small stuff, as you can see. Probably you can more than match it with your own college tales.

There was also the singing of bawdy songs, lustily delivered in the dining room after dinner. A parody of the Canadian national anthem, for example, went something like "In days of yore, / From Eden's shore, / Eve, the dauntless harlot, came, / And planted firm / Sir Adam's sperm . . ." and so forth; the chorus was "The fig leaf forever! / Hurrah, boys, hurrah!"

This campus version of *The Maple Leaf Forever* was penned by a charming boy named Sandy, who chose to believe that he was living in the 18th century. He wore a jabot at his throat and buckles on his shoes and, on dress occasions, a wide, black ribbon at the back of his head and a red one slashing across his gray-sweatered chest. He dated all his papers 1746, or the like, and wrote his senior thesis with a quill pen. He had lovely, gracious manners.

Sandy put tacks in the felt stops of the old upright piano in his dorm, so that it sounded like a harpsichord when he pounded out "Rule, Britannia" or coaxed out Handel's "Where'er You Walk." He also had a small, round cannon in his room. He would fire it out his window at the height of bachelor parties celebrating the birthday of Thomas Jefferson or Dolly Madison or whomever. When he escorted me to college dances, we could dance only the minuet — after he'd placed a record in the jukebox while the band was taking a break. Needless to say, we would be the only couple on the floor. My joy was great when he discovered that a rustic form of the waltz had been introduced toward the end of the 18th century.

Reed College had many oddballs. Some might say misfits. There was, as another example, the Jewish boy who could be spied perched on a ledge, high atop a four-story student dorm, meditating for hours while wearing a loincloth, often in the lotus position or sometimes standing on his head. Everyone called him the Yogi. I did not personally know the Yogi; he never came down, in my recollection. When his friends told me that the Yogi had an erection while meditating, I thought they meant that he levitated.

The Yogi was not the only one to brave the heights. We girls had our own way of expressing our individuality. (We didn't think of ourselves as women then, because most of us weren't.)

If you lived, as I did for a time, on the top floor of the freshman girls' dorm, you would not be surprised when, in the dead of night, a tiptoeing parade of girls would cross your bedroom with whispered apologies and creep out of your window onto a narrow stone ledge. They would sidle carefully along this ledge and then wriggle through the mullioned window of a bedroom in the sophomore dorm, which was adjoined by a stone bridge over a sally port, there to engage in revelries for hours. The pedestrian approach, so to speak, would have been to traipse down many flights of stairs in one's pajamas, then head through the sally port and up another endless set of stairs. Well, who would have chosen that alternative?

Of course I joined the parade; how could I not. Once settled in a circle on the floor, we would take turns reading aloud, often regaling each other with the adventures of Winnie-the-Pooh. Our giddy giggling at the antics of Piglet, the trials of Kanga, the adorableness of little Roo, provided a nice counterbalance to our classroom struggles with Homer's "rosy-fingered dawn" and the fall of the Roman Empire. So did *The Wind in the Willows*. As you can see from our escape to childhood comforts, we were far from being adult women, at least in those carefree, regressive hours.

Some in the community at large considered Reed students to be radicals in "a hotbed of communism." Though we thought of ourselves as daring, it was never clear where this notion came from, exactly, because our escapades were really all so tame.

Laughter, and the frivolity of our youth, were magic shields. Hamlet's slings and arrows did not touch us. We knew, you see, that *we* would go on to real lives in the real world.

And so we did not wonder what would become of Tom Kelly.

An amateur tennis champion before the war, Tom would take me to the courts on late Saturday afternoons. Rallying gloriously with him, on and on into the deepening dusk, endorphins blazing,

I could do no wrong, because he never tired and never failed to return my ball with that easy stroke of his. I found this a very good way to be with Tom.

We students were always in love in those unencumbered days. I found time for everyone. Various serious boys during classroom hours. An intense poet in the coffee shop in the afternoons. A handsome, beer-drinking chum in the evenings — the swing shift, as I thought of it. And my sturdy roommate for the graveyard shift. But Sunday evenings were for Tom Kelly.

Every Sunday evening, he would come to collect me at the dorm, dress shoes gleaming, and off we would go, by bus, for the steak dinner. I felt uncomfortably guilty about this, in view of my feelings about his also gleaming ankles. But I quashed those feelings because the college dining room did not serve meals on Sunday evenings and because I loved steak and because I could never afford it on my own. I wondered, though, if he could. I wondered what he gave up, to spend money that way.

He didn't seem to *want* anything from me, beyond my company and my appreciation of the meal. This shook up my notions of boy-girl relationships. Were it not for the guilt, it would have been liberating, if not exhilarating.

He would talk to me about what it was like to be him. About the dreadful loneliness of being forgotten for months in the white snow and the cold. And about his youthful, prewar desire to just play tennis. By the time the United States Army finally realized that this soldier was all alone manning a base in the frozen wastes of an Aleutian island, Tom's mind had been sabotaged.

Nowadays, to be in his head was to be able to sit on the ground for uncharted periods, engrossed in the movement of an ant across the pavement, and to know that this experience of time was as valid, as real as any other. He shook up my idea of what "consciousness" is all about.

Tom Kelly's was hardly the dogmatic academician's definition of the life of the mind. Like justice, the established order is blind to individuation. So of course he found congenial the Reed College, somewhat laissez-faire approach to learning.

I began to see dimly in Tom the rarity of the person who is to such an extent original — uncontaminated, unstructured by abstractions telling us how to think, how to behave, what is important, what is to be valued. He didn't give a damn about degrees. Or standards. Or careers. Thoughts of these things didn't even enter his mind.

One night, an incident occurred. Tom Kelly was arrested in front of the college campus. He was out there in the middle of the quiet, tree-lined street reading a poem by Shelley in the light of the full moon. Not that bizarre, you might think. But the police force undoubtedly shared the prevailing public viewpoint that Reed College was a hotbed of free love, of free thinking, of communism.

So the cruising cops, ever vigilant, decided . . . I don't know . . . that this student was probably reading *The Communist Manifesto* and was probably drunk and dangerous, too. They trundled him down to the station, where he was queried for some hours. Then they threw Tom, gentle Tom, who never drank a drop, into the drunk tank. They released him the next morning, deciding he was by then sober and probably harmless.

The next night, beyond the massive shade trees that fringed the campus, a hundred students gathered to stand in the moonlight reading the poetry of Percy Bysshe Shelley. Of course, someone tipped off the press and they had a field day. Headlines. KELLY READS SHELLEY BY MOONLIGHT: Reed Students Out in Numbers to Protest Arrest. Photos of a large knot of motley students, open books in hand. Photos of Tom, solo. Editorials, now promoting a large community laugh at the expense of the philistine police force. Along with everyone else on campus, students unaccustomed to being presented to the public in a favorable light, I applauded Tom as a hero.

A few nights later, my beer-drinking buddy and I were trudging home from the neighborhood pub. Instead of illegally cutting across the golf course, as was our custom, on an impulse we illegally thumbed down a passing car, hoping for a lift to campus. Dismayed, we watched a squad car pull up beside us. One of the two cops in it leaned over and opened the door to the back seat and motioned us inside. Our feelings are easy to imagine. Anticipation of profound embarrassment was perhaps the dominant one, combined with the customary undergraduate fear and loathing of such authorities. Imagine, then, our equally profound relief, when, rather than being carted "downtown," we found ourselves deposited at the entrance to the campus. In the moonlight. "This is for Tom Kelly," said the cops as they drove off, chuckling. It was a shock to find that cops had soul. So we, too, were startled into a new view.

Sometime after all this, Tom Kelly disappeared from Reed. It is only now as I write that I am moved to wonder why. And where did he go? How did the world, this world of ours more virtual than real, encompass such a man? Where are you, Tom, dear Tom?

We all have our little rebellions. And we all have our mind-joggling insights. Books, or paintings, or music, or movies, or perhaps drugs can do this for us — shift our perspective in hard and novel ways. And we love them for it. Perhaps we all have our Tom Kellys. Perhaps we have even learned to treasure that rare person whose whole being, like Tom's, embodies his singleness. But who among us can say we have had the courage, even once, to free our minds of all conventional thought and find, at a deeper level, who we really are?

‡ ‡ ‡

Heavens to Betsy

A STORY IN TWO SENTENCES
APRIL 2000

Betsy heard the short rap at the door, the slightly self-conscious buzz of the bell — expected and yet so unexpected — but, startled though she was, and even thrilled, she did not rush to open, not wishing to appear too eager, and also, having just climbed out of bed, feeling totally unprepared — physically, that is — for a significant encounter, important though it was not to keep the poor soul waiting, not waiting too long anyway, just because of her own vanity, which required and insisted that she at least comb her hair, yes, and of course brush her teeth — oh, dear, there it went again — and perhaps she should pull on something halfway decent because, well, because she really did not know the person all that well and did not, heaven knows, want to occasion a heart attack with the sight of her bare body, when at last she would fling the door open with a glad cry. Ta-da.

Don't be giddy, she told herself, and giggled as she flew about the apartment, straightening this, fluffing that, and, in spite of the acknowledged need for speed, not being able to resist a furtive peep through the little spy-hole in the door to confirm (as it jolly well did!) that her visitor was indeed the one she had wished for and (yes, it is important to face it) half-dreaded — though dreaded is perhaps not the *mot propre*, when, really, what she felt was fear of her own possible inadequacy, her own inability to rise to the challenge of such a . . . what was the word . . . such a heaven-sent opportunity to reconnect to the outside world, to connect, after all that had happened, with a fellow creature, with a person who could conceivably come to love her and accept her adoration — which would not be clinging, never be clinging, *that* was not necessary, because what was really necessary was just to come alive again, to feel — oh, my Heavens, there's the bell again — whole.

‡ ‡ ‡

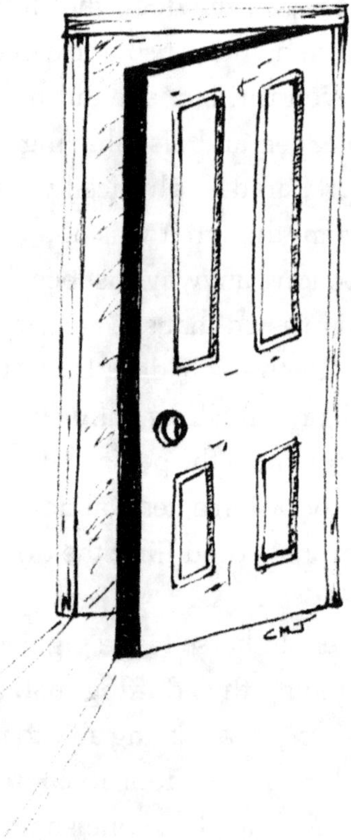

Midnight Reflections

A RUMINATION
SEPTEMBER 2005

These days, practically anything will make you cry. The level of emotion is already so high, like the floodwaters of New Orleans, of New Jersey, of Bangladesh, that it takes very little to lift it over the top. You'll be sitting watching the U.S. Tennis Open, say. Agassi or Federer or Serena or whoever wins a spectacular rally, and your eyes well up. Or you are watching Annika or Cristie Kerr or Juli Inkster make an incredible putt, and you find yourself crying out *yes*! During the ads, you peek at the news but steer away from the sob stories because the media are looting, exploiting, and polluting the genuine. And the genuine is too much to bear anyway.

How much of what you feel is the flooding up of your own dammed flotsam, your toxic chemicals, your inner runaway fires? And how much is the accumulated misery of the people of the globe? Is it your own flood tide bursting through, or is it that, being human, you must sop up through osmosis the floodwaters of humankind?

Whatever was Hamlet thinking of? How can you "take arms against a *sea* of troubles"? If Shakespeare had been to the gulf — either gulf in its time of terror — he would never have mixed that metaphor. And he's all mixed up between the sea of troubles and the slings and arrows of outrageous fortune. Well, so are we all, it seems. Eruption, corruption, overflow, overthrow . . .

Perhaps the television is a box filled with the collective unconscious. Perhaps it is like Pandora's box, whence all the evils of the world come spilling. Perhaps we should take arms against it.

Is all life a metaphor?

We see as through a glass darkly.

We grope toward the light.

‡ ‡ ‡

A Paradoxical Conversation

(Apologies to Zeno)

A PUZZLEMENT
CIRCA 1975

"I'll meet you halfway," he said.

"No way!" she said. And then, "Halfway to what?"

"Well, halfway to an agreement, a rapprochement."

"Oh," she said. "I dunno. Maybe if together we go halfway, see where we are, we can go the rest of the way. Together."

"Great," he said. "You start. Have a little more wine . . ."

"Me start? God, where to begin? Well, to begin with, there's your snoring . . ."

"Wait, wait, wait! We've been all through that. You know I can't help it. Why won't you wear earplugs?"

"Why won't you wear one of those nose-strip thingies — makes you stop breathing or something?"

"Oh, the hell with it. Why don't we just get twin beds!"

"Twin bedrooms would be better!"

"Shit."

"Are we there yet?"

"Where?"

"Halfway. To the rapprochement."

"Oh. Maybe. Let's go on. I'll go first this time. I'll be blunt: you spend too much time in the bathroom."

"After all these years, you choose this moment to tell me I spend too much time in the bathroom? Sometimes I wonder if you love me at all!"

"Wait, wait, wait. I don't mean that. Look — maybe we need separate bathrooms? We could move . . ."

"Separate bathrooms? Separate houses is better! God. How could we afford . . ."

"Yeah. Well. Moving right along, I figure if we were halfway there before, we're half of the last half by now. Pretty soon we'll be there. How's your wine?"

"Where?"

"All the way to the rapprochement."

"Oh. Okay. My turn?"

"Go for it."

"Okay. You may not want to hear this, but it really bugs me that all our friends like you better than they like me."

"Oh, come on!"

"No, no, I mean it. They do . . ."

"Well, you know. I'm just a likable kind of guy. I can be pretty entertaining. Fun to be with? You know? And I'll admit I'm always there for them in a pinch, naturally. But, really, they don't, you know, like me *best*. We're a team, after all."

"Really. I'll tell you what. Why don't we move on to a brand new set of friends, how's that?"

"For Chrissake, why don't we — one of us — move on to a brand new town!"

"Oh, dear. Are we halfway there, yet? This is hard."

"Sure. We must be making headway. We've only got half of the last quarter to get to the last half of the last quarter. Let's push on."

"Okay. You go."

"Well, honey. You know I always think you look terrific? But sometimes when we go out? I just feel as if your clothes are, well, a bit skimpy."

"Skimpy! I wear the latest in chic and you call it skimpy! God, you are antediluvian. You belong in a different era. Eon? Whatever."

"Eon, schmeon. Have some more wine."

"Honey, have you noticed that the closer we get, the farther away we are?"

"Yeah. And anyway, if each time we only go half of the rest of the way, we'll never get there anyway. Anyway."

"Let's go grab a pizza."

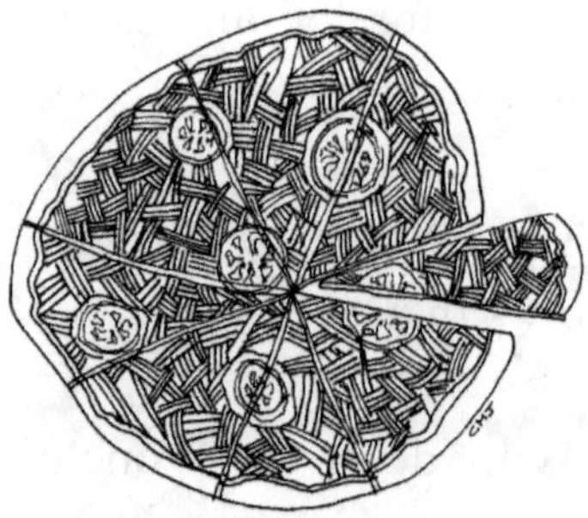

"You're on."

"We'll split it."

"We'll split it?"

"Yeah. We'll split it. Duh."

"Um. But HOW?"

‡ ‡ ‡

Winning

It was her turn, and she looked at the board with dismay;
He, for his part, was as secretly nervous as she.
Taking the plunge, she impulsively shoved at a pawn;
Heartened by this, he replied to the move with panache.
She, taking heart, whisked a knight through his dance-like routine.
Heartily bored, now he knew he would win in the end.
When it was done, she collapsed with heartfelt relief:
He, having won, would be lost in her winsome embrace.

‡ ‡ ‡

Chronicle

CIRCA 1955

Today the garbage can fell over. And all across the drive
were coffee grounds and cigarette butts and rotten cottage cheese
and bacon fat.

The dog peed on the bed
and I put the spread in the dryer
with the soap
instead of in the washing machine.
And it was my boss's birthday and I forgot.
And a wineglass fractured somehow on the kitchen floor . . .

But today is a day to dance on air.
The sun is everywhere and the treetops go on tiptoe.
And today I wrote a poem — today a poem.

‡ ‡ ‡

Door to Door

CIRCA 1964

Door bell rings. Quite jaunty,
Insistent. Who
At this afternoon
Dead-time?

How do you do —
Hand swings out like a boom.
Jaunty, insistent. I'm Margaret Smith
From England.

Eye refuses hand.
What do you want?

I want you
To vote for me in the
Savings Bond Contest.

No! — mumbling — not interested.
No need. No more magazines —
No.

Hand swings down. Mock shock.
Sullen back turns on flat heel.
Over defeated shoulder
Twisted mouth flings
revenge — I wouldn't want you
To vote for me, neither! — anyone
Who won't shake hands — flings
Despair.

Has touch,
Oh tongue, oh language
Come to this?

‡ ‡ ‡

The New God?

AUGUST 2005

For It walks with me,
And It talks with me,
And It tells me I'm not alone.
Oh, the joys we share
As we tarry there —
None other — my cellular phone.

‡ ‡ ‡

Punditry

The pundits who inform our days
Are challenged in so many ways
To keep abreast through every switch
Of who is who and which is which,
As if they knew. The latest craze
Is Slobodan Milosevic.

The foreign phrases they must spout
Whenever something new comes out,
They fold into their nightly pitch,
And never even drop a stitch,
As, oh, so gleefully, they flout
Their "Slobodan Milosevic."

They used to take a strange delight
In resonating every night
With Monica Lewinski, witch,
And Linda Tripp, that little snitch.
But now the sound they love to bite
Is "Slobodan Milosevic."

For you must know, it's no mean trick
To purge away "Milosevick,"
Enunciate without a glitch,
Without a blink, without a twitch,
The hallmark of their famous schtick,
Melodious "Milosevich."

Ah, Slobodan, what's in a name?
The surest way to instant fame.
You'll occupy this cozy niche,
Till some new Slav assumes a hitch,
And starts a fresh syllabic game,
You, Slobodan Milosevic.

‡ ‡ ‡

The Great Society

Between consenting more or less adults
War, murder, politics, rape, spite cults,
Business, and other interpersonal
Interactions are just results
Of human nature. Not quite chaste but
Not to waste a thought upon.

Only think
Of a brown-eyed or blue-eyed
Or black-eyed,
Dimpled or drawn,
Sniffling or smiling child
Looking on.

‡ ‡ ‡

And God Said

And God said, This is my Son,
Thinking, in faith, that we would draw
The line somewhere. Here.

And God said,
This is my Body, given for you
And for many, thinking, no doubt,
That this would be enough.

In every child another christ
Began. And every day another
Careless bomb turns to dust
More bodies of more sons.

And we plod
Obtusely on, razing children
To the rubble we call Man.

‡ ‡ ‡

Fireworks

They flare up like fireworks.
Wide-awake eyes are the flute-lively children,
Trumpeting drum-bright young men.
They signal a floodlight of joy
In the night. But who
Will account for their going?

They flare up like fireworks.
Showers of lights are their bomb-bitten bodies,
Firing drum-rolling men.
The silence that follows was made
With their music. But who
Will account for their going?

‡ ‡ ‡

Through a Glass, Darkly
(The Beauty Salon)

A PERSONAL ESSAY
2005

Act One. Outside the Salon.
Nobody comes here any more. None of my friends, I mean. They like to have their hair — what's left of it — trimmed and coiffed in a proper salon. With soft, golden-oldie-type music and a light, bright pastel decor. With a friendly, competent receptionist and a peaceful atmosphere. With customers who are women they know — or could know. At the ballet or the symphony or like that.

We all followed Carol from one fancy salon to another, though it was never quite clear why she left these places so suddenly. But when she set up on her own, in her own salon, everyone began to feel "not comfortable," as they put it, and drifted away. All except me. Somehow, I couldn't leave her . . .

I guess we're all pretty snobbish. Actually my friends are basically very kind and generous. They'd give their last dime to a bag lady — well, maybe not their *last* dime. And when it comes to your basic creature comforts, well . . .

But, I don't know. That's the thing. Carol is so *different*. I've never known anyone remotely like her. She has such esprit. I have to say, I like Carol a lot. Or perhaps it's that I admire her spunk?

Anyway, it's much more fun than the same old, same old. And, of course, she does do a terrific haircut. We've been intimate strangers for so long . . .

:: :: ::

So here I stand for my once-a-month "do." Stand in the street in front of Carol's shop at 10:00 in the morning, in a neighborhood not of her first choosing, but one she could afford — I mean, *way* downtown, across the street from the guys hanging out at the Amigos Market, next door to the pungency of the Thai Won On Bar and Grill, or whatever, amid various loiterers sidling along, eyeing me, eyeing my car, as I wait for her to show up, wait as always for Carol to show up 15 minutes late, minimum. Shall I put more money in the meter? Do I have any more quarters, damn it? I rummage in my coin purse. Golly, it's cold outside. I hug my chest.

Oh, but here she comes now, swinging along down the grimy street, tight jeans, really, really tight, low-cut blouse, short-heeled sandals — sandals! in this weather — long, "blonde" curls, all smiles.

:: :: ::

In the Chair.

I am sitting in the chair. I and the chair are enveloped to my chin in a boldly patterned black and white nylon sheet that has seen a lot of action. The salon is long and narrow, like a tunnel. Carol shows me enthusiastically how she's brightened the walls with the help of a painter friend. But it is a work in progress, and nothing quite comes together yet. In the dim recesses at the back, where no daylight penetrates, Carol and I have just been through the delicious, intimate experience of the hair-washing: warm, saturating water easing the tension out of my neck, her sensitive, strong fingers rummaging in my hair, gently massaging my scalp. "Ooh, Carol," I murmur, "that feels *so good*."

Now, I look in the mirror, pull at the sopping mess, as she stands back, scrutinizing. My hair. I'm lucky, I know. Naturally curly, crisp and gray, rather less of it than of yore, but still. All it really needs is a good cut, and Carol has the magic touch. "See, Carol," I whine, "this little wisp here, this one little bit that always sticks out? I'm so picky, I know." She searches about for her $300 scissors, her $200 dryer — where, oh, where does she get the money? — and scrabbles about in a chaotic drawer for a clean (I hope) comb. Rock music is providing a strong, penetrating beat somewhere in the back, and Carol's body sways a little as her feet tap out the rhythm. We settle down.

"Have you seen this picture of my boys?" The little photo gallery on her console displays four stunning young people. Beaming, she points to a snapshot of her two strapping twin boys, decked out in their high school football uniforms. "Shane has pulled his grades up, I'm so proud of him, he's not flunking out, getting mostly Cs and Ds now. And Jessie is the team's number-one running back. The paper ran a picture of him making this great catch." She reaches over and picks up the photo, stares lovingly at it for a moment. Carol's other two offspring are grown and mostly gone, now in their early 20s.

I say, "Carol, aren't you proud that they have come — that *you* have come — so far?" I look at the two grinning teenagers, their two older siblings. "Such a good-looking bunch, too," I add. I watch her in the mirror, as she stands behind me, trimming and shaping and coaxing the curls with her nimble fingers. She nods, clearly pleased and always upbeat about the upside potential of her life.

"We may have to move, though," she says.

"Oh, dear, why?" I begin, when the shop door is flung open, and in marches Liz, Carol's young business partner and co-stylist. Liz does not speak to me, does not appear to notice that Carol has a haircut going on, but engages her in an obscure round of gossip, as she sets up for a customer, who has entered the salon close on her tail.

"How about that scene last night!" Liz is saying. "Was that over the top, or what? Can you believe that guy?"

"Yeah," Carol says. "He had it coming." They laugh.

Liz is big, her voice and manner hearty. She doesn't wear leather, but it would suit her. Carol, on the other hand, is trim and composed, with a magnetic aura, a sizzling undercurrent that is just simply very sexy.

Now the two of them become embroiled in an animated discussion of tints and highlights and formulas and whatnot for the other customer, who sits in the chair next to mine and stares at herself in the mirror, obedient and quiet, clearly a longtime patron.

"Maybe a little more of the darker shades this time? You know? That new stuff we got?" Liz asks Carol.

I begin to grow irritated. Is my hair drying too fast? Will she have lost her place? Couldn't she, shouldn't she, concentrate on *me* and *my hair*? I sigh loudly and rudely and wiggle impatiently. Carol does not miss this and is at once back to work.

"The landlord doesn't like the dogs I got for my boys," she continues, as if our conversation had not been interrupted.

"How come?" I say. "Dogs are so great for kids."

"I know. And they're just puppies — cute young pit bulls . . ."

"Carol!" I am appalled. "Pit bulls! Why, for God's sake?"

"They're sweet dogs, you know, it's all in how you raise them, and that's what the boys wanted. Peer pressure, I guess. Anyway, did I tell you that Jessie has enlisted in the National Guard?"

"Oh, my God . . ."

"Shawn says he wants to sign up, too." Snip, snip. I am staring at her in the mirror. She shrugs. "I don't like it, but what can I do? They're excited about getting into the war. There are all these benefits, afterwards. And, anyway, they say they'd rather lose their lives fighting than just hang around here."

"But, but . . ." I sputter. How can I explain to her the riot of my reactions? The pointlessness of such a sacrifice of lives not yet 20, my sudden realization that this is what the Pentagon is counting on — the thrill, the allure of war, of fighting, of dying. It's my liberal politics, of course. Don't know what Carol's are. Afraid to ask.

Carol is saying, "Besides, it will be a great experience for them to remember when they come home . . ."

"*If* they come home!" I blurt. "Carol, what they'll come home with is vivid images of vicious maiming and killing, of their buddies being blown up beside them, of children, women, and soldiers alike bleeding buckets in the streets! How *can* you think they will come home with good memories?"

Carol stands very still, her hands at her side, meeting my agitated gaze in the mirror. "I have to," she says.

:: :: ::

The Plot Thickens.

Someone raps on the door. Liz goes, throws it open, and stamps on the doorstop to secure it. In comes a nice-looking guy, wants a trim. He sits in one of the worn leather chairs near the door, exchanges a glance with Carol, crosses his legs, and picks up a copy of *Motorcycle News*. He is followed shortly by a scruffy-looking fellow in need of a shave. "How much for a haircut?" he throws out. "For you, 50," says Carol flatly, and I know she's never seen him before. The first guy, though, the good-looking one . . . hmm . . . seems to know Carol pretty well; there was a kind of knowing intimacy, I'm thinking, in that brief meeting of eyes. Carol bends and whispers in my ear, "I met him last night at the Sidelines Bar. Cute, huh?"

"Well, yeah . . ." I smile. The scruffy guy sprawls on a chair. Liz leaves her customer, comes over to chat with the good-looking guy about motorcycles. They know each other, it seems. She's being pretty flirtatious. Carol ignores all this. Another woman comes in, her head carrying a huge bush of jet-black hair, sits in the one remaining chair. Liz says, "Just wait while I comb this woman out, it'll just be a minute."

The little shop is now bulging with characters, and I begin to feel that I have stumbled into a stage set, into a play going on around me. These unlikely people, these characters, these bit players with their own mysterious — to me, maybe to each other — stories. It is theater of the absurd perhaps, where nothing seems to relate to anything else, nothing is clearly defined, but everything seems to have an undisclosed purpose. And now it seems that this play is taking place in a different world into which I have plunged, like Alice falling through the rabbit hole — no, going through the looking-glass — into an alternative, coexisting universe. Our Town. And Carol is the Stage Manager.

:: :: ::

The Play's the Thing.

When I say Carol's the Stage Manager, I don't mean in the sense that she is outside of the action. On the contrary, she is at the heart of it. She is what makes it happen.

This is Carol's world. Carol's world, and completely foreign to me. I am entranced. Sometimes horrified, but entranced.

Having dropped in, the bit players begin to drop out. This is a "walk-ins welcome — no appointment required" salon. It appears, however, that an appointment would be desirable. The scruffy man shuffles out, wiggling goodbye with his fingers over his retreating back. The bush-bedecked lady tells Carol she'll be back after lunch, has some errands to do, makes her exit. Liz puts the finishing frizz on her customer, who blows a quick kiss to Carol and heads for the door.

Liz saunters over to the cute guy. He looks up, smiles. Carol watches them out of the corner of her eye as Liz bobs her head toward the door and mouths, "Let's get out of here." He rises, hitches his tight jeans over his taut belly, and says to Carol, "We're going out to grab a coffee. Bring you back anything?"

"Thanks, no," Carol says, pleasantly enough, and turns on the dryer. "Shut the door, will you?" she calls after them, and to me, "Brrr, it's cold, isn't it?" We are alone again.

The dryer hums to itself, moves, like a murmuring mouth, softly, slowly through my hair. I am aware of Carol's warm body, pressed against my side, as she maneuvers the dryer and continues to clip off tiny, calculated wisps, flicking the ends into small curls.

Someone has softened the radio's volume to background music and now, unbelievably, the song is "I'm too sexy . . ."

"That guy *is* pretty cute, Carol."

"Yeah, but I just got involved with this other great guy. He's so different. He's funny, really makes me laugh, clowning around. He's smart, too. Gets along great with my boys." She stands behind me again, continuing to shape and coax. "He doesn't have any money, though."

"Oh, well, then . . ." My irony is only part of my meaning.

"He's an artist."

"'Twas ever thus," I murmur. "Carol, you're looking awfully skinny. Is that your love life, or are you ill?"

She laughs. "You mean the hepatitis C? No, that's long gone into remission. Anyway, I'm not that skinny. See?" She steps back and whips up her blouse to reveal a firm, tanned tummy with a glittering gem in her belly button. "There *is* one guy," she continues, dropping her blouse and regaining the comb.

"I've been crazy about him for 15 years — but he's not around any more . . ." She trails off.

"Carol," I say. "You and your men!"

"Yeah. My mom used to have a lot of men around — my dad was nowhere — so I was sort of used to it. They helped out with us five kids."

"Wow. Five," I say. "But, come on, Carol, how come you really are just skin and bones?"

"Uh. Yeah. I did have kind of a bad time a couple of months ago. I didn't tell you? Yeah, my ex turned up and moved in."

"I thought he was in prison?"

"Out on parole. So, he was pushing drugs, and I slipped a little bit."

"Oh, Carol . . ."

"Just for a couple of weeks. I'm fine now. Anyway, he was robbing stores and homes to get money for drugs. Some busybody ratted on him at the boys' school, which was really embarrassing for them. My church didn't help any, either. I thought the church was supposed to help you when you're in trouble? Good works, and all? I was going to this study group at the church. We were supposed to read a part of the Bible and then come in and talk about it? I think they thought it would help me with the stuff that was going on, and I sure did need help. But every time I brought up something we were reading in the Bible that was contradictory or just plain impossible when you think about it, you know what they all told me? You've got to have faith! So, no — it's not good works; it's not what you can understand. It's faith. Faith is *everything*! Doesn't make sense to me. What's the good of faith if it doesn't . . ." She shakes her head.

". . . translate into good works?"

"Yeah. What really got me was when he tried to get the boys to steal for him. That did it. I hated to, but I finally reported him, and he's back in jail."

I gulp. "For good, Carol, I hope for good!"

"For a long time this time, anyway. He violated parole, too."

"But why did you hesitate? Why not turn him in at once?"

"Well." Carol straightens up, hand on hip. "He's really tried to get clean. So many times. He's not a bad guy. Just, nothing works for him."

:: :: ::

A World Away.

"You know, Carol, I've never asked you about your time in prison," I venture, hoping I'm not bumbling into territory too personal.

"Yeah," she says, "that was when they took away my kids. Twenty years ago, I just had the two older ones then. Me and my husband were into a lot of stuff in those days, like everyone we knew. He was doing the selling. I just got — you know, the customers. Somebody ratted on us and we got busted. That was 20 years ago. Twenty years I've been clean. Two and a half years in prison."

"Oh, Carol, where?"

"In Oregon. A women's prison."

"Just like Martha Stewart, right?"

"Yeah, right. I was in with that woman who murdered her husband and two kids — remember that case? Twenty years ago. It took another five to get my kids back, though."

We're both silent for a moment. Carol fiddles idly with my bangs.

"But," she says, "I've been doing all the talking. What about your kids? Did any of them get in the service? I know you've got four, too. "

"Yes, but . . . Well, they're all grown now, Carol. I've got seven — seven! — grandchildren." I hesitate. This feels so awkward. "But, well, at the age of your kids, you see, things were different for them. The service wasn't . . . um, they were pretty focused on college and their careers. They were studying hard in Ivy League colleges . . ."

"What's that? Oh, you mean those schools back East?"

"Um. Yeah. During the Vietnam War, my older son drew a pretty high draft number, so he wasn't called. My younger son reached draft age just as the war was winding down. And, anyway, he was an antiestablishment rebel, in college and afterwards. He was a Dead Head, actually, Carol." I look at her to see if this rings a bell. It does.

"Oh, sure." She nods.

"I guess neither of them gave much of a thought to fighting and dying for their country. Of course, now, one of them is a college professor and the other is a practicing therapist. So perhaps they're doing some good in the world?" I finish lamely.

"What about your girls?" she says, letting this go by.

"My girls? Now? They're both married, one is the art director for a major magazine, *The Atlantic Monthly* — I don't know if you would have read that one? And the other is a doctor."

Carol stays focused on my hair. She has turned off the dryer.

I say, "Different tracks, Carol, different tracks."

"You're divorced, though, right?" Her tone is gentle, tentative.

"A long time back, Carol. A long time back. He was a philosophy professor . . . And, yeah, I lost my kids, too. Three of them. Like you. But different."

How can I tell her about *my* heartache? The kind that never goes away, can never be resolved, because you can't undo the past, can you? I can't tell her. Can't fix it — so why dig it up? "It's hard to talk about . . . I . . . I don't like to go there. I try never to go there. It's just too . . . "

She nods again, pensive. Then she says, very quietly, "I never got to college. Sure would have liked to." And I realize she is about the same age as my eldest. I want to take her hand, smooth it between both of mine.

Instead, I suddenly notice my hair. "Carol!" I am almost shouting. "It's too FUCKING SHORT!"

I have shocked myself and begin to apologize — what came *over* me! — while Carol seems to be swallowing a laugh as she occupies herself with busily flicking what's left of my hair into admittedly attractive curls.

"Too short? Do you think so?" And, of course, I don't.

Looking out, I see Liz and the cute guy crossing the street, chatting, laughing, approaching the shop. Carol sees them, too. She gives my head a final cheery pat, whips off the nylon sheet, and begins to sweep up the little swarm of my superfluous and now totally irrelevant hair.

Watching Carol perform this humble, Zen-like task, I am almost engulfed by a tidal wave of feeling, filled with the reality of her horrendous past, the drugs, prison time, divorce, her children taken away from her, the long, tenuous haul back to clean and sober, the triumphant retrieval of her kids. Her courage in facing up to it all. Her tremendous courage.

Automatically, I pull out my checkbook and search for my keys.

"Oh, my God! Damn it, Carol, I've locked my keys in the car!" I stare at her, shake my head, disgusted with myself. "Now what? Call Triple A, I guess."

"No need," Carol says. "I can do it for you. Just let me get a hanger thing."

:: :: ::

Outside the Shop.
"Where's your car?" Carol says. She has straightened out a metal coat hanger and is confident she can pry open the lock.

"Just here," I say, pointing to my Honda Prelude, parked a couple of doorways up the street.

I trail Carol as she strides to my car and begins to insert the coat hanger's bent-over end between the window and the door panel on the driver's side. No luck. She moves to the sidewalk side of the car. Tries again. And again. We hear a rumbling and, looking up, see a huge fire engine advancing slowly down the street toward us, its three firemen perched on top, chatting and laughing, on their way back from somewhere to the station.

"Hey," Carol calls out, waving. The fire engine slows almost to a stop as the firemen get a look at Carol. "Hey," she calls, again. "Can one of you gentlemen give me a hand here? Do you happen to have a slim jim?"

Now all three men are alert and agog, as one of them says, "Hold on, we'll move the engine." The enormous vehicle drifts slowly down the street, turns the corner, and stops, completely blocking the side street, as the men jump down.

Carol and I walk toward them as they approach, Carol whispering in an aside to me, "We'll say it's my car."

The thing about this scene that I am finding remarkable is that Carol does not walk flirtatiously, does not talk flirtatiously, does not seem to show any particular interest in the fact that these guys are falling all over themselves to be her savior. I stand back, a fifth wheel. Carol is displaying a certain impatience, almost an annoyance, as two of the men try to pry open the door lock with no success whatsoever. The third man, who is chatting amiably with me, moves forward, takes the prying thingy from one of the others and with a quick flick unlocks and opens the door.

I am effusive in my praise of their prowess — and greatly relieved. Carol thanks them in a sort of casual way, not really appreciative enough in my view, but off the three men go, waving cheerfully, as content as can be.

Carol sighs with satisfaction, and I thank her warmly, bestowing a little hug on her slim form. "See you in a month?" she says, as I move toward my car, hop in, pull out my keys, and flash them at her. "In a month," I confirm.

I take a deep breath, reinsert the keys, turn on the engine, watch her returning to her shop.

There she goes, swinging down the street. Carol. My hero.

:: :: ::

Act Two.

A month has gone by, and I am back at the salon. This time it is 2:30 in the afternoon and I march right in. Carol is attending to a woman customer with long, long, very, very golden curls. I sit down and pull one of my perpetual crossword puzzles out of my purse, a trick I use in lines at the post office, the supermarket, the service station, and such-like places, so that I can enjoy rather than deplore the wait.

Liz is working on a guy in the other chair. Not much hair. None on top.

Nice, eager face, though. He's leaning forward, toward the mirror, as if to get closer to Liz, who is standing behind him. He's saying, "I don't ever call it 'conflict resolution,' see?" Liz grunts. He's — he seems to be some kind of therapist? Marriage counselor? Business consultant? What? "Because that already suggests there is a conflict! I call it — ever read a book called *Getting to Yes*? That's what I call it." Liz mumbles something. "And we're already on the way to a solution, see?"

Carol has ushered out the woman, who left with the same long, still very long, even more golden, goldie locks. She moves over to me, peers at my puzzle. "Whatcha writing? Oh. Exercising your mind, right? Come on back."

She leads me to the semidark back of the shop, where the washstands are. No music today. She tucks a towel around my neck, inside my collar, and I lean back in the chair, relaxing as the anticipated soft, warm stream begins to flow over my scalp. I close my eyes.

"So. How you doing, Carol?"

No answer. Then, in a choked voice, "I got into trouble." I look up. Her eyes are big and brimming. Her face is blotchy, her mouth taut and twisted, like the mask of tragedy.

"Oh, Carol, what?" I reach up awkwardly to pat her arm.

She says, "You promise you won't leave me if I tell you?"

"Of course, I promise. I wouldn't leave you, Carol. No matter what."

"I got busted. Right here, around the corner . . ."

"Whatever for . . .?"

"For selling dope. I sold dope to a cop." She shakes her head. "It was a setup. I think Liz's boyfriend set me up. But my boys, my boys. I'm so afraid . . . what if . . ." Her eyes well up again.

My heart turns over, and I find my thoughts glued to the one thing that seems more important than anything else. "Oh, Carol, but . . . but were you using drugs yourself? That's my real fear for you . . ."

"No. No. No, I'm not using. But I had to say I was . . . These other cops came, cuffed me, took me down to the station. The boys came and bailed me out. Luckily, I had some money in the house, so they bailed me out with $500. I told them to save the money, I'd spend the night in jail, but they did it anyway. I go for my arraignment Friday."

I am stunned. The whole story is like a nightmare. These things only happen on TV, not on Fourth Street! Not to Carol. "But I still don't see why you had to say you were using?"

"Because if I'm using, I'm pushing to support my habit. If not, I'm a big-time dealer."

"I can't believe it," I snort. "You mean, two crimes are better than one?"

"That's a laugh, isn't it?"

"I suppose it wasn't just pot . . .?"

"Speed. It's just . . ." Now she cannot contain her tears. Her face is wracked as she says, "It's just I'm afraid for my boys. We've got to move, in two weeks. Yeah, the cops searched my house — cop cars all over the neighborhood. Took all my credit cards. They think they'll find that I've got a lot of money! So the landlord's throwing us out." She wipes at her eyes with the back of her hand.

I am finding it hard to get a coherent picture.

"I was so much in debt, afraid I'd lose the shop, could hardly pay the rent. I just didn't want the boys to find no food in the house. I didn't know what else to do. I met this guy who got me enough speed so I could put a few hundred together. When I did, I wanted to stop, but this guy — this guy who turned out to be a cop — I sold to him three times, but he — he kept calling me, kept pleading with me, just one more time, one more time — so I said okay, one more and that's it."

"Did he trap you, Carol? Was it . . ."

"Entrapment? It's his word against mine — what do you think?"

"Oh."

"Jessie and Shane said, 'Why don't you just get a little apartment for yourself, and we'll get out of your way.' In three months' time they graduate. They'll be 18. I begged the landlord, couldn't we stay for three months? Wouldn't you think he'd let us stay for three months?" It's thinking of her kids that brings the tears.

What can I say, what can I possibly say? "One thing I know for sure," I offer. "Your boys love you very much. And they're going to want what's best for you. You know that, don't you?"

She's following her own train of thought. "Jessie's already in the National Guard. Shane's changed his mind, though. There's a guy he's working for who builds race cars. His family has been so good to Shane. They like him a lot, and they want to take him in." Then, with great emphasis, "But I don't want anyone else to take credit for my boys! I brought them up! I'm so proud of them. It's been 20 years since I got out of prison. And now this."

She finishes washing my hair, wraps the towel around my head, and guides me like a sleepwalker to her chair in the front. Liz has gone out, apparently. It is only the two of us. The shop seems cold and very empty.

"Liz went out?"

"I guess. She thinks the shop is bugged." Carol looks around, shrugs.

Lowers her voice. "They raided the shop, too. Found a pipe . . ."

"What was *that* doing here?"

"I don't know where it came from. It was in a drawer in the back with a mess of Liz's things."

"Liz, again!" I say, with no charity at all.

"She's had a rough time."

The black and white plastic sheet envelops me, and the haircut begins, though neither of us is paying it much attention.

"Well, then, so what happens at an arraignment? Do you have an attorney? Or will the court appoint someone or what? Don't you have any friends who can help you? What about that guy, the artist?"

"He's out of the picture — so to speak," Carol spits out. "He turned out to be a terrible person. He was a leech. He used me. But remember the guy I told you about? I've been crazy about him for 15 years, on and off. Remember? Well, he just got out of jail. He's got a house out in the country. Wants me to come live with him, but it's too far away, how would I get to the shop? He was there when I got busted. They took him in, too."

"Oh. Well." This new news is disorienting, and again I seek a coherent account. "But the arraignment, Carol, what will happen at the arraignment?"

"They'll appoint an attorney, set a date for trial. If I'm lucky, I'll maybe get probation or maybe four months. I want to get ahold of my old parole officer; she'll speak up for me."

"Oh, Carol, you, in jail again? I can't bear it. And what about the shop?"

"Anyway, Prince — that's his name, Prince, that's what his parents called him — he's inherited a lot of money. He thinks we should go to work for the narcs; turn in the guys who ratted on us; keep our friends out of trouble."

Somehow, this does not seem to me to be a solution, but by now I am past reasoning.

"Anyway, things always work out for him. He's a Pisces. He's always optimistic. Says I'm a worrywart."

"A worrywart!" I begin to laugh; Carol, too. I say, "You're about to be arraigned on Friday, thrown out of your house in two weeks, maybe go to prison, maybe lose your kids, your salon — and he calls you a *worrywart*?!" I am caught between wild laughter and uncontrollable tears.

She inspects my hair. "Did I take off enough?"

"I don't know." I sigh. Does it matter? What will become of Carol, what will become of her . . . "May I call you next week? See how it's going?"

"Sure."

Carol's face is a study; so close are the mask of comedy and the mask of tragedy.

:: :: ::

Epilogue.

I stand in front of the shop. The salon. The beauty parlor. Whatever. It is 10:00 in the morning. I do not have an appointment. I have tried to reach her on her cell phone, but there has been no response. It has been only a week, but . . . well, my hair doesn't need it but I do. So this time I am a "walk-ins welcome."

I wait. I wait for 15 minutes. Half an hour. The shop is dark, closed tight. I peer in. Darker, it seems, and tighter. I look down the street. Soon she will come swinging along. Won't she?

I begin to walk slowly up and down the street. Something is wrong. Have they taken her away? I am becoming alarmed. Worse, I am becoming doubtful. Uncertainties, discrepancies come flooding. She said she wasn't using drugs. Is this really true? Perhaps she just didn't want to disappoint me, to undermine my good opinion of her? Or perhaps — more cynically, as my doubts begin to feed on themselves — she just didn't want to drive me, a customer, away? And why is she so skinny? And what of the expensive things she has? The scissors, the hair dryer, the purebred pit bull puppies? How has she paid for all of these things? *Was the sale to the cop her only drug dealing*? And how come she left those other salons? Could she have been asked to leave? I want so much to believe her, to believe that she is real, is true to herself, is heroic in her courage.

And now it can no longer be avoided. The big question. *Why do I care so much*? Why is she so important? Not why is she important as a person, we all are that. But why is she so important to *me*? Because. Because? Because Carol is my dark, my hidden side! Carol is the part, the deep-down part that never sees the light. Carol *lives* it. She is really living, every minute of every day. She lives in the light. And I, I am simply attending the play. I have become a looker-on at life. A voyeur. Groping for a glimmer of understanding.

Then what am I to her, I wonder? What could that possibly be? Maybe simply a customer. Or perhaps . . . perhaps . . . the future she never could have, never will have: *her* own unrealized potential? Perhaps we are like the yin and yang of it, opposites forever needing to turn into each other, for wholeness. The light and the dark forever entwined.

Perhaps she'll never know this.

People brush by me in the street. I look again for her approach. I am standing beside my car. I must face the real possibility that she has been arrested and taken away to prison. What a waste, what a wicked waste that would be. I open the car door, climb in, so easy, no problem this time.

I sit in my car. Waiting.

‡ ‡ ‡

PART V

Nature: Food for Thought

Bamboo 156
Barrier...157
Bee Worlds: Introduction 158
Bee Worlds: I and II 159
Changing Seasons...161
Destiny 162
Mystery: I, Sea and Rocks 163
Mystery: II and III 164
Mystery: IV 165
Ninth Month 166
Projection 168
Resurrection 169
Rock Paintings 171
Salmon River Wilderness 172
Teatime with Children 173

IDLE THOUGHTS

Language, love, and laughter are life to me.

Bamboo

The bamboo is restless tonight.
So agitated . . .
All flying fingers, sparkling
Green starfish; darting
Wet minnows. Arms flinging
Everywhichway,
Excitedly groping,
Searching the blackness . . .

Blind man's bluff is the game
They are playing — with the million
Flitting, whirling,
Teasing snowflakes.

‡ ‡ ‡

Barrier

For David

Fish fighting upstream, fins walloping water,
Wind-lashed fir trees, hissing back.
Bird swoop swinging on air, riding the wind,
Even the still rock, stubborn back to the rising stream,
Even the stream, the wind, the air,
Carving, plunging, slipping, soaring
Burst continuous into existence —
As the bright, eager crocus
Breaks through earth to light.

Is it thought or self or sin
Prevents my breaking in . . .

‡ ‡ ‡

Bee Worlds

JULY 2010

Introduction

The queen bee's single purpose in life is to make more bees and provide cohesion and purpose in the hive. She takes a matrimonial flight with her swarm of bees and mates with a sacrificial drone, thus propagating the hive. The drones vie for the honor and the privilege, though success brings certain death.

Is it too fanciful to enquire into how the sacrificial drones feel about this? Perhaps there are bees who follow the romantic literary tradition — the Wordsworths, the Lord Byrons, the Shelleys of the bee world — in love with nature and with sacrifice for love and honor in the service of their amorata. Or perhaps they follow the classical Greek mode, or earlier, a world of goddesses and female rulers, as depicted in the ancient Greek fertility myths and legends, where a peasant is chosen to be a ceremonial "king for a day," to mate with the Queen and die.

Well, let's try. Here are two little (appropriately) poems exploring this theme.

‡ ‡ ‡

Bee Worlds

I. The Romantic Bee

I fly
to break
the screen
of this thick
pulsing blue,
the whole world sweet
beneath the sky,
bright hopes, opaque,
beckoning to woo.

Quick
Let me here now
take
my queen
and die.

II. The Classical Bee

In the image
Of the Goddess
She will fly,
Yellow prelude
To the coming Day
Of Night
When She herself
Escapes the sky
And soaring free
Explodes
Into pure light.
We, brief replicas,
Will spiral with her
In her flight.

Bright light
Of all my skies,
O, let me be
The chosen
Sacrifice.

‡ ‡ ‡

Changing Seasons

A Pathetic Fallacy

1960

Falling blossoms glaring?
Striking each other as they fall,
To settle single, a sullen heap
Beneath an indifferent tree?

No and no. Nor should we now
With bitterness reject as we recall
The small sweet days
We spent together on the bough.

We shared a scent, a hue,
Admired a common view.

‡ ‡ ‡

Destiny

Thin veins line pink fingers of a maple leaf
Arrested, stretched like parched clay,
Etched in red upon the golden air.
A mite, clinging beneath that seeming flaming sky,
Suffused in a dire gleam, a world awash in a red dye,
Would will no more brief stay
Before the fall, than I in paradise,
Were I, before the Fall, suspended there.

‡ ‡ ‡

Mystery: I

Sea and Rocks

Skittering jewels explode,
run to air.
White rivulets of glass,
racing sea icicles,
torrents of tears, stream
down scarred brown faces.
Pearls selfless merge,
a massive sheet withdraws —
an instant of unity
before the next explosive resolution.

‡ ‡ ‡

Mystery: II

A vast canyon
the width of a gull wing
cups seven grains of sand.
Snug under pea-sized
boulders, an instant
fern breathes.

Mystery: III

Under the pistol crack
and thundering roar,
under the always coming and going,
sounds
the silence
of the sea.

‡ ‡ ‡

Mystery: IV

To the starry eyes
of a sudden-smiling child
rush the riddles
of the spheres
and all discords dissolve
in two
blue orbs.

‡ ‡ ‡

Ninth Month

Summer sails out on a high wind,
silver on the underside of leaves, the backs
of gulls, white upon the waiting river.
Stretching, the river bellies wide and flat, flexes
silver muscles under rippling skin.
Veteran gulls veer and skim, wheeling down
their long, unwinding spiral slides, dipping
indifferent wing tips in idle salute.

Poplars bend and swing. Upon the soft,
ecstatic wind, maples whispering satisfaction
spend — why not? — everything.

‡ ‡ ‡

Projection

Three jumping beans
On an orange metal tray
And I, in bed, between then
And then, listless,
Listening
As they click
Like castanets.

Do they know I'm here?
My god, are they
Talking to me?
Do they never sleep?
Or, for each other,
Do they do this little
Tap dance all the time?

‡ ‡ ‡

Resurrection

Not heaven but hope
The loss of is,
White blossoms unfolding
Upon the black branches,
Flocking like crystals,
Mingling with the spring.
Now, the flowers appear on the earth
And the plum remembers the day
Of birth, of blooming
And cannot bloom.

The time of the singing
Of birds is come,
Of the jubilant chorus,
Shrill heralds of miracles
Piping their eager participation.
But no bird cries now
In the wilderness; even the voice of
The dove is still.

For the winter is past, the rain is
Over and gone. Gone, too, the cool
Breeze in the plum tree
Tingling the sun-warmed skin,
Kindling the mirroring sun within.
Bleakly a black sun hangs, holds
Only glints of light echoing still —
Gone shepherd, gone king, gone desert sky —
Reflected from a dead star.

Easter day is dawned;
But still Good Friday stays,
And the black silence
Not heaven but hope
The loss of is, of those
Remembered springs,
And the time when the plum stirring
Rose to sing,
White blossoms unfolding
Upon the black branches.

‡ ‡ ‡

Rock Paintings

For Carl Morris

Being led deep
Into rock,
Mind beholds
The canvas contains it all.

The shell-skin
Enfolds the sea.

Into thought flows
The puzzle. "All things
Are reducible to the one, but
To what is the one
Reducible?"
The artist
Wills a crucible, distills
Stone, bone, earth, spills
The rich emergent. Flowing
Line, liquid light
Circle like the wrinkles
In a shell, like the lines
Upon the Kyosai tiger's skin.

‡ ‡ ‡

Salmon River Wilderness

Tour Guide

APRIL 1960

Enter soft inside an emerald
Cushioned all with moist green sponges;
Glide among the towering columns
Frosted green with porous mosses;
Pass, like light through glass, through dampness,
Quiet slipping through the stillness.

See the greenly tinted sunlight
Touch upon a sparkling trillium,
Shimmering eerie fairy shamrocks
Pattern velvet fern-fringed carpets.

See — the stars are yellow violets.

See swift-flowing liquid emerald,
Winding world within a world,
Within the flow still filtered sunlight,
Lily trillium, mosses porous.

Watch the green god part the waters,
Enter soft the emerald goddess.

‡ ‡ ‡

Teatime with Children

Children, silently staring, absorb
You — sipping tea — with their eyes.
Siphoning, they suck you dry.
Convulsively perhaps you clutch,
Uncertain of the napkin on your knee,
Your slipping soul, subsiding,
As surf tide-drawn from shore,
Ebbs out to sea.
Handing sandwiches
You contemplate with bleak surprise
The stranded crabs, the weed waifs
Beached, your underwater life providing
Nourishment for children's eyes.

‡ ‡ ‡

PART VI

Comings and Goings

Sermon Off the Mount 176
Of Saints 178
Absurd 180
Family Tree: I 182
Family Tree: II 183
Delivery 184
Child of the Future 186
Coming Alive 187
Mamba 188
The All 190

IDLE THOUGHTS

The universe is change; our life is what our thoughts make it.
Death, like birth, is a secret of nature.
—Marcus Aurelius

Sermon Off the Mount

On Disobedience

ASSISI, 1993

"Thine eyes shall be opened
and ye shall be as Gods."

With Eve, the unconscious was born.

But let's go back . . .

Here's Adam,
serene and dutiful,
tending the Garden,

Naming things. Names the plants,
the beasts, the dog, the cat.
It's a job. It's peaceful here.
It's perfect here. It's
Paradise.

Except

It's don't touch this
and don't eat that . . .
and stick with naming,
Adam.

And, God, it's lonely.
And suddenly it's too much
And up rises Eve!

So now we know.
There is in us something
will not be tamed,
must find its own ground
of being.

Unless we disavow Eve —
and how can we? —
we will always and ever be
cast out.

Name of the game,
says Adam.

‡ ‡ ‡

Of Saints

Cool and Hot

SEPTEMBER 1997

The woman watches the lanky boy lope by.
His uniquely *his* Levis will not fall off, she concludes.
His lopsided, oversized, much inscribed T-shirt gleams white,
Is wildly awry. His Nikes say, "Man, have we seen action!"
He looks exactly as he wants to look.

We pass for who we are, she recalls Emerson wrote.
Maybe. Maybe not. The boy wants one to think that, too,
But she is not taken in. There is the matter of the persona,
Which he has traveled too short a road to know about.
When you become aware that your persona is
Only your persona, you are on the way to who you are,
She silently tells him. He does not hear her, of course.

Young Joan of Arc — sporting her armor all aglow,
Flashing her scarlet cape, her seductive sword, her uniquely
Her own flames — looked exactly as she wanted to look.
And in that final burst of light, did she become completely
Who she was? Did the person she presented to the world
Fuse with the person she was inside? Did she manifest
The outward and visible sign of an inward and spiritual grace?
Did she eclipse time and arrive in her youth
At the end of her intended growth?

Perhaps it is only saints who really round out the journey.
And even they only when they have seen all the action.
And who knows who are the saints? The woman watches
The boy round the corner. Going somewhere. Cool.

‡ ‡ ‡

Absurd

People exist —
Or so they say —
Who while away
The world, wailing,
Sighing, flailing,
And pulling anxiety up
By the roots like each hair
Of their head,
Expose despair.

There is one distress
They cannot bear:
They find it unfair
To expect to be
Finally
Dead.

And yet I know of a lady
Who, on her final bed,
Was heard to express
A contrary view.
"It's all been
So lovely," she said.

The lady referred to in the final stanza is Graham Greene's mother.

‡ ‡ ‡

Family Tree: I

For Judy

Trees squeeze babies out
Through the pores. But what
Is the difference? A little while
They linger on the bough, drawing her
Into their skin, and then they, too,
Slip into an alien stream.

She makes with her limbs akimbo
A circle. Akin, the Madonna
Sits and pretends all is
Between them still. Birth
Is the bane, our one joy of
Oneness gone. Love is the balm.

Love is the blood, flowing
From mother to child, to mother
To child forever — until the end.
And then it is anguish pressing
Through endless selves, onward to Eden,
Where Adam has yet to be born
And Eve awaits his waking dream.

‡ ‡ ‡

Family Tree: II

Consider the magnetic field:
It coils not, neither does it spin.
And so the apple falls,
But man does not
Without the garden,
And the garden snake, and sin.

Well, Adam was no child, but even in our spring
Of days was ready made and manned.
And so the bounty of the autumn yield
Was none of his, nor sown in joy,
Nor reaped in pain.
We earned the child, unplanned.

It was no part of the arrangement,
Sun and earth and creatures grown,
To have this breath, this innocence
Blown in. But here, bud, babe, to each
A new and unaccounted life. Our heritage,
The fearsome, unpredictable unknown.

‡ ‡ ‡

Delivery

For Robert

The angel robe hung limp and damp.
I was a bowstring drawn and drawn
and drawn again. Legs bent were
white dried wishbones, back arched
leaping up pulled my will along.

Thin line of energy intent
drew a concentrate at last;
muscle, sinew, bone spoke, broke,
opened a hot, an outward-pushing flush,
bearing in its red release
a fresh, a new, an un-known self.

And in the bustle following,
flurry of white cloth, cold enameled basins,
by twos, warmed forceps, embattled
steel stirrups withdrawn,
after all those months, from next to naught
two hands offered —
His eyes grew wide.
His flesh moved, still tried to mesh
with mine, still clung. They placed him on
my sprung-elastic chest, my son.

‡ ‡ ‡

Child of the Future

For Sally

1973

Child of the Future,
Be born today.
Let no din of yesterday
Drown your heart's beat,
No drought of circumstance
Drain your blood's flow.
You know, centering there,
Nothing is wanting
But the will to go.

Go forth from the mother
As a star in the night.
Be your own light.
Child of the future,
Let the future grow.

‡ ‡ ‡

Coming Alive

It is not approval of what we do
But authentication of who we are
We seek. Not good! But yes!
We come alive in bursts,
A drumroll, each tap
A beginning. We come
To live in time.

But, oh, we come
Each time from
Out of time. Each tap —
Bird wing, raindrop, sunbeam —
A summons.

And every beat we measure back,
And every tune we also play.
We orchestrate the universe
With our tumbling, thundering
YEA!

‡ ‡ ‡

Mamba

In Memoriam

OCTOBER 25, 1985

Into fall they ease,
the leaves
still ablaze upon the branch.
Each tree sports
its gallery of rogues,
on the faces of the leaves
the family resemblance.
The leaves like pages code
the message of the forebears, "We,
we, too, passed here . . ."

And the mother
in her passing swells the archives,
ever adding ". . . and will pass . . ."

‡ ‡ ‡

The All

1998

We have a yearning
backwards, back to when consciousness
began, and before, back before the knowing
of things, the naming of things,
back to when time began
with the stars. We have a yearning
back to the peace
that passes all understanding,
back to when we were not we but one
with the All.

We have a yearning
back to the womb, and before the mother,
back to our father before the joining,
back to our father who holds the knowing,
the naming, our father not yet a man,
before the Fall.

We are made of stardust, and when
at the last our consciousness leaves us,
it leads us back, back, back, and back
to the beginning of time, back
to where we, in the All,
began.

‡ ‡ ‡

FIN DE LA PREMIÈRE SECTION
DU LIVRE — THE THING IS

CONTINUEZ POUR LA DEUXIÈME
SECTION DU LIVRE — THE THING WAS

APPENDIX

The Thing Was: Living With the World

FOUR AMERICANS INVADE EUROPE

A Memoir (England) 196

Letters to My Mother, a.k.a. Mamba (Italy and France) 210

The Memoir Resumes: The Unforgiving Minute

(England Again) 235

(France and Italy Again) 236

(Another Season of Returnings, Lovings, Leavings) 242

SIX AMERICANS AT HOME ABROAD

Mostly Burma, With Smatterings of Several Other Countries

(Letters to Mamba) 245

(Patsy's Letters and the Kids' Say-So) 298

(Independence Day: A Children's Story for Grown-Ups) 304

CAPTURING CHINA

In Eight Little Poems 309

THE GREAT GETAWAY

A Grown-Ups' Holiday at the Florida Keys 317

IDLE THOUGHTS

Live with the world to understand the World.

About the Appendix

The Thing Was is for readers with a curiosity about living abroad in the 1950s. Such readers may be few and far between, but the experience of actually living in rather than just visiting a place has its own distinct voices that cry out for sharing. I hope *The Thing Was*, if not wildly entertaining, will at least provide the occasional chuckle or tear.

The Thing Was gives a sampling, in letters and memoirs, of the adventures and misadventures of an academic American family doing just that. On one trip, we lived for just under a year in Oxford, England, and undertook shorter ventures into Italy and France. On a later trip, we explored a bit of Asia — Hong Kong and Japan — before settling down in exotic Burma, in our own home-away-from-home in Mandalay.

There is also a little set of verses about China — the mysterious East?

‡ ‡ ‡

My four children, from the left:
Robert, Judy, Sally, and David.

Four Americans Invade Europe

A Memoir

(ENGLAND)

Judy was just turned four and David was barely five when we set foot in Oxford, after an exhilarating crossing from Quebec to London on an Italian ocean liner. The time was September of 1954.

Edwin, already a distinguished professor of philosophy at Reed College, had come to England with our two small kids and me, his young and bedazzled wife, to engage with his peers at Oxford on a Rockefeller Foundation grant. And, oh, were we green! These were our salad years, and I shall treasure them in memory forever.

This memoir is drawn from my running correspondence with family at home about our adventures over our 10-month sojourn abroad. I've plucked out a few episodes that largely focus on the children, in England and more expansively in Italy.

A word about the world into which we stepped might be helpful here, as it was, after all, 60 years ago. At that time, hardly anyone we knew had traveled in Europe. Today, there's hardly a one who hasn't.

At that time, the aftermath of World War II was still having an impact on British society, its adjustments and attitudes, none more in evidence than the Brits' warm and accepting feelings about us.

We Garlans reaped the benefit of their gratitude for America's role in the war.

There was another reason, too, for their ready acceptance of us raw Americans that came clear to me long afterward. It is something that Americans have to be taught, because it does not come naturally, as it does to the Brits. The class system in England, though somewhat modified during the war, was 100-percent the arbiter of behavior in relationships in every walk and aspect of life, from royalty to the aristocracy and all the way down to the lowliest chambermaid. Antiquity of one's lands and breeding took precedence even over money and power — unless these were also part of one's inheritance. And often, the more exalted and secure the position, the more charming and self-effacing the personage. It was often subtle, but it was there.

One simply did not work for a living. But there was an exception: members of the professions — denizens of the church, the law, the military, and the great universities — were welcomed into the drawing rooms of polite society and sometimes even into its ranks. These would often be the younger sons and daughters of the gentry, or their dear friends, or sometimes just plain persons who were schooled at Eton and Harrow and Oxford and Cambridge.

So there was, in short, a certain cachet about our little family, both because we were Americans and because Edwin was a professor. To the aristocracy of Oxford, we were socially acceptable.

The war still loomed in the memory of the Italians, too, and we were showered with warmth and affection everywhere we went, but for a very different reason. It was partly, I do believe, because Italians love *bambini*, and our two were of an age to be petted. But it was also because, as one Italian woman told us, the Americans were the least objectionable of all the forces that invaded and transformed their world.

These were the social waters into which we Garlans, with innocent abandon, threw ourselves hook, line, and sinker.

:: :: ::

Our first week in Oxford was devoted to an almost totally disheartening experience known as house-hunting. We were staying at the only "gentil" hotel we could afford in Oxford, a temperance hotel, no less — the other being the Randolph — and though the children liked the resident cat, and there were lovely local people who were friends of friends in the States inviting us to tea until it was coming out of our ears, we were increasingly eager to get out of there and into our own digs.

So we put an ad in *The Oxonian*. "American college professor and family seek to rent an apartment or small house, close in . . . etc." We decided that the children would not accompany us on our house-hunting forays. It seemed best to leave them to the willing care of the hotel staff. They were picking up new words like mad, and all with lovely English accents. The cat, named Oscar, was called "Osca" by Judy, and lovingly lugged around. Osca was the first of the friendly, contented cats all over England that got a sharp jolt when they met with Judy's passionate attentions.

Happily, we received a myriad of phone calls in response to our ad, inviting us to come and take a look — but, unhappily, nothing we saw was at all right, and I, for one, was becoming a tad panicked. We tried, however, to focus on various compensations of the hunt. We had storybook views of the countryside from every angle and intimate glimpses into the homes of all varieties of Oxonians.

For instance, our first look was into a terribly depressing home belonging to a retired professor who could have been Alec Guinness being a retired professor. The house was dingy, sunless, fussy, filthy, and small (and very damp in the walls). After seeing a few other houses that were uninspiring, sometimes to the point of absurdity, we reached another low point when we found a brand-new, clean, single-story bourgeois house which answered all the objections we could think of. It was easy to run, close in, inexpensive, big enough.

But it was so *very* much *not* what we wanted. We finally admitted to each other that it was just too damned American and, with a sigh of relief, turned it down.

Our spirits brightened after we stood firm against that capitulation and responded to an ad for a manor house, no less, in a little village just outside Oxford. It was a lovely day, and we decided to bring the kids along, all just for fun.

Well! It was really *so* grand. We were invited by the Lady of the Manor to visit first the Great Room, where coats of arms on red velvet hangings and crossed swords bedecked the walls. There were elaborate fireplaces everywhere and views of the village and the inviting countryside. Outside, we wandered in the manor's expansive gardens and encountered a real donkey in a field bordered with hedgerows, situated on a private lane not far from a little stone country church.

It was so very, very England. We would be renting a suite in a private wing. And, of course, that was the rub. It was so lovely it was heartbreaking, because we had to acknowledge we couldn't afford it.

So we decided to give it one more go on what was actually a cheerful, sunny afternoon. We had been invited to look at a "cottage" recently "left" by a Sir Reginald to the 20-year-old daughter of a Sir and Lady T-Bone, it sounded like on the phone, when a nice-sounding guy, a Sir David Monteath, called about our ad. It just might be something, we hoped, but it was probably too small.

HALLELUIAH! Success at last. Our home in England was to be this very cottage, Black Hill Copse on Old Boar's Hill; it was *not* too small and it was just right in every way and it was snuggled on a hillside amidst its gardens, conveniently just outside the University, looking out over the complacent Oxfordshire countryside, with its occasional tiny stone villages, with steeples and whatnot dotted here and there, just perfect.

What the Brits seem to mean by "a cottage" is "a dwelling that is *not* a mansion or manor or abbey or castle." It is, in fact, what we call a house. A sweet little house, with a nice front hall sporting a divan and a white telephone, a comfy living room that had a cozy nook and a fireplace and lots of bookcases, and windows looking out over a terrace and rockery and rose garden to the green-flowing hills and fields. It had a pleasant dining room, also furnished in the best of taste. Two large bedrooms were up carpeted stairs and were most inviting — with good beds and blankets and electric heating throughout. There was also a fireplace in our bedroom — so cheery for a snowy night. Fresh flower arrangements greeted us in the hall and throughout the cottage.

But, ah, the kitchen! Here is where the adventure really began. We had been greeted with a gracious smile at the door by Lady Monteath, who explained that she was the mother of the young woman who had been bequeathed the cottage and who was living at present in London, and would we mind awfully coming out to the kitchen, which she and her husband, Sir David, were in the process of painting to freshen up the wooden walls. Perhaps we would like a cup of tea before she showed us around?

It was a large kitchen, an add-on, Lady Monteath said, with a "boiler" for warmth and to heat the teakettle; you fed it with coke that was delivered periodically to the bin. There was a large breakfast table, an old davenport, and rugs on the floor. There was also a real stove. The Monteaths seemed very proud of this stove. It was an Aga, they explained.

The gardens pretty much took care of themselves, Sir David informed us. He said that the large vegetable garden in one of the lower stretches of land had been let separately to a man named Anthony Sprent. Sir David said that he presumed that Mr. Sprent was a gentleman, because he was "on the phone" — which is to say, he *had* a phone and was on the phone service.

There was also a garage, pronounced GAR-age. And in that garage was a ridiculous-looking huge box of a car, a 1934 Morris

Oxford sedan. Sir David explained that it had been left to Sir Reginalds's "man," who was eager to sell it and was asking £53. This, in U.S. money, was about $26, so we bought it on the spot!

Edwin's trials were many and varied, learning how to drive this imposing monster on the wrong side of the street on the wrong side of the car, with the brake and accelerator reversed and the accelerator between the brake and the clutch and four forward gearshifts. All this was complicated by not being able to see out the windows, which were frosted and hoary with age. But his manly efforts were well rewarded with the freedom it gave us to go anywhere. Well, almost anywhere. Not readily up the steep hills of Wales, if at all, as we discovered in a later adventure. It was so big — big on the outside and bigger on the inside. But the seats of soft, green leather; the copious back area capable of accommodating both children, sitting or standing; and the built-in tray and picnic basket were a clear invitation to explore our new world.

And explore it we did. We also acquired two bicycles with little chairs — also of green leather, with side arms and everything, for the two children — David's strapped on the back of Edwin's bike and Judy's on mine. These did nicely for short, half-day tripping, reserving the Morris for longer undertakings. Off we would go, Judy and me in our nylon dresses, me with stockings and heels, Judy in her Mary Janes, whizzing along to the Derbyshire for lunch — usually trailing the boys by about a block.

Anthony Sprent and his wife, Mary, and their two children became our dearest friends in Oxford. We four grownups had many near-delirious times together, tooling about the countryside in the Morris, belting out lusty songs Anthony taught us, and downing pints of beer and sausages and Scotch eggs in pubs along the way, where we would argue about such controversial questions as whether the British toilet tissue, which was totally nonabsorbent and scratchy, was, as Anthony insisted, a good thing because it built character. It didn't pamper one, the way the American version did.

The children accepted everything with a ready enthusiasm. The only off-note was one struck by Judy when she inquired at one point whether we were all through with England yet. But that was before the discovery of school! Old Boar's Hill was studded with the dwellings of Oxford dons and other notables, like Masefields' at the top of our lane and Lawrence of Arabia's down the road. The dons' offspring were sent to a small prep school conducted by a Miss Skerry and so, too, were the two young Garlans.

It was only a short ride from our cottage on the bus that would transport the children to and from the little school each day, in their English prep-school uniforms of grey flannels, knee-length grey stockings, and navy blazers and caps, emblazoned with the St. Michael's emblem in gold and magenta. They were to be taught manners and how to read. They were to have Scripture readings, arithmetic, singing, painting, acting in the Christmas pageant, history, and a little French. Miss Skerry was about 108 — in both years and weight — and didn't seem to see or hear very well but gave the clear impression that she would be able to cope. "At least they will learn how to speak properly," she said.

Lady Monteath had explained about the deliveries we should "organize," and it turned out to be quite an undertaking. The elaborate arrangements one had to make in order to exist were a blessing in the long run. She had asked a neighbor of ours, the Bursar of Pembroke College, to call and make us welcome. He came and also promised to have his fish man call by. We arranged for the groceries to be delivered from Oxford, milk to be delivered from Wooton village, and newspapers from the village and for the bread man to come three times a week and the coal and coke man to come once a week. She recommended, and I hired, a woman from the village to come two mornings a week as our charlady to deal with the fireplaces and do the cleaning.

The Monteaths were both so charming, and, in fact, we saw quite a bit of them during our time there. Sir David and Edwin hit it off, chatting about men's interests — I don't know, fishing and libraries and the like — and Lady Monteath filled us in on the local inhabitants and festivities. We learned, too, about the history of Old Boar's Hill and that during the war Black Hill Copse had housed 17 children.

They introduced us around among their friends and neighbors, and we became rather sought-after. People would invite us to tea, a bit smugly upstaging their friends with, "You must come and meet our Americans."

Their own country estate was not far away and included a large manor house. It was so large, in fact, that when Lady Monteath invited us for Thanksgiving, she herself brought the soup course to the table (her cook being on holiday) in thermos bottles to keep it warm during the long trek from the kitchen. Of course it wasn't Thanksgiving for them, and she apologized for not serving turkey, so we made do with pheasant, which, she said, was the closest she could come to it. It was close enough!

We rented a radio, which turned out to be one of our main delights. One's home becomes more than one's castle. With the BBC to pipe it in, it becomes the world. With our sturdy old car, our bicycles for four, the children ensconced at Miss Skerry's, and a multitude of new friends and acquaintances, we were jolly well prepared for it all.

:: :: ::

The children settled into a routine, charming to behold. They learned to play endlessly together with almost no props. Their relationship was very beautiful. Judy was a little ego-booster for David; he represented for her the essence of manly competence and ingenuity. She was very stabilizing for him. They stimulated each other's imaginations in games and conversation. They got themselves ready for bed at night and up and dressed in the morning, doing each other's buttons and tying each other's shoes. David sometimes combed Judy's hair and was patient with her fussiness about it. He could make it look like an Indian girl's, which she liked.

At school, it was a big deal when David learned to read. He had some goodish words. About the Boston Tea Party, he asked if the English were "very annoyed." And about medieval times he said, "I shall ask Father Christmas for a book about knights. I'm very inter-stress-ted in knights and armies and things like that."

They were also taught arithmetic, which Miss Skerry called "sums" (and Judy heard as "thumbs," because she, Judy, counted on her fingers).

It is wonderful how children of that age fall into everything new as if that is just the way things are. No quibbling. Just embracing. When they were introduced to new children, such as those of our charlady, Mrs. Webb, their icebreaker would be "Do you have any songs?"

Language — the importance of it — loomed in practically every nook and cranny of our interactions with the Brits. The children's English accents did, indeed, take on an upper-crust cast for words they learned at school, as Miss Skerry had hoped. Not so in chats with the children of Mrs. Webb.

Mrs. Webb and I also had a terrible time with language. It was so gratifying how she worked like a beaver. She had high standards about the cleaning and waxing, and on top of that suggested that she be allowed to do the sheets "because the laundry gets them so hard." This was where the tangle came. The Webbs spoke a sort of Berkshire dialect, and my barbarous American English was quite baffling to her. So when we spoke to one another, we would stare intently and intuit. When she said "hard" about the sheets, it sounded like "odd" to me, which of course they would pronounce "awed," so I thought at first it was "ironed," which comes out rather like "ah'd." Sigh.

When Miss Skerry said at least the children would learn to speak proper English, she meant not like Americans and not like the charlady. Here we have class raising its not-so-lovely head. And it recalls two memorable conversations in particular.

One eye-opening exchange was with Mrs. Webb, when I was going on about how the war had introduced a new democracy to England. The landed gentry were finding it impossible to keep up their country estates and their mansions, and were seeing their maids and chauffeurs and stable-hands and farm-workers go off to manufacturing jobs or jobs in the cities, and wasn't this new freedom from servitude a good thing. Much to my surprise, she interrupted me sharply and proclaimed that it was a terrible thing. What would become of everybody? People got their status, their place in society, from being attached to a grand house. When that was gone, they became nobody!

The spirit of democracy with which Americans are so imbued didn't touch our charlady. The other memorable exchange involving language and democracy was very different in this regard.

It took place in a tiny pub in a little inn in a tiny village called Trebarwith Strand on the coast of Cornwall. Edwin and I stayed a few days at the inn, which was actually embedded in caves (with a pirate history) that cradled the Strand. In the evenings, we would pop into the pub for a beer or a whisky and to listen to the local chatter. When the barkeep would call out, "Time, gentlemen, please," it was the standard cue to customers to order their last beer before closing time at 11:00 p.m. While most of them would shuffle out after this, three or four familiar locals would be allowed to remain after the heavy doors were closed to the outside world. Edwin and I were touched and honored to be included among the little group that remained.

Inevitably, we got around to personal stories, and one man began to talk about his son. The boy had been a brilliant student at Oxford University and had pulled down a "first" but couldn't completely shed his broad Cornish accent and speak what Miss Skerry called proper English, of the Oxford-educated variety. Still, this was a wonderful accomplishment, we said admiringly. But, no. The father was sad and bitter. Because of his son's Cornish roots, he had found it impossible to get a position worthy of his education. And because of that education and his somewhat English accent, he no longer fit in at home in Cornwall.

For these Cornish folk, the spirit of democracy was embraced in the depths of their independent souls. But little good it did them.

Another small revelation about Brits in action — or inaction — came when Edwin and I drove to London to get our three trunks out of hock on the docks, where they had been languishing since their arrival because of a dockworkers' strike. The office said, though they couldn't check the contents because they had lost a key, they thought we could retrieve the trunk containing our books if we drove the car down onto the docks to do so. With advice to "run 'em down" if pickets attempted to stop us, we drove onto the docks without incident, where a rather nervous officer said okay and assisted in the removal.

We drove off with our spoils hidden under coats and the friendly recommendation that in case of trouble at the gates, "'Ave the lydy do hall the tawking." Having just seen *On the Waterfront*, we were hardly in the mood for exchanges with picketing dockers; they play too rough. But the pickets had all gone to tea!

:: :: ::

As December rolled around, Edwin and I firmed up plans for the four of us to spend Christmas "vacs" (vacations) in Italy. At Miss Skerry's, they began early to rehearse and perform the little school's annual Christmas pageant. We were very pleased that David and Judy would be able to experience some yuletide festivities in England before we ventured forth to the continent.

They became deeply involved in the pageant, Judy going around reciting all the parts in her excellent English voice. "See! It is the palace of the king, and we will find him whom we seek." David was a servant, and at first there was a line that went, "We will leave our camels and our servants at the city gates," but they couldn't leave *him* at the city gates, he told us, so they amended it to just the camels. And they warbled Christmas carols incessantly. They knew all the words of "O Little Town of Bethlehem" and "We Three Kings" — "bearing gifts we travel *safar*," Judy insists. And "Little Jesus, Sweetly Sleep," with the most wonderful lines in it, like "snugly round thy tiny form," which Judy sang as "tidy form."

:: :: ::

During all this, Edwin and I were plunged into a dizzying whirl of activity. From September, when we arrived in Oxford, till late in December, when we took the children on the trip to Italy, and again on our return in mid-January, in addition to our many day trips throughout England on our bikes or in the Morris, we grownups went frequently to London and twice to France, where we had our own cherished adult adventures. (The children, meanwhile, stayed with a young family in nearby Wooton Village, where they picked up head-lice and rather unsavory words from their playmates.)

And there were all the goings-on at home in Oxford. Everyone was so extremely kind to us we were practically overwhelmed with social activities. Teas, concerts in college (as musical events at the university were termed), museum trips, lectures, and a bit of pub-crawling and such with compatible friends consumed a great deal of my time. All of these invitations required a complementary return, naturally, so I did a few teas of my own for the ladies, and dinners for the couples and families. Surprising, even distressing to me, was the fact that when husbands were included, the conversation was steered away from areas that smacked of thought, like philosophical ideas, serious books, politics, or learned projects they might be working on, as being unsuitable in the presence of ladies!

Fortunately there was also the occasional American student studying at Oxford who was pining for a taste of home and whom Edwin took under his wing and brought to Black Hill Copse. One such was an American who was a Rhodes Scholar just finishing his thesis and trying for a D.Phil. I happily agreed to help him with his bibliography, he having no wife of his own. Another was a Reed College student who was at Oxford studying in the same field as Edwin. When I introduced him to Judy as an Oxford student from Reed, she confided to him, "Daddy is a student." And when I said, "Well, not exactly; Daddy is a teacher," she came back loyally with, "Pretty *soon* he'll be a student."

Another Judy-ism comes to mind. One evening, when I bawled her out for putting her pajamas on over most of her clothes instead of troubling to remove them, she howled a bit and then burst out with "God makes me do all these naughty things!" And when I somewhat coolly asked her to elaborate, she said, "Well, God makes us," and then, ruminating, "I think God is two Gods: a good one and a naughty one." She hadn't heard that the naughty one is not called a god. She was picking up all this God business at Miss Skerry's, of course.

Judy always seemed so, well, casual in her thought processes; she didn't seem really to *think hard*, the way David did, or to carry a thought on long. We took David and Judy and two little friends to see a new film, *Richard and the Crusaders*. Pondering it afterwards, David said he couldn't understand why, when one of the knights was stripped of his knighthood by Richard, he went and put on Turkish clothes. "He could have been just *nothing*, like me and you." (Yes, I'm afraid he did say "me and you.")

Edwin was spending increasing amounts of his time in university, at one college or another, with various dons and heads of college. His fundamental purpose here was, of course, his scholarly pursuits in one of the cradles of civilization.

Oxford would be, I think, quite appalling to the more naïve of

American educators in its degree of anarchy. Actually, nobody really looks after the scholars; they jolly well fend for themselves. But it is quite common for a bewildered American scholar, say, to find after two or three years there that he has been going after the wrong degree. There are some rules, of course, governing living conditions, but often, if not always, they are archaic. At one of the colleges, the curfew, which was originally at 10:00 p.m., as at many of the others, has for the last few centuries been at 10:20. This is because long ago, when a riot broke out between a couple of scholars and some townspeople, the scholars dashing for safety arrived at the gates at 10:05 and, not being able to get in, were killed by the townsfolk. So ever since, the gates have closed at 10:20.

It would take a tome to describe the colleges' many quaint or outdated customs, as faithfully observed as any rule etched in stone. The practice "in hall," at mealtime, of arranging the student scholars on benches at a long, I mean very long, table down in the pit, dining on very simple fare, while the dons lived it up at High Table, far above them at the front of the hall, like Henry the Eighth, at a table sparkling with crystal and silver and brilliant candlelight, with an array of fine wines and roast pheasant, is an example. Students pacify their yearning tummies with "Mahs Bahs" (that's "Mars Bars" in plain American).

Edwin dined twice in college, once as the guest of a distinguished philosophy professor at University College with whom he had been pursuing their common, though somewhat differing, philosophical persuasions. Of course, I don't think they discussed such matters at High Table. That would be like talking shop, which would be perceived as a vulgar and deplorable practice. The dons wore their robes; Edwin wore his tux. It was all very grand. At the request of his left-hand dinner partner Edwin took snuff from an ornate silver snuffbox but couldn't sneeze. He was very embarrassed.

The other time he dined in college was at the guest table of Queens College, in the pit with Oxford students, whence they ogled the masters' High Table. He brought a couple of them home afterward for ale and chatter and healthy laughter and engrossing shop talk.

:: :: ::

December having set in, winter was upon us and vacation time was upcoming. We had by then become accustomed to the snow. Our first inkling of it was one evening, when Edwin and I were reading by our cozy fire in the drawing room. I became suddenly aware of a ghostly quiet encircling the cottage. Opening the front door for a look around, I was positively enchanted to see snowflakes whirling delicately like tiny dancers through the hushed air.

But with the snow came cold and a persistent dampness, so the prospect of the sunny climes of Italy propelled us eagerly into the arrangements for our trip.

Letters to My Mother, a.k.a. Mamba

(ITALY AND FRANCE)

As I sit at my desk rereading my letters that form the basis of this memoir, letters lovingly preserved by my mother, who served as Information Central, letters written 60 years ago, I conclude that my youthful enthusiasm at age 28 is really part and parcel of the experiences I am trying to describe — especially we four on the Italian trip and, later, a separate bike trek through France, just Edwin and me.

Though I blush at parts that would now be seen as way over the top, they were heartfelt and motivated by the desire to communicate, somehow, these marvelous moments — moments that today bring on a nostalgia I do not need to share. So, selectively, here are the unadorned letters. The account has the voice not of a seasoned old lady but of a frisky, young married woman, out on a spree.

So off we went to the Côte d'Azur, starting with a quick stay on the French Riviera, and then on to our destination on the Italian Riviera, the bitty little town of Laigueglia. But getting out of England proved to be our first challenge . . .

Off to the Continent
December 17, 1954

Our first glimmering of the Italians had come in a wire from the *pensione* I had written to on the Italian Riviera. My letter was written in English — with apologies in English for writing in English — to say we were coming and hoped they would have room for us. The evening before we were to leave Oxford we received their response, signed "Giacomella." One word: "WAITING." Lovely?

Our plan was to stop in Menton on the French Riviera near the border for a few days, because this enabled us to take advantage of the excursion rate on the French train. We were thoroughly packed — crammed, I should say — into three huge suitcases, liberally lined with books and sprinkled with Christmas-y items. We set the alarm for 5:30 a.m. and went peacefully to sleep.

Next morning, we scrambled into clothes, scrambled eggs, scrambled into a zillion coats, and scrambled into the waiting taxi at 7:00. I forgot to mention that we also had a small canvas bag with overnight things and toys. And a typewriter.

We caught the first train out of Oxford at 7:30, changed at Reading with much help from other commuters. The train from Reading was really jammed full, and we got separated — David and Edwin in one car, me and Judy in another. You should picture us in our marching order as we proceeded from conveyance to conveyance throughout these changes. Edwin came first with the two heaviest bags, followed by a staggering David, going choppily along with the small canvas bag, whose handle kept coming apart. Then a lopsided me, lurching along with the other heavy bag and the typewriter, and last the lighthearted, skipping Judy, who bumped into everyone on the platform and kept disappearing from view.

Our only serious worry was would we be in time to catch our boat train out of London; after that it would be clear sailing, if you know what I mean. We arrived at Paddington at 9:10 and were due to depart from Victoria at 10:00, with passport, officials, customs, and weighing inbetween.

We were helped out of the train at Paddington by a very nice man who split a gut carrying my load along the platform, while I carried his newspaper and umbrella, on which I speared my ankle and snagged my stocking.

After frantic waving, we procured a taxi, got to Victoria at 9:35, and put ourselves in the hands of a tiny but competent porter who hurried us to all the ticketing windows and got us on the train with a good three minutes to spare.

The train to Dover was painless, then a very pleasant crossing, lunch on board, and then the train *Côte d'Azur* to Paris and to Menton, arriving 10:30 next morning. Very quick, the whole thing. We had three couchettes in a compartment of six.

The couchettes were long and narrow, really just for stretching out; there was a blanket and a pillow. We were very lucky in having first a nice young man — English schoolboy — as our companion, and from Paris an utterly charming young Frenchman, extremely good-looking, very clean and aristocratic (or is that tautological in France?), and very accommodating in the matter of couchettes. He took the top one and lay on his back motionless, first reading, then sleeping till morning, when he rose, or, I should say, descended, looking fresh and smiling, wished us a cheerful "bon voyage" and walked out of our lives.

When we woke up, dawn was breaking, the sky was clear and blue, and, my God, I thought it was California.

Menton, France
Saturday, December 18, 1954

We were a bit worried about Menton. We had forgotten to bring the *Michelin Guide*, and we hadn't the remotest idea where to stay. At the station I asked the magazine man if he had a *Michelin Guide*, and he said no but sold us a pamphlet about Menton, with hotels in it. It had the same classification system as the *Guide*, four stars down to one star, so we weighed and considered and finally took the plunge, picked out a likely looking one-star which fronted the sea, and got a taxi.

We didn't regret our choice for one moment the whole stay. They had economized in just the right ways. The place was unpretentious but charming. The paint was coming off the front of the building but our room was huge, with tremendous French windows opening to admit floods of sunlight and a beautiful view of the sea.

The food was simple and delicious. A typical meal? Well, our first, lunch, consisted of *hors d'oeuvres variés*: tomatoes, delicious other cold veggies, egg with mayonnaise, sardines, etc. Then came a creamed turkey dish with rice, green salad, assorted fruit, nuts, and *fromages*. And of course, *vin du pays*. Or a typical dinner: soup (clear), followed by a sort of savory (a little glazed pasty filled with creamed mushrooms), then roast beef and chips, peas, a sweet pastry, and coffee. For breakfast? *Café au lait* (*chocolat pour les enfants*) and rolls, served in our room when we rang.

The *pensione* was quite small — about 18 rooms. There was one chambermaid, who was also the waitress, with whom we got quite chummy. She kept an ear open for the kids when we went out in the evenings. She didn't know a word of English, so I had much practice with my French, hashing over the children's menu, for instance. They fed the kids their supper early, at our request. Fortunately, the young proprietress spoke English very well and had a cousin staying with her who is from Palo Alto — an American. The proprietress had a little boy just David's age, who knew no English, but with whom the kids played.

The cost, by the way, was very reasonable — always a nagging concern — but still gave us a little worry about Italy, because we could not afford the $15 a day every day. Still, as always, we made do. (If I seem to dwell on money a lot, it is because of the paucity of it. I dwell on food, too, for the opposite reason — the plethora of it.)

Menton itself is a very nice town. I think I definitely prefer it to Monte Carlo. Monte Carlo is about 10 minutes by bus; it's terribly fancy, of course, especially the Casino; we spent Sunday afternoon wandering around there. The season is just beginning to get under way. English with poodles all over the place. Menton is frequented mostly by French people on vacation, though I suppose lots of English come, too, as a jumping off point for Monte Carlo.

Laigueglia, Italy
Monday, December 20, 1954

We set off Monday afternoon just after lunch for Laigueglia. It was a three-hour bus ride, with interminable goings-on on both sides of the border. But, hoo boy, the minute we crossed the border and the Italian passport officials got on board, I realized that ITALIAN WOULD NOT COME EASILY, as I had confidently been expecting that it would, what with having my bit of French and Latin. But I didn't even know how to say *grazie* and, Gods, I felt totally impotent! Edwin had been boning up and did a bit better. He is also better than I at sort of intuiting people's meaning. Still, the funny thing is that, while English is the second language on the French Riviera,

French is the second language at Laigueglia, and I have been leaning very heavily on it.

We were dropped in the road, somehow got a taxi, and were taken to the Pensione Giacomella. Another surprise: it is a tall, modern, very new building, in a group of ditto. Apparently everyone here looks to the future; they want to be just like Nice, which I gather is fairly ugly, and they scorn the lovely old parts of their village. Anyway, being new it is clean, which I suppose is something to consider in Italy.

The *pensione* is less than a block from the sea, but unfortunately across a road that is treated like a highway — a turnpike — by the wild Italian drivers.

Well. We rang the bell at the *pensione,* and an assortment of about 10 people came to answer it. They all took us in — both literally and figuratively — nodded heads a lot, talked, smiled a lot, counted us, knew who we were. Some of them went away calling out "Americanos — bla, bla, bla." We felt very good, for some reason. I think it was because they expected us and because they were so friendly. And because we had arrived!

Then the daughter of the house came and asked us if we knew a *petit peu de français;* she did, too, so she explained that her mother would be back soon, and she spoke a lot of French. Then she showed us up a thousand stairs or so to two rooms. They were — well, just rooms. But they said would we like coffee, and you know the answer to that in any language.

Then we asked about *mangiare per bambini.* (Everybody, of course, exclaimed over the *bambini.* Even customs officials, who looked rather fierce otherwise. I think we heard the word *bambino* a hundred times before we were in Italy for an hour.) We had a wonderful "discussion" with the daughter about the menu, during which she spoke Italian and French, gesticulated, laughed, and mooed at us. We didn't know if the "moo" meant meat or milk, cows being so versatile.

A very young serving girl went to see the cook about it and came back a bit later, touched her tummy, stuffed her hands into her mouth, pointed to the children, smiled, nodded, and beckoned.

At last, the French-speaking woman came, and also the real boss of the establishment, the Captain, who, hooray, speaks English. We had a big talk while the children ate at our table in the large dining room, which is also a sort of lounge. People write letters there at their table and read and in the evenings gather at one end to watch the *pensione*'s one television set.

They moved us down a couple of floors to two rooms that are much nicer, one quite large, with a balcony on one side of the building, and across the hall a nice one for the kids, so that one room or t'other has sunshine during the day. The balcony has a pleasant view of the sea and of the village of Alassio, which is along a point, an arm of the harbor, while we are in the trough. Very agreeable. AND we are on the same floor as the bathtub!

Then, while I got the children ready for bed, Edwin had a business discussion with the management, and the financial situation is good. We are paying about $6 a day for (almost) everything — rooms, service, food, except for evening coffee, wine, and extras, for all of us. (It's about half the season price, I think, and less than half the tab at Menton.)

The Captain told us another American family is staying here. He's a philosopher from Yale, about Edwin's age; two kids — a girl, three and a half, and a boy, nine. Very good news, somehow, and very nice they all turned out to be.

It's 12:00 midnight, and what a day it has been.

Italy is *the* place for children! Judy (Judita) and David (Dah-vidh) are of course known by everybody in the *pensione* and made much (too much) of in many languages. They have learned to say *ciao*, pronounced "chow," which is all that is expected of any *bambino* in the way of both salutation and valediction. And *grazie* (for "thank you") and *ancora* (for "more" or "I'm not finished yet") and *basta* (for "finished"). And David is working on *non capisco* and *sono Americano*. And, of course, the very useful *ecco* (for *voici*!). This is about the extent of Edwin's and my working vocabulary, plus *quanta costo, buon giorno, buona sera, prego, permesso, scusi,* and *mangiare*.

But do not form the impression from this that we do not converse with people. *Au contraire*. I think we have talked more here than in all our time in England. The language barrier is simply ignored by everybody. Many people have a little French and a word or two of English; one guy we met has French and German. But mostly they speak Italiano and communicate their meaning by gestures and by willing it.

The normal complement of guests is about 20, I think. But beginning Christmas Eve, which it has magically become — as I'm sparing you the pre-Christmas frenzy of buying and wrapping and secrets — the place has been hopping. Lots of kids, too, who have all adopted Judy, as usual. They say "Judy," like everything else, with their tongue way forward in the mouth, touching the top front teeth.

And now it is December 27th, we are on the beach, and I am attempting to write about Christmas, but I am considerably hampered by a small puppy, who is playing ball with his young master and David, and who seems to consider the crevice between my back and what I'm leaning on his goal.

We had quite a good stocking opening, though the Santa Claus here did not have as much ingenuity as the one at home, particularly for us two grownups, who received many *noci* (nuts). Then we went down for breakfast and exchanged many *Buon Natale*s with everybody and back upstairs for the "big" opening. Since we each had something for each, it was really not bad.

Judy had a drum for David, a game for Daddy — the puppy is now vigorously undermining me from behind — and a black belt for me. David had a pen for Daddy, a little lamb for Judy, and a scarf for me. Edwin and I had bought in England lovely, soft, huggy animals for the kids: a fluffy lamb for Judy, a sleepy-looking dog for David. I got for my two men a *basco* each: a black beret, like the ones everyone wears, and for Edwin a lovely, I thought, grey silk Italian scarf (so did he think).

Our other major present for the kids was, for David, a grey wool sweater with two red dragons on the front, black trim, high neck. With his grey stockings and shorts and his new black *basco,* he looks wonderful. For Judy, I had such a business. I must write about this, because it will tell you something I found very touching about the Italians and shopping in Italy, at least as I experienced it.

A few days before Christmas, I looked in all the shops in Alassio for a sort of spectacular, native-type dress — Judy loves that sort of thing — and finally, two days before Christmas, found a shop that was displaying a red felt flary skirt with white-felt appliqué. Well! But it was too small and too expensive. Then the drama began; I won't say comedy or tragedy; you must decide for yourself. The woman whose shop it was had very little French and no English, but she somehow conveyed that if I were to come back tomorrow afternoon she would have more of a selection. She asked what kind of thing and I said blue, full flary skirt, and a blouse.

Next day (Christmas Eve) I returned and found the shop closed. I inquired at a shop across the street, and they went and found her somewhere, and darned if she hadn't been *making* a skirt. I think she had closed the shop to devote her time to it. (I had specified *pas trop chère,* and she stuck to that, bless her.) It was almost done — a lovely blue, with a soft flannel effect inside and a gentle sort of gabardine outside. We had a huge discussion about various kinds of trim; she had some little colored felt figures to sew on, just Judy's cup of tea.

About then in the proceedings a young man came in who spoke French very well and had very good taste. He thought a subtler kind of trim than we had chosen would be prettier and would tie it in with the blouse she was going to whip up. A woman came in to shop who spoke French and of course contributed her views, and I kept trying to explain what I thought Judy would want. We all got very confused with our languages; they would find themselves speaking French and gesturing to each other and explaining to me in Italian, and I found myself going blank from the waist up.

Finally, the young man suddenly said, "Do you speak English?" I sank gratefully to the floor. After that we got all straightened out, settled on the appliqué figures, and I said I would return that evening for the skirt and blouse.

Edwin returned that evening, and she actually had the skirt done. The blouse didn't get finished, so she sold me (him) the more expensive one for the cheaper price: white with blue trim.

I was in a panic about whether it would all fit. But of course it did and looks darling and is a tremendous success.

Christmas dinner in the dining room with the other guests of the *pensione* became a feast by the addition of *antipasti* and *ravioli* to the usual fare, after which all the kids played contentedly together and watched TV.

The Italian kids are the *nicest* I have seen anywhere. They are really lovely to David and Judy, and they are very sweet and affectionate with each other. They are up till all hours (ours are not) and are omnipresent but are beautifully dressed, clean, and pleasant. We haven't heard one cry or speak harshly, and their manners are lovely and from the heart.

We became deeply attached to the dear Italians at the *pensione*, particularly the French-speaking manageress, Madame Capriotti, who by the end of our stay was lavishing special attentions on us — butter for breakfast, grapes for Judy, special dishes for me because they got it into their heads I wasn't eating. I especially liked their *risotto alla Milanese* and asked for the recipe; it really is delicious, but oh dear, we did have a lot of *risotto* after that, and I was, despite my protestations, invariably given two bowlfuls!

The children spent the mornings at the beach. Edwin actually found himself able to work and knocked out a good part of the paper he is to deliver in Bruxelles in a couple of weeks. We had wonderful fun with the American family, who turned out to be very simpatico. We developed a most pleasant custom of having a goodnight coffee and *Strega* with them at the little *ristorante* on the corner, about 10:30 each evening.

One evening was particularly enjoyable. A rather tipsy Italian at the *ristorante* was unable to restrain himself from bursting into song, though he tried. He would sit down but suddenly leap up again and begin to sing, striding about, then stopping suddenly and subsiding again.

At first everyone was a little embarrassed because of us, but we smiled and nodded and said "*Bravo*" and "*Ancora,*" and everybody relaxed — except for four card-players, who couldn't concentrate. He had a very good voice and he was a natural comic; there was much more clowning than singing. Lots of fun. And towards closing time, everybody sort of drifted over to our table and stood around and were pleased that we were pleased.

We also met a nice Italian senator and his not-so-nice American wife. At least she is nice enough, but apparently *persona non grata* with the Italians. She is always complaining about the goings-on in Laigueglia, and threatening to "write to Rome"! Once, she threatened the *pensione*, because of some smoke coming from their chimney. She received a reply the next day, she claimed, which greatly amused the scoffing Italians. Madame gave us a pantomime of her whooshings of the smoke and a demonstration of her condescending-type walk, with her large derrière swinging.

But the senator was nice, though he had been in the Senate during the whole Fascist period. Rather a puzzler. Italian senators were appointed by the king and may not have played any role, but one wonders. Our friends of the *pensione* suffered from the Fascists, from the Germans, from the French. Awful.

Rome
January 1955

Well, we were having such a peaceful, economical sojourn at Laigueglia that, paradoxically, we couldn't resist the temptation to run off to Rome. We had four eye-popping days in Rome, and two superb ones in Florence, then back to Laigueglia for four days, and then home to England. So I have three categories to write to you about — plus all the sloppy edges, like a quick stopover in Assisi.

We decided to take the night train to Rome, it being the only practical, convenient, and fairly economical option. We got Judy free, David half-fare, and a shared apartment with two bunks. We left Laigueglia (Alassio, really) at 9:00 in the evening and were in Rome next morning about 7:30. A very comfortable trip.

We were overwhelmed first by the huge, handsome, modern train station, through which we wandered till we found a *ristorante* for breakfast. Here we had an extraordinary stroke of luck. Sitting next to us was a huge, handsome hunk of man (sort of a cross between Brian Donleavy and Uncle Joe), who, having observed us struggling with the order and the waiter, straightened us out through the medium of French. He turned out to be a professor of law at Trieste and a charming man.

We asked if he could recommend a hotel, which he did — *"economique et gentil"* — where the teachers and priests stay. Very old and centrally located. And, indeed, it was just in back of the Pantheon. He also gave us an excellent tip about places to eat, which we followed to our delight. He said go to the *trattorias*. They are the kind of *ristorante* that features old-style Roman cooking, unprepossessing-looking, usually very cheap, and often the best food in Rome. All of which we found to be true.

We taxied immediately to the hotel and were given one large room for, I think, $7. No food. Bathroom across the hall. Baths extra, of course. It worked out very well for us. It was so good to get settled in immediately. We rushed right out, bought a book about Rome and had a look at the Pantheon. Thence we hoofed it over, through the fancy shopping area, to the Spanish Steps and a little section where a lot of restaurants are. Couldn't find a *trattoria* on that occasion but had a delicious though rather expensive lunch.

We seemed never to be able to calculate the bill in advance. There are always items you forget to add in. The most pernicious is *coperto e pane* (cover charge and bread) which is often quite flexible, particularly in our case, because we never knew how much it would be for the kids.

But enough of these generalities. Let me get specific about FOOD — here in Rome and at the *pensione*. I'm sure that fancy people in Italy have a different experience, because the Italians have a fully articulated cuisine, with fancy pastries and all, but simple (and cheap) folks like us had the common fare.

Lunch always starts with *pasta*. Lunch is the big meal usually, I think. Of course you can have *antipasto*, but we usually didn't. The kids adore the pasta, especially Judy, who continues to call it "pasghetti." Pasta is any one of a hundred different shapes and sizes of spaghetti, with anything from butter and cheese to an elaborate sauce. You eat masses of it. We became quite good twirlers, even Judy, who resented having hers cut up. This is followed by some form of meat, and vegetables. One may have rice or ravioli — as on special occasions at the *pensione* — instead of pasta.

The meat is some sort of cutlet usually, fancy or plain. At the *pensione* the vegetables are odd; don't know what any of them are, except the raw artichokes with oil and vinegar. After this, you have a green salad, or not, then assorted raw fruits, cheese if you like, gorgonzola probably.

The slant at the Pensione Giacomella is, we were told, simplicity and wholesomeness of ingredients and purity of cooking. Garlic is used sparingly. At least, it is used extravagantly when used, but that's not often. Soup, meats, pasta sauces, etc., were without. Sometimes the strange veggies had it. This may be the governing principle at the *trattorias*, too, and, of course, south of Rome is a horse of a very different color, unknown to us.

For supper at the Giacomella, and mostly in Rome, too, one has soup — delicious, wonderful soup, either minestrone, which is thick and busy with vegetables and things, or, what was better, *brodo*, a bouillon-type deal, with any one of a number of pasta things in it, quantities and quantities, and grated cheese on top. Then fish, *omelette*, ham, or meat and salad. Then fruit and *caffè*.

Well, back to Rome. We were considerably restricted in our movement, as you can well imagine, having brought our two little ball-and-chains. The best solution turned out to be tours. We had always scorned that sort of thing, but they were awfully good, and with the kids it seemed the only sensible arrangement. (The tours are not cheap, but the kids were free, so that helped.)

Our first afternoon gave us a thrilling series of glimpses of ancient Rome — the Fora Romana, old temples, the Circus Maximus, Coliseum, etc. Exciting beyond words. I was prepared to be staggered, but I didn't expect to be all *that* staggered. Every step you take brings into view some work of art or other. Statues, statues everywhere. Hundreds of fountains. And, of course, once one gets started on the churches . . .

We did, I think, five tours in all. We saw many, many, many churches. You've never seen churches till you've seen Roman churches. Just to mention high points: of course, St. Peter's is really overwhelming — it is huge, too big to be imagined, to be believed — and, of course, each chapel as you drool down one side and up another has its own gasp.

We spent most of one morning in the Vatican Museum (gave the pope a miss). We had an excellent guide, who led us through infinite corridors of mouthwatering stuff, pausing to concentrate on only a few masterpieces, and swallowing the rest in great gulps, whole. As the guide pointed out, it takes two days just to walk through the whole museum, two weeks to study one hall-full, and three months to become vaguely familiar with what's there.

It is charming the way the Christians helped themselves to what they wanted from all the Roman stuff! (Read "outrageous.") Hadrian's villa, which we visited one day, has most of its contents in the Vatican Museum. The bronze and marble from the Coliseum is to be found in various churches throughout Rome.

For me, the thrill of a lifetime was, I'm afraid, not a discovery precious to me alone, though my ignorance of what's considered good, and rightly famous, made it possible for me to be struck dumb as by a fresh discovery. I refer to the ceiling of the Sistine Chapel, which is too beautiful, too perfect for words. The soft colors, the grace and rhythm of the whole, the delicate, sensitive detail of each part, the scope and variety of the theme, the unparalleled taste and excellence of Michelangelo's artistic vision are too lovely to be true. The breath-stopping moment when the outstretched finger of God touches the tip of the searching finger of Adam. I had a crooked neck for days. If only one could remove one's head and put it on with the eyes aimed straight up.

The huge end wall, which is the Doomsday of Michelangelo, would have been disappointing if I had been expecting anything. He painted it (or his apprentices did) some 30 years later, when he was quite an old man. The pope's secretary didn't like the idea of the figures being naked and had everybody draped, for which Michelangelo painted the secretary in one corner of Hell. The pope defended Michelangelo when the secretary complained, saying he couldn't help him, having no jurisdiction over Hell.

An utterly bizarre experience awaited us at the Church of the Capuchin Monks. Again, this is probably generally known, but I didn't know it and led the children innocently down into the crypts without a qualm. Apparently, the tombs through the years had gotten all filled up with Capuchin monks, and facing a — shall I say it? — grave shortage, they dug everybody (every *body*?) up, dismembered the skeletons, and made the most fascinating artistic designs all over the ceilings and all of the tombs with the bones — much as one would do with marble or plaster.

Again, it needs to be seen to be imagined. More than that, postcards won't do; they won't do for most of what we saw in Rome. It needs to be seen to be *experienced*. The ceiling looked like those elaborate 18th-century gold-embossed ones; except that the intricate tracery was more of an ivory color, of course. Occasionally, in nooks, there were still lifes — or should I say "still deaths" — featuring a reclining skeleton clad in monk's habit.

The children, being children, took it in stride. It didn't bother them at all.

David was an absolute angel throughout this Rome junket. Judy was a dud. A good sport, however, bless her heart. But David was actually interested, even fascinated, most of the time. Of course, everything we saw entailed vast explaining. For instance, the Michelangelo sculpture of Moses with horns, which meant all about Moses, and then why the horns, which meant all about translations, and so on.

David was awfully good about not asking us loud questions while the guide was talking. I suppose he discovered that if we were permitted to hear the guide first we would have more information to pass on to him. (The guide would speak in English, but the accent was too thick for David to follow.)

Judy was terrifying at first. She talked while the guide talked. She had to tie her shoe, or fell, or examined something while we were supposed to be hurrying along. She had to go to the bathroom when we were in some old church or ruin (the wall at Hadrian's villa received an offering from both young Garlans). In one magnificent church, I guess she felt she had really had enough, for she began to run, skipping and singing, up the nave and discovered a huge bronze pedestal and started to shake it. Its gentle rocking set me into pretty fast action, and I dare say a great number of interested saints were leaning down from the walls to catch it; I didn't take time to look. Judy couldn't understand why I waited till we got outside to inform her of my feelings.

But that David — I hope I shall always retain the image of him, standing in some huge, ancient church, staring up, pensive and absorbed, at a portrait of the Virgin or a sculpture of the Crucifixion.

We took the children one afternoon to the zoo and one afternoon to the film *The Living Desert*, which fell rather flat, I think, though they were very polite.

Florence
January 1955

We left Rome early in the morning, off to Florence, to travel by CIAT, the excellent bus service. It was a daylong journey, arriving in Florence about 7:00 that night. It was a beautiful bus trip and a pleasurable one. There was a very nice hostess, who took the kids absolutely off our hands and whom Judy immediately adored. We stopped for lunch at Assisi, a charming old town high up on a mountainside, as all the villages in Italy seem to be — so different from England, where you find them tucked away in valleys. We had a look at the basilica and the monastery and at St. Francis's tomb. The children, who had heard about St. Francis at school, think he is a girl and won't be shaken. (The name? The long robe?) "That girl who loved the birds, *you* remember, Judy," David would say.

And then, and then: Florence. Ah, Florence. Florence is as reserved and unspectacular at first as Rome is brilliant and extravagant. But you soon find that you can't take a step or open an unprepossessing door without stumbling on the Renaissance.

Arriving in Florence, we were really feeling the pangs of our empty purses and were determined to put up in the cheapest hole we could find. We marched into the CIAT office, told the young clerk we were broke, and asked him please to get us full *pensione* for the four of us for as close to $10 as he could come. His heart didn't seem to be in it, but he got on the phone and after some lively conversation with it in Italian told us the Ariela would take us for $15 a day.

We thought that wouldn't be too bad if the food was good. The food was excellent, he said, and the accommodations had a private bath. That did it, and off we went in a taxi, getting thoroughly gypped by the driver — who claimed we hadn't tipped the man we hadn't seen put our bag in the car, so he'd have to take him a couple of hundred lire — and helped himself on top of that to his own tip! We got out of the cab, quite reconciled to the thought of the impending dump, just to be rid of this dreadful man.

We turned to find the huge front door of a stately old building being opened by a uniformed little maid, who led us up one flight of a very grand staircase and into what we later discovered was one of the most elegant *pensiones* in Florence! It looked like a posh private home, in exquisite taste, which, it turned out, it had been until a couple of years ago, when financial pressures resulting from the war had obliged the mistress to turn it into a *pensione*.

The *signora*, who spoke some English, met us in one of the large antechambers we were shown through. She was chic, stylish, in a smart black dress and enormous stole, youngish, smiling, and blonde. They had waited dinner for us, and it was to be served at 8:15.

The maid took us to our room, which turned out to be a suite with a little sitting room at our disposal, then a couple of little antechambers, just right for the kids, a huge beautifully furnished bedroom, and the loveliest bathroom we'd seen since America, with a real toilet that didn't smell, two washbasins, and a huge tiled tub with shower.

Well, it was a bit of all right! I don't want to give the impression that it was showy or cold — not at all. It was tasteful, spacious, and dignified, with a feeling of peace, comfort, and smooth management. Of course, though I felt I'd come *home,* Edwin was a bit worried and felt he should have a heart-to-heart talk with the *signora* pretty promptly to be sure there was no misunderstanding about the $15. But *that* turned out to be all right, except that she thought we might like to leave a little something for the servants; but, then, we always do that anyway. It appeared that, its being out of season, and the Pensione Ariele being quite new, they really needed the business. We were the only people there, besides the family, as we discovered when dinner was announced and we sauntered into the charming dining room.

We were helped into our seats by the waiter. But I can't call him a waiter. He was a young, baldish, smiling butler, a dear, who had placed little cushions on the chairs for the children. Our table looked lovely, with delicate linens, beautiful, thin colored glass, etc. The children were enthralled with the glassware and made loud exclamations about my red ones and David's blue ones and Judy's yellow ones and Edwin's green ones.

The butler came round with a huge silver tureen of the most heavenly soup, from which we helped ourselves and from which he adroitly helped me do the children. The meal was food for the gods, and, though we had been eating well, was quite the best I'd had anywhere in ages — including Paris. And all the dishes came around twice! We had three desserts: a sweet, fruit, and cheese. The sweet consisted almost entirely of sweetened whipped cream, with parchment-like rolls of cookie.

I'd love to write and drool about all the delicious dishes we had during our stay there, but I must restrain myself. It was truly a gourmet's paradise, and, withal, beautifully served. Well, here's one instance. One luncheon dish was a cold fish salad, basically, but it came out of the kitchen on a long, fine china platter, and was shaped like a fish, with a real fish-head and smooth, pale, yellow back, all tightly decorated, with bits of olive and carrot, as scales.

Wine was extra and damn good. We nursed along a couple of bottles of old Chianti, the least expensive they had, and did very well for ourselves.

After the first evening, we arranged for the children to have dinner early (ours was at 8:00). They were extremely accommodating about that sort of thing. And, on their own initiative, they wheeled the kids' dinner into our room, which was ideal, and the little maid officiated. (We saw only two servants, fortunately, though there must have been a wizard or two in the kitchen.)

Breakfast was also the best we've had on the continent — *real* coffee, real butter, delicious rolls and preserves, hot chocolate for the kids (also wheeled in when called for in the morning: not the kids, the breakfast) — and appetizingly set out, with clean, crisp linens, etc.

Well, I'm not ashamed to admit it: I do adore all that sort of thing. And it was so unexpected, which added much to the fun.

So, Florence. I haven't written about Florence. Except that I do think this *was* Florence. Centuries-old Florentine families living graciously in centuries-old Florentine houses, beside the timeless Arno. We were a block away from the Arno, by the way, a very ugly river on the whole, I thought. Except, oh, the Ponte del Vecchio. What a gem, the only bridge left from before the war, the others having been bombed by the Germans when they left. The Germans had been camped on one side of the river, the Americans on the other. Awkward for everybody, we were given to understand by our *signora*. She was the one who said the Americans were the least unpleasant of anybody they had to put up with.

The Ponte del Vecchio has little bobbing houses lining it, all the way across, like a regular crowded market street. As you walk across, you go by masses of jewelry stores. Florence has leather goods and linens at very good prices, but as we had no money, who cared. We did yield to a long-nourished temptation to get me one of those long, slender umbrellas. They're terrifically smart; mine is very long and black, with a straight, decorated, real-silver handle; ooh, it is smashing. Judy got a little red plaid one. An onlooker could see us two swaggering down the streets of Florence, while our menfolk interested themselves in monuments and *objets d'art*.

There is so much to write about Florence, but I won't, except just to say that all the famous names took on *meaning* at last — the Duomo, Santa Croce, San Marco, the Annunziata, the Piazza Signoria, etc., etc. It is a wonderful city, and I think could easily, easily be preferred to Rome.

We arranged to train out of Florence on the third day, starting us on our way back to Laigueglia. We had to leave at 12:00, and the *pensione* served us a heavenly lunch before we left. The butler gave us some fruit to take along.

We signed the guest book and said goodbye to our hostess. The *signora* urged us to come back and said that, now we were clients, even if we came in-season we could have a special price. I weep to think that we probably never will. I truly cannot bear it, but the way our money has simply gone we probably won't get back to the continent in the spring. This was one reason why we grabbed Rome while we were there. But — oh dear, oh dear — it was only a taste, a mere sip; I can't bear it.

And not only Rome and Florence and dear Laigueglia, which I feel we *must* see again some day, but to think of all the places we didn't even peek at — Naples and Venice, not to mention Sicily, and all the little untrammeled mountaintop villages that do so need to be stayed at! Oh, damn money and the way it vanishes.

The staff turned out, and we got *huge* smiles in exchange for our tips, so they must have been adequate. The butler carried our bags down to the waiting taxi and with glistening eyes kissed the children goodbye.

Back to Laigueglia
January 1955

On the train to Genoa, our first lap to Laigueglia, we got into the worst rat-race we've had. Poor Edwin, what a time he had with the five great helpless lumps he had to dispose — me, the kids, and the bags. We had second-class tickets, but they don't seem to label cars, though everyone except us knew what was what. When we finally jockeyed our way into the second-class carriage, we found it bulging at the seams, so simply collapsed in the first-class car, which was cool and contained — containing, I should say.

So far, so good, right? But then Edwin had to deal with the conductor and pay the extra fare. It was terrible, because the conductor simply couldn't get across, in Italian, what he wanted to tell us. They struggled for about a quarter of an hour, and, finally, a French-speaking passenger offered to help, and Edwin got me, and we all straightened it out in a jiffy. But this was the deal, and you can imagine getting *this* straight in a language you don't understand: We were to buy first-class to Pisa, but at Pisa our train was to be joined with the train from Rome, and in Genoa the Rome part would proceed to the station from which we were to depart via another train, to Alassio. The rest of the Florence train stopped at the other station in Genoa, and if we were in that part we would have to taxi across the city. So the deal was, be ready as soon as they switched the *voitures* to make a dash for the second-class compartments on the Rome train, where we might find space.

Making a dash was something our little party was really not designed for, but Edwin did as he was told and leapt onto the Rome train as soon as it was coupled, only to find the car already packed — but our French-speaking protector smilingly saving us a bunch of seats.

Well, all this is neither here nor there, but it does give an idea of the kind of problem that arises. And poor, over-worked Edwin, fighting his way through endless corridors and heavy doors, holding up two bulging bags, one before and one aft, and piloting his worried little family along. Except that I tend, in these stressful situations, to get laughing fits. They are so ludicrous, and one's getting to where one wants to go is so haphazard, it seems an extraordinary piece of luck always.

Arriving in Laigueglia at 9:00 that night, we were cordially welcomed by the whole staff at the Pensione Giacomella and offered dinner. We were starved, so I said to hell with the children's bedtime, and we all sat down to a large meal. Buckets and buckets of Christmas mail from the States had been forwarded to us from Oxford, so we gobbled food and letters and slurped wine and talked with our *pensione* friends and found it a lovely homecoming.

We re-arrived in Laigueglia on Saturday evening and had planned, however reluctantly, to depart Monday afternoon because of our, shall I say, straitened financial circumstances. But we had not reserved sleeping accommodations on our train home. So, Sunday, we asked Madame if they would let us send them a check when we got back to England, saying we would like to stay until Thursday. (We would have just enough lire to get across the border, francs to get through France, and our return tickets from London-to-Oxford glued to our cuffs.) They agreed, and we were so glad.

In England, blizzards were blizzarding, and there were 10 inches of snow around our cottage. Of course, David was champing at the bit to get at it. None of this puttering around on the Mediterranean for him, when there was fresh snow in England.

When the day for our departure came, we were all very sad, and Edwin was sick with a cold. We made a little presentation to the management, just trifles, and I created a little poem. I think they were quite touched. We were served an early lunch, and when Madame waited on us, she was quietly crying.

I guess I've not described Madame Capriotti, so now is the time. She's not the crying sort. She's a large, strong, competent, matter-of-fact, handsome woman — an Anna Magnani — rather stern and frightening at first, but with a lovely, dry sense of humor. And the sternness is from sadness and affliction, her husband having been crippled by a fall and now residing in a rest home, all their money (apparently having been considerable) gone for that and for educating her two kids, now grown. She had lived in Rome for 20 years and adores it but will never go back or keep in touch with her friends now. So she is sometimes sad. But, as she says, it is necessary never to look back; one must always look to the future.

She seems to be doing a good job of making the *pensione* pay. All the others in town are empty at the moment: everyone, as she says, comes to Giacomella. After the war, she and the cook teamed up with the "Captain," who had been able to salvage some things from the little *pensione* he had before the Germans came. He found the piano 50 yards from the house, in the bushes.

The Captain is most amusing, describing and demonstrating how he hid from the Germans. Each day, he would pop his head out and see Germans. Then one day, he peeked out — no Germans. So out he came and was plucked by the back of his collar off to jail, or somewhere, by the French! He gave a demonstration, carrying himself off by the collar.

Here's one more glimpse of Madame Capriotti, this one regarding her cuisine. She explained that she gives *omelettes* to foreigners but very seldom to Italians because Italians all have livers due to too much passion, and *omelettes*, everyone knows, are death to livers. Foreigners, not having livers, are all very fond of *omelettes*. So that clears that up.

The farewell was a delicious Italian farewell. Everybody came out into the hall, smiling, tearful, kissing each of us on both cheeks, embraces, *arrivedercis*, clatter, and the moving of suitcases and children into the Captain's tiny car. He insisted on driving us to Alassio, though he had to put us down a block from the station so as not to anger his friends the taxi-drivers.

Oh, dear, how I hated to leave. It is one thing to say goodbye to people you expect some day to see again. But it is desolating to say *arrivederci* to people you expect never to see again.

Home to Oxford
January 1955

Madame's picnic lunch lasted us to the second day. We had a scrumptious lunch on the French train, too. *Hors d'oeuvres variés*, then a sort of creamed-fish-and-shrimp-on-biscuits dish, then rare roast beef with a mushroom sauce, apple cobbler, cheese, etc.

It was a fairly gentle crossing on the ferry; David felt a bit collywobbly, but we docked at Dover just in time. Old hands now, we were the first off instead of the last. Hopped on the best train to London, because it was supposed to be fast and we anticipated a devil of a scramble to catch the 7:25 to Oxford.

Of course, the train to London ran late and we got to Victoria about 6:45. We had to claim our other three bags, which we'd sent on ahead a couple of days before we left. We got a dream of a porter; some of them are really good, and you do have to depend on them absolutely. He got our bags out of hock and got us through customs quickly, the guy being "a decent sort," said the porter. The porter took us up the baggage lift ("the little chaps looked as if they needed a ride"), found us a cab, and sent us off posthaste to Paddington. We made it with time to spare, and anyway the trains were all running late; it was pea soup outside.

Got to the Oxford station an hour late and waited a while for a taxi. So what? We were dead-beat. But we were home.

It was a delightful trip and a great success. It is rather odd to look at England through Italian-colored glasses, having had only America to compare it with before. But, as Madame Capriotti said, "It is necessary never to look back; one must always look to the future."

The Memoir Resumes: The Unforgiving Minute

(ENGLAND AGAIN)

The ensuing months flew by. There was so much going on. We were now meeting people in Oxford at a great rate — now that it was almost too late to get a friendship going. The continent continued to lure us, as did other parts of England, sometimes with the kids, sometimes just *à deux*.

And, boy, do these academic aristocrats live it up. We went to a terrifically posh sherry party at the home of the Master of University College and, along with everyone else, were announced!

One morning we discovered that there was to be a party we should attend that very evening — for American friends sailing the next day — in Ealing, at the edge of London, not far from Windsor Castle. So we pulled the kids out of school at noon, hopped in the Morris, took them to see the castle, and then bedded them down at the party.

Another time, without the kids, Edwin and I squeezed in a memorable five-day trip to Devon and Cornwall. I mentioned earlier the charming little cove on the northern coast of Cornwall called Trebarwith Strand. We did love it, with its caves, beach, rugged rocks, smuggling legends, terrific Cornwall characters, and delicious food. Cornwall has much to be independent and protective about.

(FRANCE AND ITALY AGAIN)

Edwin and I took one further short trip to the Continent during those last, precious days. It was a bicycle trip in the South of France, to Avignon, Arles, les Baux, les deux Sainte-Maries, and the Camargue, all the way through Provence to Nice and — almost — to the Italian border.

(And I began to wonder whether, being so close to the border and all, we could possibly pop across and return, however briefly, to Laigueglia? I'll get to that presently.)

The train ride from Paris to Avignon was quite fun. The scenery was lovely, and the train itself gave the lie to much of what one heard about the misery of third-class travel. We felt most gratifyingly like natives when, at lunchtime, we brought out our loaf of bread and hunk of cheese and jug of wine — just like everybody else.

On arrival at Avignon, we successfully got ourselves settled at Jacquemart, the inexpensive hotel recommended to us by an English friend, as our base. Of course, from then on we had to rely entirely on our French.

Avignon, dripping with antiquity, has very high forbidding-looking city walls. The main item of interest there, the Palais du Papes, is a huge, impressive structure that housed the popes during their exile from Rome. Its effect was spoiled a bit for me when we discovered, just below it, in the shadow of its walls, the most incredibly broken-down slums that I have seen anywhere, and it was difficult to reconcile such unsettling discrepancies in the southerly reaches of Europe. And, of course, there is the Pont d'Avignon, which walks right out into the middle of the Rhône and just stands there. The Rhône is lovely, lovely. And it follows you everywhere in Provence.

We picked up our bikes, which we had sent ahead, and had a sort of trial run with them across the river to a beautiful old town with a fortress. We were made deeply aware, there, that Provence is very old and has been the scene of much bickering and fighting and was once Italian and, long before that, Roman.

In fact, in the course of our trip, everywhere we went was alive with history, villages and farms and bridges and monuments and museums, and we reveled in the breathtakingly lovely French countryside and, toward the end, were breathless and exhausted. It is so tempting to describe our many and varied adventures, but all I will say is, if one can, one must go there. Preferably back in time to 1954, when it was perfect.

On our detailed *Guide Michelin* map of the area, places looked awfully far apart, viewed with bicycle-conditioned eyes. These distances, I suppose, are nothing to seasoned young bicyclists, but as deteriorated old married folk we were very conscious of our deficiencies. At least, I was conscious of mine, but Edwin was sanguine, and as we studied the map he kept explaining that it was deceptively large and that in miles it was only half what it was in kilometers. So after much cogitating, we decided that we could get fairly comfortably to Nimes that day — about 40 kilometers, which was still, however you looked at it, 24 miles or so.

A little, self-inflicted problem was all the stuff we had brought. Though we had cleverly left one of our suitcases in Paris, to be picked up on our return, unfortunately by the time we had loaded everything we thought we needed into the suitcase we were taking, the other was practically empty, and the one we took was so heavy it was almost immovable. And it bulged ominously.

In violent reaction to this situation, we decided to dispense with *everything* for our overnight jaunt to Nimes. So we took only bicycle lights, puncture kit, plastic macs against rain (which we didn't once use), toothbrushes, and a pair of shorts for me (no pajamas or extra undies) — oh, and of course our cameras and our *Guide*. Once on the road, I discovered to my distress that I had forgotten my dark glasses and later, to our sorrow, our Michelin restaurant and hotel guide. There was, too, a discrepancy between us in our choice of wearing apparel. Edwin took no sweater or jacket, and I was dressed in my wool ski pants and warm windbreaker.

Oh, but it was lovely, tooling along in the hot, baking sun, with the cool breezes urging us on. Except for tangling with the occasional hill, it was smooth going through little villages and pretty scenery to the Pont du Gard, which loomed up at us, immense, as we rounded a bend in the road.

This structure presented one of *the moments* in our Provence experience. It is gigantic, it's beautiful, it's utterly practical, it's ingenious. In sum, it's Roman. How can I describe it? It is constructed of two-ton rectangular stones, on an archway principle, with three layers of several arches each, each layer as you look upward smaller than the one below it. It spans the river, which goes through a wide, green gorge at that point, so that the top of the *pont* is way high above. The road you come along is about halfway up the side of the hill and crosses the *pont* at, I think, the lowest level. It's a soft gray-yellow color and fits beautifully into the scenery, which is clean and foliagy. From the bridge, one can look for miles up the curving gorge.

Settling down in a cool, friendly spot under the bridge, we dove into our elaborate picnic of cheeses and *saucissons* and olives and tomatoes and ham and a baguette and wine. Then we had oranges. And then we had a big, fat siesta.

On the road again, we had a pleasant, uneventful ride to Nimes. On dismounting, however, I almost sank in a heap, much to my astonishment. All my muscles and bones and things protested querulously about this change of posture. But I found, on remounting, that my various parts were equally reluctant and quarrelsome. And my bottom was awfully sore. However, we had arrived in Nimes and quickly hunted up a cheap hotel and a good dinner and lived to tell the tale.

We sopped up history and culture and just the feeling of being in *la belle France*, so difficult to convey. But, I felt, oh, if we only could *talk* to people. If we only had the courage to seek out an unspoiled *café* or to walk into someone's farm and ask for hospitality — or at least a glass of water. But we never did. I think if we had each been alone we might have done it, but being together made us shy, somehow. It's the paradox of the tourist who wants really to be a part of the country, of the peoples one is visiting. But, alas, as with the cultural anthropologist, the very fact of one's being there changes the situation. And no matter how much one may empathize in fancy, one is an outsider in fact. This feeling weighed on us, and we retracted a bit and sent postcards to the kids and felt lonely.

(And I thought again of Laigueglia. If I could possibly manage to go back, would it be like that? But returning is so different, isn't it? Isn't it? One must never look back, said Madame Capriotti in my head.)

We were in the mood for the Camargue. This is the barren, desolate, mistral-swept area that spreads to the sea from Arles, the "gateway to the Camargue," as the posters say. The sea has flowed over this land again and again, till much of it is hard-baked, white, salty earth and part is marshes, where people grow rice and white flocks of flamingos and egrets make their home. Wild, white horses and *taureaux* — black, shiny bulls — graze here. Bullfighters come from Spain to pick their bulls. I think I have never been in a place with such a daunting, haunting impact.

Naturally, there is a nadir in any undertaking, and ours hit us in Nice. Edwin and I both came down with a nasty cold or flu or something and felt ghastly. Our trip was coming to an end, and in three days we would be loading the bikes and ourselves unto a train to Paris and thence home to Oxford. So the sensible thing was to stay put now and rest up for a couple of days in Nice.

Well, *of course*, that was the sensible thing. And Edwin was being very sensible. And I was thinking, a simple little bus ride and, *voila*, the Pensione Giacomella, wow. So I pointed out the bus idea, and Edwin, though unconvinced of its wisdom, was, as usual, very sensitive and generous about my feelings. You go, if you wish, he said, but I just can't do it.

I left early in the morning the day after our arrival in Nice on my overnight pilgrimage to Laigueglia.

What a treat it was to be back in Italy. The customs man and the passport man and everybody around were so wonderful and charming and alive. A nice young man at San Remy had arranged with the bus driver where to let me off, so, at about 2:00 in the afternoon, I dismounted just a block from la Pensione Giacomella.

A new girl opened the door. I asked for Signora Capriotti and walked in. First came Mariola, who greeted me warmly with the double embrace, and then the Captain and then my dear Madame, who peered unbelieving through the dim room. She kept muttering in Italian, and I kept laughing and saying "*Parlez français, Madame, parlez français.*" Finally, she came to life and hugged me and rushed to her desk to get a letter of mine that she had out to answer and rushed to her bedroom to bring out the pen we had given them when we left. She had taken it away from the Captain and reinstated it in the envelope we had presented it in, *"pour souvenir, pour souvenir,"* she kept saying.

Well, really, it was all one could wish. Of course, I was immediately asked if I had eaten, was I hungry? I said I hadn't, that I'd like a *petit peu.* She gave vast directions in Italian to the new girl, who went off to the kitchen. Everyone asked questions at once. I was brought a large *apéritif.* Then some soup came, and the Captain and Madame sat down to watch me eat and to talk. Madame would constantly get up and bustle out to the kitchen. I had a huge lunch and a bottle of their best wine — a somewhat sweet *spumante.* I simply could not manage all the food they brought me. Truth to tell, I was not hungry, being still feverish and all excited. But of course they clucked and said, *"Vous ne mangez pas! Vous ne mangez rien!"*

Then I said I would have a little siesta and let them get back to their accounts that they had been doing when I arrived. So Madame took me upstairs, pummeled a few beds till she found a good one, and installed me in my room. She turned back the covers, *"comme votre mère,"* and after some more affectionate embraces and gabbling, she went off, and I went to bed and slept till 6:00.

Well, and so on. We all walked by the sea before supper. I had a table next to the family and the almost undivided attention of the new girl, who was an excellent waitress. When I asked, during dinner, for my coffee *"subito,"* remembering that if you say *"subito"* you get it about 20 minutes later, she actually brought it *subito,* and Madame said it would be *freddo,* and I said, *"Non, non, ça va, grazie, grazie."* The evening was pleasant but short, because Madame discerned that I had *"la fièvre"* and made me go to bed early. She sat on the side of the bed, and we had a wonderful chat, though I did feel only half there and welcomed bed.

Next morning I had to leave, and it was cruel, cruel hard.

I go into all this at great length, partly because I love to remember that happy time, but partly to demonstrate how wonderful it is to go back to places — especially in Italy. Some day, some day, we will go back to Europe and not as a stranger but as a friend.

I returned to Nice in time for lunch, and afterwards we went down to the beach. It was pleasant.

The trek home, through France to Paris and London, involved the by-now familiar hassle with the bicycles, customs, various necessary papers, and snafus of one sort or another. We caught the 7:30 p.m. out of Paddington to Oxford and walked into Black Hill Copse about 10:00 to find the kitchen warm and the cottage fresh and fragrant. Our competent charlady had been busily cleaning and had just left. She hadn't expected us yet and was utterly chagrined next morning when she came, to find that we had returned before she had finished. She had put her children and her husband to work in the garden, and it was beautifully neat and "kempt" and had burst into riotous bloom while we were away.

We gathered up David and Judy the next morning from their sojourn with the charlady's family in Wooton Village, pleased to see that everybody was happy and well. They came running to meet us and hug us and were glad we were back, though they had had a lovely time. Ah, the joys of returning.

(ANOTHER SEASON OF RETURNINGS, LOVINGS, AND LEAVINGS)

"Turn! Turn! Turn! (To Everything There is a Season)" goes the song title, and now was the season for leaving. We had reserved a really good cabin on the Italian Home Lines ship *The Homeric,* due to depart from London on June 23 — unless the perennial dock strike goofed everything up — to arrive in Quebec on the 29th. It was a two-class ship with lots of deck space, a private bath, and good Italian fare (nothing wrong with *that*). We were booked to fly from there to New York, where Edwin had a lecture series engagement, and thence later in the summer to Santa Barbara and then home — our American home — in Oregon.

We began a frantic packing, and the place was a hurrah's nest. Our stuff for the ship had to get off in a week, unless, worry, worry, the train strike intervened. We were frightfully busy in a social way, too. Last glimpses of everybody and all. And we had to sell the car. That turned out well: a nice man came and offered us more than we'd paid for it, so that was one less concern. And, somehow, somehow, we pulled it all together and said our final, wrenching goodbye to Black Hill Copse.

Another season, another leaving, another returning. And the thing is, all was well.

‡ ‡ ‡

Six Americans at Home Abroad

Mostly Burma, With Smatterings of Several Other Countries

(LETTERS TO MAMBA)

Herein follows a sampling of letters to my Santa Barbara-based mother — known affectionately to her grandchildren, and thus to us all, as "Mamba" — about the Garlan family's life and times during our 1960s sojourn in Burma and our ventures thence to points east and west. These letters Mamba assiduously, devotedly typed, on her rickety old typewriter, from my handwritten scrawls. By now there were six of us: Edwin, 47; me, Patsy, 35; David, 12; Judy, 11; Robert, 5; and last, but very much not least, Sally, 2 years old.

We began this marvelous adventure with the excitement of a nightlong flight to Japan, a new experience, and brief stopovers in Tokyo, Kyoto, and Hong Kong, before pressing on to Burma.

We lived in Mandalay for nine months (mid-June 1961 to mid-March 1962) and followed that with travels to India, Greece, Italy, and Spain, all made possible by a grant from the Fulbright Commission, an inspired program set up by Congress to enable Americans to work and live abroad, broaden our minds, and be good ambassadors for the United States. Edwin's work was teaching philosophy at the University of Mandalay. Mine turned out to be working for

USIS (United States International Service), helping Burmese students with their English.

I need to explain that my frequent references to "Joan" are like references to a *deus ex machina*. She is my mother's cousin, the unsung angel who often eased our path during our Asian sojourn and in Europe. Because her husband was a high-up executive of Sterling Pharmaceuticals International, the two of them had deep diplomatic and personal connections throughout Asia and Europe, which she unobtrusively would activate on our behalf. Lucky, lucky us.

:: :: ::

Tokyo, Japan
Thursday, June 1, 1961

Full moon all the way (14 hours from San Francisco to Tokyo); jet very large; no fear; stop at Honolulu in middle of night (2:30–4:30), no fun in spite of their trying to persuade us it wasn't the middle of the night but only 11:30. This bizarre change of time and loss of a day was a most queer feeling — combined with not much sleep and children eating and sleeping at screwy hours. Hoping to get all straightened out today.

Met at Tokyo airport by a variety of men — a Fulbright one, a Joan one, a hotel one, etc. Taken by the hotel chauffeur to the Hirano Inn, as arranged for us Fulbrighters. (As I write, Robert and Sally just hup-two-three-foured down the hall, from their bedroom to ours, with the child's Japanese sword Rob was given by Joan's man over his shoulder, the sheath over hers. It is 5:30 in the morning; I'm afraid this will have roused the whole household.)

The Hirano Inn turns out to be completely Japanese-style. Nobody ever heard of it except a PanAm official who told me it was of the best. Prices seem high ($24 for our two rooms, and $12 or less for food — two meals for four) but are not, apparently, out of line.

While the rest of Tokyo is bulging with Rotarians, we are quite snug and smug in this peaceful little inn, in the center of the old Geisha section, with an eager, beaming, delighted cast of thousands tending to our needs.

We had tea and little matchbox-like candy cakes served us immediately; sat upon pillows for it; Robert's samurai sword accompanied him to table, to bed, to everywhere. We had decided to keep negative remarks to a minimum; so if one feels it necessary to say something one says, for instance, not "God, it's hot!" but, with heavy irony, "Nice and warm, isn't it?"— thus avoiding compounding one's own discomforts by six. The reaction to the tea and gelatinous matchboxes was therefore registered only in silence and rather queer facial expressions. It is also understood that everyone must taste everything, but no one must eat anything he doesn't like.

We then had an American-style breakfast (soft-boiled eggs, toast, and coffee). This sounds pretty straightforward, I suppose, but you have no idea what an undertaking it was for Edwin, who was trying to arrange for it to be brought from the kitchen, whence everything edible derived. He kept trying to order this, in his travel-guide Japanese. They kept sending up what they thought they heard, or, when that failed, what they thought we would like — the most astonishing being cold coffee in cups with a raw egg in each. Finally, however, the connection was made and all was well. We arranged ourselves around a very low table that sat in the center of our living room and tucked our legs down into a shallow, tatami-matted trough under the table.

Then baths. This was wonderful, the real shakedown that quickly settled us in. I should say "bath," since we all had the same one — the boys first, of course. The bath was huge and terribly hot; everyone soaped and rinsed with water in little wooden tubs first, in the large tiled bathroom, and then boiled themselves communally in the tub. Then beds were put down for naps; the four kids in one room and Edwin and me in t'other. We were given blue-and-white kimonos ("kinono," Sally says). There was much tittering and giggles when Edwin mistakenly put on mine and me his. I couldn't have felt more comfortable and "at home," with the soft, white-covered beds, the springy caress of the straw floors on bare feet, and the feeling of deep cleanliness and ease.

After naps we had tea again, the inn manager joining us, showing much interest in my Duke smokes. He has a collection of cigarette wrappers from all over the world and was delighted to add a new one. The inn people speak a little English, but not enough. The little maids are almost hysterically cheerful and make a great to-do over Sally-san. In their little kimonos, Sally is too fetching in hers, and Robert, with his blue kimono and sword and very confident barefoot swagger, is a little warlord.

We had not expected to plunge so suddenly into Japanese-style living, but — except for the kinks in my back, which I expect I shall leave in today's bath — it seems a wonderful stroke of luck that the Rotarians gobbled up all the American-style rooms.

Edwin went out to get money, thinking it a few blocks to the Imperial Hotel, where they convert one's dollars into yen. It turned out to be a 15-minute taxi drive, and he almost didn't get home; street names mean nothing in Tokyo, and the Hirano by name drew a blank. But he bumped into Gary Flint, an old Reed student, whose address we had tried unsuccessfully to get in the States! This was extraordinary and such a rescue, because Gary was able to get him a taxi — very scarce, raining, rush-hour, Rotarians — and give the driver some indication of where to look for the Hirano.

Edwin called cousin Joan's friend Burridge, and we were simply overwhelmed by the way he assumed on his shoulders all our little arrangements. He and his wife came to the Hirano at 4:00 and caught me just in the act of popping across the street with the manager to buy cookies and milk for the kids. What they must have thought when they saw this great hulk (I mean from the Japanese perspective; I don't really consider myself a hulk — it's not my figure but my height, a mere 5' 7", that gives them pause) flapping and clomping across the street in a flamboyant, blue-and-white kimono and wooden shoes! The Burridges — his most charming wife's name is Ann, but he seems to be just Burridge — have planned a wonderful-sounding three days for us, offered their maid as baby-sitter or to have the children to come to them, put their car and driver at Edwin's disposal, plan to take us sight-seeing, are finding a better booking for us from Kyoto to Hong Kong, etc. We couldn't seem to stop them from going to all this trouble, so great and powerful is Joan's name.

Incidental intelligence: One should not ask for things until one is ready to have them. Unlike the Italian *subito*, which could mean now, presently, or later, here the mere mention gets immediate results; e.g., if you ask about baths during breakfast, you will be led to the bathroom right then. I think it would be very easy for Americans to upset the Japanese by asking for too many things at once.

I asked the manager, "Bath, now?" And he said, "Tokyo General Station." We stared at each other for a while, and then I saw he thought "bus," and he saw I meant "bath."

After this first day or so, we were whirled away by the Burridges and painted Tokyo the appropriate color. We saw all sorts of drama, including a Noh play; the Burridges did not come to that but sent a Japanese friend with us, a very aristocratic gentleman who was a Noh fan. Perhaps the most fun was seeing *Madame Butterfly*, yet, at an elaborate Chinese nightclub, done by a Japanese opera company, while we gorged on superb Chinese duck, shrimp, chicken, etc., etc., etc., and danced between acts. Museums, exhibits, department stores, Tokyo Tower, the Zoo, marvelous restaurants, and a night-club with girls on display and to rent for the evening — interspersed with respites and highballs in the Bs' very comfortable apartment, where we saw Robert not at all from the moment he and their son

Lewis met (he slept, ate, and thoroughly enjoyed himself at their apartment)—gave us a spree we hadn't in the least anticipated. We liked the Burridges so much; and though we felt very guilty about accepting all their hospitality, there didn't seem to be any way of stopping it, so we just settled down and had a blast.

Kyoto, Japan
June 1961

Our exquisite little inn in Kyoto is snuggled in a miniature landscape of gardens, lovely to behold, with pathways among rocks and ferns and ponds with tiny waterfalls. The sliding rice-paper doors of our suite all but vanish when we step out into the gardens, so interwoven are the inside and outside of this serene dwelling.

I find it very difficult to write about Japan, to record my impressions, or say anything thoughtful. For one thing, so much of what one sees or experiences is so obvious, once one has seen it, that I feel it must have been a failure of imagination that prevented me from anticipating it. For instance, the people and black oxen preparing the paddies for the rice planting, the excessively gaily colored streets of shops (pinks, reds, blues, purples, blacks, and whites, fluttering flags and signs and what-all, mostly paper junk), the cool artistic settings of the rooms and gardens of the Japanese inns. On the other hand, the impressions that cut deep are on the whole pictorial, and one yearns to be able to catch them with sumi ink and brush, not with words. Or, rather, it would require such an effort to render them with words that I run from the task. And then again, I feel more and more strongly that experiences must be direct and immediate to be real and not shadows; so that even a poem would catch not the experience itself but something else—it would itself be a direct experience, but a different one.

There is, however, one aspect of our inn life I would like to think through on paper, and that is the general aspect and effect of living in a tatami room. The first thing that strikes one, of course, is the tatami mats; they are so soft, and when one is shoeless and kimonoed, one walks or sits on them at will, and the sense of distance from the floor (in western rooms, the floor is for the feet) is obliterated. One has, rather, the sense of living in a box — a box, however, whose walls disappear sometimes, or recede, or are transparent, so that there is no sense of being hemmed in, but rather set off, like a three-dimensional picture in a frame. The ceiling, walls, and floor are considered all of a piece and felt that way, perhaps because the proportions or areas of all are broken, or, rather, subdivided, by wooden strips or the clean lines of sliding rice-paper walls, so that one finds rectangles repeated everywhere, with restful variations.

This sounds very busy; it isn't. For one thing, there is always a focus of attention in the flower arrangement and scroll, or perhaps in a view of the garden beyond. The absence of furniture and clutter permits the space of the whole room to operate as space, and, in fact, one has the sense of inhabiting with one's whole body the whole space — rather than being compartmentalized from top to bottom as in a western room.

There is a pleasant shock in finding that the Japanese are cheerful, friendly, responsive — I suppose one should have known this, too. (Beware of hasty generalizations; yes, I know, but then I would be mute — "a good thing, too" did I hear you say?). I think I hadn't realized how much my notion of the Japanese was formed by the wartime image; how false this is. The paradox to me, however, is that this apparently natural ease grows in the context of the highly conventionalized, disciplined character of their upbringing. It is comparable to the Japanese "love of nature," which again involves such a different view of "nature" than our own.

Japanese nature doesn't just grow but is enhanced by the control to which it is . . . I started to write "subjected," but that is not the right word. In the Japanese aesthetic, "wild" nature lacks beauty until its beauty is revealed by the hand of man. There seems to be little that is allowed to be wild — in nature — including in human nature. It is hard for me to discern, or at least determine for myself, the relationship between art and nature. Rather stale questions arise, like doesn't art falsify nature? I suppose an answer to this might be: no, all human experience of nature or of anything is selective, and one unconsciously organizes and structures, according to often unexamined and perhaps indeterminate kinds of preconditioning. Japanese art (any art?) simply makes this process conscious and projects into the natural objects themselves what we ordinarily do in the mind. Thus, nature copies art.

I had never taken very much to the more elaborate forms of Japanese décor — screens, scrolls, paintings, or to the indiscriminate jumbling of harsh colors one sometimes sees. But here, one can digest much more of this, because it is absorbed with liberal doses of its opposite — the very simple, clean, open areas in scroll, screen, or sky; the extensive use of rich, dark browns in softly polished floors, rooftops, recesses of the temples; the soft blending of the pervasive natural straw and wood colors. Against these, the brilliant orange and white of the temples (the orange-painted wood pillars and beams, the influence of China) is both memorable and mellow. Perhaps all this points to the notion that, beautiful as a scroll may be when looked at and drooled over in one's living room or at a museum, its beauty moves in depth, range, and significance when it is seen as part of the integrated living pattern from which it grows.

We dug up Gary Snyder (poet and Reed College pal) on our last day in Kyoto — regrettably not sooner, as it turned out. We saw him in his dear little monastery, and in the evening he and his delightful wife came to our inn, bringing a bottle of Japanese whisky and some crunchy things that were wrapped in little papers with ancient obscene poems written on them that even Gary couldn't read because the Japanese was an old-fashioned kind. We sat on the tatami mats around our low table and consumed the whisky and crunchies and each other. It put the cap on a delightful glimpse of Japan.

Hong Kong, China
June 1961

In Hong Kong, we were squired about by Elaine and Joseph Chow, Joan's people. They were perfectly lovely and gave us a superb Chinese dinner at their home.

The Chinese women in Hong Kong are gorgeous. They all wear either the *cheongsam* or a sort of dress that is shirt and pants — stunning in silk — the shirt long-tailed, form-fitting, and very high-collared like the *cheongsam*. The latter is the most successful dress style I have ever seen, perfectly suited to the slender, small-breasted, handsomely legged Chinese woman. It is in all kinds of silk and cotton, very tailored-looking, simple and elegant, both dressy and informal, with the high collar and the slit from knee halfway up the thigh characterizing it. The skirt is tapered, tight under the bottom. The tailoring is always so good that the dress fits every curve, accentuates the small waist, etc. A tremendous amount of leg is displayed when she walks or sits.

Actually, there are tailors who can whip you up a *cheongsam* overnight, perfectly tailored to your measurements! You pick your silk, he takes a few measurements, and voila! — the next day you pick up your featherweight silken dress, and it fits like a glove. How do I know all this? Well, Edwin got me two of them (and a string of pearls). One is a deep blue, the other a fire-engine red, and while I can't claim a figure like a Chinese lady's, and insisted that the slit be less extensive, we found that the style is quite, quite flattering, even to the less-than-perfect form. I adore them and wear them everywhere.

I think I could like the Chinese best of anybody so far. The

Japanese have exquisite taste but are lacking in imagination and flair. The Chinese have both. Witness, for instance (or, better, eat) the Chinese cuisine; I think I would even set it up against the French for variety, subtlety, style, and just plain deliciousness. I wish I could take the time to describe the elaborate dinner the Chows fed us, from shrimp to chicken to beef to Peking duck to a whole fish, etc., etc.

In Japan, on the other hand, one may have *tempura* (which is terrific and can be very varied) or *sukiyaki* (which is too sweet) or raw octopus, salmon, squid, etc. And then you go round again. Their other dishes are quite ordinary. They do have wonderful beef in Japan, but there are only two or three places that know the best way in the world to cook it, and in Tokyo the Burridges took us to one. These are establishments that have a huge, hot steel plate; you sit on one side of it, and the cook stands on the other. He butters it slightly and then cooks, very quickly, cubes (about 2" by 2") of beef; he shoves these to your side of the griddle, with perhaps a mess of bean sprouts done the same, and you pick up the pieces as they come along, with chopsticks. This, with maybe a little bowl of soy sauce to dip in and maybe a bowl of rice and a glass of beer, is hard to improve on. Specially at the end of the evening, after a few hours of revelry with pleasant company.

Rangoon, Burma
June 1961

We are in Rangoon at last, being well taken care of by the Fulbright Commission. They popped us in a very nice house for our brief stay here, before we head upriver to our home-to-be in Mandalay. (Actually, we will journey north by land, but did you know that "the road to Mandalay" is actually the Irrawaddy River, "where the flying fishes play"? I didn't. Do now.) Here, we have a cook who is a doll; also, he is a tremendous cook. If I weren't so lazy I would attempt to describe him; he is so young and beautiful. He glides about in his bare feet, with a serene expression, and is at his very best at dinner, when he makes an elegant, smooth, swift tour completely round the table, bearing the roast lamb or chicken or whatever before he presents it to me to serve myself first. We have, too, a slender young nanny who smiles and does the washing and ironing and cleaning.

We have also in our ménage here a gardener and a guard, who paces up and down outside at nights, looking very fierce. He has run away from his people in one of the hill states (Kachin?) because he is peaceable and they are warlike and insurgent. We have also little tan lizards, geckos with beady brown eyes, who run about on our interior walls gobbling up bugs; they make loud kissing noises, very inspiring. Outside are crows — more than three — who make a tremendous tropical racket all the time, and huge lizards that make a noise at night like goats.

Everything seems very natural and normal now we are here in Burma. The heat is as expected, but the ceiling fans help a lot. There are mosquitoes, but not malarial, and actually we have been bothered less than in Kyoto; of course, we sleep under mosquito nets, and the house is screened. Occasionally, things happen that are a little out of the way but not awfully; e.g., night before last I looked out and there was a woman sleeping in our driveway in front of the house, straw pallet, cover, and all, with a chair beside her. The guard had brought his wife to keep him company, I think. Every once in a while, he sat in the chair and watched her sleep. And when he paced around, he seemed to be guarding her more than us. Yesterday morning, a man came and said his child had died and he needed money to bury him at 10:00 a.m. But our cook said that it wasn't true, so Edwin said he was sorry, but no. Then the man asked for a bag of food.

There is a huge, tall pagoda, the Shwedagon, that quite dominates the landscape — a great inverted ice cream cone. I wondered how they could ever build something so tall. Our guide said that there is a Burmese saying that if a man builds one layer at a time, he can build a whole pagoda.

So far, the one unique visual delight here in Rangoon has been the monks in their saffron robes, wandering everywhere. You can't imagine, at least I couldn't without seeing, how vivid and gorgeous these robes are — a very intense yellow, almost orange — and the greenery everywhere and hot sun to set them off; they are most effective at the pagoda, against the gold, and walking among the red-painted pillars of the scores of small shrines that higgledy-piggledy cluster at its feet, each housing at least one garish, gold-painted, white-faced Buddha. To one large, rather surprising, reclining Buddha, stretched comfortably out, smiling face propped on one arm, Judy said "Well, take it easy, why don't you? You're supposed to be helping the people, I thought."

I've said practically nothing about art, or Zen, or the children's reactions to everything, I see. Oh, well, I hadn't really meant to write all this stuff. If you care about the larger picture, you would do much better with a travel book!

I really don't feel that we are as far away from you as you probably think we are. It's funny how actually covering the ground (or air) oneself brings it all so near.

The commission has lined us up with house, staff, and car for Mandalay, and soon we will be off.

Mandalay, Burma
Near DSP's House, Old Civil Lines
July 1961

Two weeks in Burma. We arrived in Mandalay on June 24, David's birthday, and now I must write before the honeymoon is over — but who writes letters on a honeymoon? — to say that I have found myself high-spirited and cheerful from the moment we landed in Mandalay. The heat is immense, rains abnormally slight, the sky high, wide, and handsome, with great cloud activity. After the bustle of Rangoon, the peaceful town quality of Mandalay is very pleasing.

Let me start with the early-morning scene before my eyes. Between the bright green trees, among the mimosa with its million tiny suns, glides a monk, his saffron robe flashing orange among the green as he enters a gate and stands very still in front of the red-brick house across the road. A little boy comes running out with a dish from which he spoons cooked rice into the monk's large black-lacquered bowl. The monk turns and moves on to the next fortunate house — it is a favor he is doing the house, by providing the opportunity for giving and thus earning merit toward *nirvana* — and the scene is repeated, with another monk coming, to be met by a little boy, with monks coming to houses all over Burma. (I have been told that when the people have fallen into bad ways, the monks come by with bowls turned upside down, and this is usually enough to bring the people to their senses.) A herd of cow families goes by, a man with a long stick ambling behind them, calling to them; women with huge baskets on their heads, chatting; an oxcart creaking; a bicycle careening. And so the day begins.

For us, it begins with coffee in bed at 6:00, brought by our bearer, Aung Hla. I have mine under the mosquito nets, which are not proof against the human critters who creep under it; we sit about under the tent and discuss the state of our bowels and other pressing matters.

Aung Hla is a cheery fellow, a bit of a devil, they say, very good at everything; he is our bearer, chauffeur, messenger boy, gardener, etc. He is quick, intelligent, alert. When I yell out "Aung Hla! *Deego la sah,*" he comes tearing around the corner — "He running," says Sally — and smilingly presents himself. He lives with his wife, Ohm Ghi, who cleans for us, and their three children in the quarters in back of the main house. Living there, too, I think, is the guard and his son. In the other half of the servants' quarters (the whole thing smaller than our living room) lives Lewis, our cook, who is Indian and Catholic, his wife and four children, and his young cousin, who just came from the convent in Rangoon and wishes to be our nanny. Lewis is an excellent cook and a sweet man; he is conscientious and reliable, has worked for foreigners, and was brought specially from Rangoon for us. He is very small; his children are, too; the oldest girl, 6 years old, is about Sally's size. Perhaps this is just as well, in view of the size of their quarters. Lewis's salary is K140 (about $28; "K" is for "Khat," pronounced "chaht") per month; we spend about K140 a week for food. His English is fair — but quite good enough, because he is teaching us Burmese so fast we won't need English. The nanny's English is minimal, Aung Hla's wife's nil.

We hope to have the nanny, Salina, sleep in the house, if all works out. But we are waiting to see if Sally will condescend to make the adjustment. (She has been allowing no one to minister to her except Judy, Edwin, or me, without substantial bribes; this will not do as a way of life.) And whether the doctor gives her (Salina) a clean bill of health.

We are particularly fortunate in our servants, we are told. Many Fulbrighters and other Americans have squabbles and civil war breaking out among the servants, etc. Ours seem to get on well. I am so pleased with the household — so far. Lewis knows how to cook American, Indian, Burmese, Chinese, and, of all things, Yugoslav food. He and I are eagerly awaiting the arrival of the new stove, which will permit him to actualize all these potentialities.

We have been having chicken in various forms, lamb leg, duck, fried rice — all agreeably seasoned and done up. (Yesterday, I realized for the first time why the chickens are so fresh and nice; I went into the kitchen, and there they were, two of them, under the kitchen table, quite live and be-feathered and all, waiting their turn. Ew. Lewis doesn't trust the dead ones, he told me.) With the spices, they all taste the way perfume ought to. The mangoes are particularly nice — though treacherous, we found to our inner distress, except when served quite firm — rather like a cross between nectarines and cantaloupe, not at all like the icky (probably overripe) mango I tasted and harshly rejected into the shrubbery as a child.

The Fulbright Commission has taken wonderful care of us. The Burma Commission is rightly reported to be the most generous in the world. They have provided a house and furniture and a budget to augment the latter; arranged for our staff; are actually buying a car — Jeep station wagon — which we will rent from them; and have supplied us with a Morris Minor in the meantime. (In contrast to a horrible tale of a Fulbrighter to Pakistan, whose year there cost him $5,000 and no end of misery; in Japan, too, I understand, the Fulbrighters fend for themselves — not at all easy to do in crowded Tokyo or Kyoto.)

The house is new and sparsely furnished, which I rather like. It is screened, thank God, and we have not been badly pestered by mosquitoes; in Japan, we were almost totally consumed by them. Mosquitoes are, on the whole, nonmalarial in Mandalay and in Rangoon. The water is not reliable, but Lewis is and boils it for drinking, dishes, washing vegs, etc. The heat is our cross, but even in this, with ceiling fans and sometimes a breeze and sometimes a downpour and many shower baths, we welcome the variation from hot to not-so-hot, as at home we would welcome the snow. Also, our tummies are complaining of the change in water, the climate, the mangoes, or something, but not too loudly.

We have met many people whose affable welcome and thoughtful consideration of our needs and pleasures made us feel at home immediately.

We had chosen to fly from Rangoon — in preference to driving, which is uncertain because of bandits, and to going by train, which is uncertain because of insurgents who blow up the trains sometimes — only to find that these dear old Burmese planes have a way of falling to pieces in midair. Ours didn't, however, as you may have deduced. We had a bumpy but mostly monsoon-less two-hour flight, during which we Garlans, I'm proud to report, were almost the only ones to keep our stomachs in place.

We were met at the tiny airport by a fourth-term Fulbrighter, known to Rangoon and Mandalay and pretty much throughout Burma simply as Maryjane. (As we crossed the lobby, she pointed out the CIA man, whom nobody is supposed to know about but everybody does; I think he was scouting for drug dealers.) She teaches English in the Teachers' College here. Meeting us, too, was her friend U Sein Tu, Edwin's colleague and boss at the University of Mandalay. Maryjane had with her a basket containing a bottle of Scotch and bottles of lemonade for the kids — you can tell at once what a dear sort she is — and we all repaired at once (why repaired, I wonder?) to our house to look into them. Lewis was in the kitchen whomping up a birthday dinner for David's birthday celebration.

We sat and gabbed of this and that. Maryjane is a nice combination of down-to-earth and lively, generous, warmhearted, and independent. U Sein Tu, after four years of Harvard, talked academy with Edwin, and it sounded just like home. Maryjane is putting out a series of books on teaching English to the Burmese and will let me help, I think. I have just the qualifications she needs: I know nothing whatever about the formal teaching of English! So I'm to read her stuff and tell her critically and honestly whether I could teach from it.

Maryjane threw a cocktail party for us where we met many charming Burmese and a couple of not-at-all impossible Americans. People keep dropping in, and our neighbor, the district superintendent of police, whose wife is our landlord, sent us presents twice. The first time, it was a tray of mangoes. We reciprocated with (Lewis's idea) from the commissary, 1 pkg. Jello, 1 pkg. Kool-Aid, 2 small boxes cornflakes. But yesterday came a huge tray of assorted fruit. Gad.

There is so much to tell, about the town, about the Burmese, about our Burmese tutor, about the children's schools, and about the little things — like the beautiful feather brooms that Edwin wanted to put on the wall for aesthetic purposes and the "fly swatter" that looks like a cow's tail (and probably is) — but this letter is far too long already. I will content myself with three little anecdotes. One concerns Robert, who was looking out the window with me one morning. I said, "Oh, Robert, see the monk going by!" He looked for a long time and then said, "I see a red boy, but I don't see a chip-monk."

The second illustrates one of the baffling things about people here. Our Burmese tutor — an elegant, cultivated, older man, well versed in Buddhism, who as a tutor deplores what he snootily calls our (admittedly casual) "bazaar Burmese" — is also, like Lewis, Catholic. One day, when we were seeing him out after our session, we found that his Catholicism did not preclude his warning us about the *nat* spirits — the ancient animist belief that spirits inhabit everything in nature — that can come into your house, on your shoes, if you are not careful; this is why you leave your shoes outside the door on entering. He said that he did not believe in the animist spirits, but once you let them in the house it is hard to get rid of them.

The third will give you, I hope, a little of the flavor of Lewis. I suddenly began to wonder why we haven't yet tasted Burmese curry — quite different from Indian curry, as we know it at home, I take it; less curry power, more like a very interestingly spiced stew. "Lewis! Why haven't we been having curry?" "Yes, madam, I am just now thinking. I have all the spices, but I am needing a stone. I want to grind the spices myself, madam, then curry be nice. Because, you see, madam, if I am buying already mixed, they put in everything, curry not so good, madam. Sometimes stomach ache is coming." "Do you need to buy a stone to grind them on?" "I'm go see at my village, madam. My mother is knowing where to get stone."

I see I must give you a fourth anecdote, because it is an outcropping of the Nat spirit phenomenon alluded to above. It concerns our worry over a rash Sally developed on much of her little body and sweet face. Actually, the entire household shared our concern, by which I mean the servants, who were full of helpful suggestions. After the local miracle powder, *thanaka*, which all the ladies use as a beauty powder, failed to alleviate Sally's condition at all, the prevailing view was that we should get a seer, a sort of medicine man, to diagnose the problem and propose a solution.

As it turned out, Aung Hla had an uncle in a nearby village who could serve this function. So the seer came and explained to Edwin, whom he rightly perceived as the person in authority, that Sally's affliction had probably occurred because — again! — the *nat* spirits, the household gods, were annoyed by the family's wearing of shoes in the house. It showed disrespect. That was the diagnosis. And the cure? The thing to do was to put out a basket of fruit in the holiest place in the house, which he reckoned to be the desk in Edwin's study, and leave it there overnight. No one must go in, in the meantime. The gods would come and be pleased and APPEASED.

We ran this by our erudite Burmese teacher, who frowned on the plan, for the above-mentioned reason about how pesky it would be to get rid of them.

Still, something had to be done. So, enormous quantities of fruit were brought from the market, the seer came and shooed everyone out of the study except Edwin and performed a little ceremony with various incantations in Pali, in the privacy of the all-male twosome. Then they came out, and Edwin locked the door.

Now, I suppose you think I'm going to tell you that the gods ate the fruit. But, no. I am going to tell you that Sally's rash went away — for the time being. The gods just sniffed the fruit, and in the morning when Edwin opened the door, he invited the servants to divide up the fruit among themselves, so that everyone could share in the good luck.

I don't know at all whether all this is of any interest to anybody. But if you love us a little, and love life in all its forms, perhaps you will bear kindly with this small offering.

Patsy

P.S. Here is Edwin's letter to Mamba, giving a whole different dimension to our experience.

Mandalay (Edwin's letter)
July 1961

Like any traveler to foreign lands, I see the familiar as the strange and the unfamiliar as the impossible. Today, I for the first time participated in what would be called, I suppose, an official bit of academic behavior. I marched in an academic procession onto a stage amid hundreds of faces looking on, in step with what is comparable to Reed's "traditional" horn group. It was convocation. Like convocations, it was full of praises, hopes, exhortations to duty, to God, and to country. Learning for its own sake was extolled, with adequate compromises for the fact that not one in ten of these students was here for any better reason than that he sought to obtain a job some four or five years hence. The many speeches, including the traditional one by the student leader, droned on and on as they do elsewhere. Everyone but the girls, all segregated in the front part of the "auditorium," became duly restive within the half hour and then struggled unsuccessfully to keep still to the end. Respite was given by the very occasional opportunities to laugh or to applaud, and finally it was over, we marched out, and everyone felt better about having done his duty, including myself as I rushed away to meet with our tutor, who was waiting, as far as I knew, at our house. (Though he wasn't, not having arrived by the time I got home.)

Yet the whole operation both seemed and was strange. Of

course, all but one of the speeches was in Burmese. The banal, thus cloaked in strange sentences, seemed even more monotonous and ritualistic than it would at Reed. Professor Singh, dean of science, the only one who spoke in English (in a high, solemnly thin voice) revealed to me — with surety — that all the speeches were along the same line, for they all had the same effects as his did on the students and on me. Nonetheless, his English really seemed more foreign than the Burmese to me; and the Burman syllables, nearly all of which are, from our mode of articulation, slightly off center — like making every "g" into "ng" and every "h" a compromise between ours and the German "ch" — kept one sensitive to how foreign even the elements are. (Their spoken language is like their color patterns — like bad color photos.)

The students were all "freshers"; they have no hall that would hold more than that — about 700 I would guess. As indicated, the girls were all up front and comprised about one-fourth of the audience. All but one wore a *longyi*, the traditional long skirt secured with a twist of the fabric at the middle, and a sort of corset-cum-bra setup, and thin, transparent, long-sleeved blouses. Both *longyis* and blouses were in all colors of the Burmese color pattern. Actually, the outfits were quite fetching, the hair tightly coiffed, and the girls lovely to behold. The boys appeared in row upon row to the back of the room almost faceless, and the whole effect was something like that of the Hall of the Thousand Buddhas, which we visited in Kyoto (the Sanjusangendo, to be one up). This effect occurs in part, I suspect, because the girls all sit with their hands in their laps (there was some variation toward the end), Buddha fashion — the palm of one hand forming a cradle for the back of the other. They did not give up this "hand stance" even to applaud but sat there immovable while the boys got all the exercise.

The procession, by the way, which moved from one main building to another across a dusty road, was presumed to start at 9:00 a.m. I happened to arrive five minutes early only to find that the procession had already started, and, indeed, the whole speech ritual began at least three minutes before nine. (There were only some 16 of us in this august group, and this included about six of us foreign visitors; only department heads were supposed to participate.)

The University of Mandalay's summer program was scheduled to start about the 15th of June. Since we arrived in Rangoon on the 19th, one would have thought I was in the way of being a bit late. But, no; everyone urged us to "recuperate" from our trip to Rangoon (which we did, until the 24th) and that it would be all right for us to come "late." On arrival here in Mandalay, we were in effect told to "recuperate." I thought all this was a matter of courtesy to a Fulbrighter, but I was wrong. The starting of the university is something, I gather, like the starting of a four-motored plane: one motor starts, then another; one rolls out to the takeoff, warms up and tests, and waits; and finally the whole thing starts down the runway. Or perhaps the model is that of these loose-jointed, two-wheel oxcarts which seem never to start as one piece and only move at all after very slowly overcoming inertia. At any rate, it is only this coming Monday that I actually meet my classes — the students to which have not all showed up yet.

Philosophy is part of Psychology — or vice versa, one can't tell. The department head, U Sein Tu, however, is a psychologist with a Ph.D. from Harvard, where he spent four years (and one year at Columbia). He is young, enthusiastic, anxious to build a strong department, and one of the best bison, tiger, leopard, and wild boar hunters in the area. So far, we have had about five gallons of tea, three gallons of beer, one gallon of coffee, and 30 *cheroots* together. We have shared much of this with a friend of his who teaches "Commerce" and who spent a few years at NYU. (We have also had lunches brought in, on occasion — almost any occasion — by the bearer, who seems to do nothing but wait around for orders to go get us something to drink or eat.)

One other member of the Psych team has just returned from study under Klineberg at Columbia. The Philosophy "group" consists of a very unhappy Indian (he was done out of the headship — by politics — he feels) who teaches metaphysics, epistemology, and Eastern philosophy; and Daw Gyi Gyi Hla, a young married gal with three children who doesn't show it in the least. She was, I understand, Miss Rangoon and also Miss Mandalay — and looks it. Her specialty — most unlikely — is symbolic logic. The rest of the staff consists of "tutors" and graduate students who carry on some kind of quiz sessions for the large courses taken by the "pass" students in the first two years.

My office was, I am afraid, something of a disappointment to David. It has huge 12-foot doors padlocked on the outside. Opening these, one meets with swing doors like the old-time saloon. Opening these, I can see the legs only of the students passing by along the arched passageway onto which my office opens. Indeed, I can practically stick my foot out and trip them. (The ceiling, by the way, is about 15 feet high.) My big, padlocked doors seem to be for show, since at the side of my office is a doorless passageway to a Psych reading and seminar room which appears to be open all the time.

Apart from my padlock (made in China), my big doors, and my frontage on the arcade, my main status symbol is a mechanical bell which permits me to call the "bearer." All I need now is a loyal following of students!

Edwin

Mandalay
July 18 or so, 1961

As I sit cross-legged on my bed starting this letter, our little nanny, Salina, Ohm Ghi, and Sally are all three playing about on the floor at my feet. Sally is rolling herself up in the straw mat, and Salina is chortling and peeking at her; Ohm Ghi peeks, too, as she absent-mindedly brushes the floor with her feather broom, waddling about like a duck. Aung Hla is gardening outside the window and calling out teasingly, "Saaa-lly? Saaa-lly?" Salina tells her, "Say *Shin*?"— a politeness meaning "Sir." Sally has a white powdery stuff on her face and arms, which, after all, controls what turns out to be the prickly heat that keeps visiting her. It beats Johnson's Medicated Powder hollow. When I first saw little kids, their faces all whitened, scratching away at their scalps, I thought they had some horrible skin disease; it's only a combination of insect bites, prickly heat, and *thanaka* — the latter considered, I may have mentioned, a beauty effect as well as a facial. Dolled-up ladies riding along in pony carts or on *tri-shahs* (a bicycle-taxi with a sidecar for passengers) wear it.

This *shin* business, by the way, as opposed to *kimb-ya,* is the female version of "sir" or "madam"; it is how a woman says it. Similarly, "I" — *Chinma* is what girls say; *Chindaw,* the men say. Thus I would say *"Nay kaung yeh-la, shin*?" for "How are you, sir (or madam)?" E. would say *"Nay kaung yeh-la, kimbya*?" to which the answer is, in case you're curious, *"Nay kaung bad eh, shin"* (I say). Or *"Nay kaung bad eh, kimbya"* (E. says). Or, on occasion, *"Nay ma kaung boo*!" ("Ma boo" is the negative, usually.) *"Cheh-zoo-tin-ba-deh"* — "Thank you." *"Kesa ma shee boo"* — "It's nothing" or "Don't mention it" or "Pas de tout." *"Kaung"* — health, good will, sun.

The beauty of this language is its simplicity, in that words are usually only one or occasionally two syllables. To change tense or shades of meaning you just throw in another word designated for that purpose. There is one word to create a negative (*ma-boo*), one for past tense (*bee*), one for politeness (*bah*). So, for example, the word "go" in English requires a different word for past tense ("went" or "gone"). In Burmese, go is *"thwa,"* and it's always *"thwa"*; the past tense is *"thwa bee."* If you are playing tennis and a ball is hit out, you call out, *"Thwa bee*!" ("It's gone out!")

Our tutor will be here presently, and I haven't been practicing.

He comes for 1 hour–1½ hour, four or five times a week. Then Aung Hla gives us a workout at mealtimes, so that we know everything on the table, plus orders such as *"Pankah pwen-lik"* — "Turn on the fan." And requests such as *"Chey-zoo pu-yu-ee"* (please), *saa* (salt), *pyau-ba* (give) — thus "Please pass the salt." *"Ba"* is put in for politeness. For instance, as above, *"Kesa ma shee ba boo."* Bazaar Burmese, indeed, and just what we need.

Well, I didn't mean to give you a language lesson. Judy, by the way, is learning the alphabet at St. Joseph's. David is getting no formal language training. I think we shall arrange for French lessons for him and Judy, considering they'll have five months of travel later when they can really use it.

Robert has a special friend at school. A Burmese boy of his age walks along with him, hand-in-hand, to and from school and just around. It is a sweet sight, and a common one among the young boys. Somewhat older girls do this, too. They look so pretty and happy, in their laughing, charming intimacy.

Robert has a deadly fear of snakes. And, one might say, rightly so. But of the three kinds of poisonous snakes in Burma, only one is to be really leery of. The cobras always coil before they strike, so you have time to skedaddle. The other big, green ones, I forget their name, are very shy, so it is good to shuffle along, if you are in the grasses, to warn them that you are there so *they* have time to skedaddle. But the adders! These are the baddies. They coil not, neither do they flee. And they really, really don't like being disturbed.

So one morning, when Robert, David, and Judy were getting ready for school, Robert came barreling out of his room to say that there was a big snake in his schoolbag, which he kept hung on one of his bedposts. He was desperately distressed when no one believed him. We all scoffed because it was like the boy who cried wolf. Still, I called Aung Hla, who said, *"Kesa ma shee ba boo"* — "Madam, I think maybe a pencil; I go see." So we all of us traipsed into Robert's room.

We gathered round Robert's bed, Sally's chin resting on the edge of the mattress, and Aung Hla lifted down the schoolbag. He reached into the bag and, soothingly to an agitated Robert, said, "See, Robert? It's just a pencil." And then, pulling out a ruler, "See, it's just a ruler." And, with a great show, he dumped all the bag's contents onto the bed. And, you guessed it, a largish snake came writhing out! I grabbed up Sally, we all jumped back, Aung Hla quick as lightening gave the snake a mighty whack on the back with the ruler, grasped it behind the ears (I suppose they have ears), and hurried it outside. And we all began to breathe again.

There was not then, nor has there been since, consensus of any sort about how the snake got into Robert's schoolbag. Some — me, for instance — thought that probably one of Robert's school chums had put it there for a prank. And it was probably therefore not a poisonous kind. Some thought, "Well, or maybe it was the servants, for fun" — though it was not much fun at the time, somehow.

But Robert thought that it came there on its own, slithered into his room and onto his bed and up the bedpost and into his schoolbag.

I have often considered answers to questions I'm sure you would put, but usually I'm not sitting writing at the time. Like (1) Does the *dhobi* beat the clothes on rocks, and what then of one's nylons and treated cottons? The answer is yes, he does, with a stick in the Irrawaddy. The first time we sent our laundry out, all Judy's underwear had the elastic beat out of it, and it became twice its width, just giant panties. But now our sweet Salina washes our nylon things and Edwin's socks and Robert and Sally's clothes. (2) What about mildew and mold? This is no problem in Mandalay, because it is dry here. But when Edwin came back from a conference in Rangoon, everything in his suitcase was quite wet just from being there.

It seems to me David and Judy have grown up a lot on this trip. Doing things together as a family has brought out the best in both of them. David has now separated himself from the younger members and prefers to sit and listen to the adults whenever permitted; he loves to accompany Edwin places — they did a lot as a twosome in Kyoto — and he copies his father in everything. Judy has been perfectly lovely, very helpful with the little kids (refusing sometimes to leave them with a nanny in Japan or Hong Kong while we sightsaw, feeling Sally needed her), positive in her responses and generous to a fault in sharing things, treats, and goodies. Her keen perception and distinctive perspective of what is going on make her an entertaining companion. (Is modesty appropriate in discussing one's children? I don't think so — it's not my fault they're the way they are.)

A word about the *dhobi*: he is so wonderful-looking — a mustachioed, turbaned Indian, dressed all in white robes and with a wrinkled, sad-looking face. He refused to set a price for his services, saying I should ask the other *memsahibi*. So I asked and told him my figure: K50 per month (many pay much more, but this is what the Burmese pay). So he said it wasn't enough. We thrusted and parried a bit and finally, with a great sigh of resignation, he accepted the deal.

(Note: In Asia, we've learned, if you don't haggle and bargain over prices, in the bazaar or wherever, you take away all the fun of the interaction. It is expected.)

It is quite an event when he comes. Ohm Ghi turns to, and she and Aung Hla or the *dhobi* or Salina strip the beds and replace the dirty sheets with the nice clean ones he has brought; these are carefully inspected. Then they spread the nice clean tablecloth on the table and give it the once-over. Then Aung Hla gets his book and, piece by piece, checks off everything the *dhobi* has brought. Then they gather up all the dirty clothes and the *dhobi* sits in the center of the living room in a great pool of dirty sheets and clothes, and Aung Hla counts them and writes them down in his book. After half or three quarters of an hour of this, the *dhobi* sits in the kitchen and has a little chat with Lewis. He then goes off carrying the huge, white bundle, the size of a calf, on his head.

Since my last epistle, a small bright star rose and set in our household. This is the heart-rending saga of our nanny, Salina, as it has been unfolding. Have I described her? She is about David's height, 16 years old, a slender beauty, with dimples and a merry, captivating chuckle. She is Sally's slave, I'm afraid — cares for her with solicitude and tenderness. When Edwin and I are cross with Sally, Salina becomes very frightened and tries to get between Sally and us to ward off our anger. If she only realized that it is we who need support against the little critter, who can protect her own self. (I'm not sure Salina apprehends that I love Sally to pieces.)

Salina calls me "Auntie." "Yes, Auntie" — so solemnly. It disconcerts me a little. I don't mind being madam-ed and even sir-ed (with only one word for both in Burmese, they get mixed up). But Auntie! It makes me feel so old-lady. But it also makes me feel very responsible and mature, and I shall go about with my hands folded over my bosom.

She can be quite firm with Sally. "Sally bath, Auntie?" she will say and bundle her, kicking and screaming, into the little tin tub. Or "Eat, Sally! Sally good girls, no?" "Come, Sally. Powder. Then we go playground."

I will say, "Salina, have you had any dinner?" With a smile, "No, Auntie." "Well, go have your dinner, dear, for heaven's sake." "Yes, Auntie. Thank you, Auntie." She has her meals in the servants' quarters with Lewis's family. She sleeps in the house — we bought a bed for her — with the two girls.

She is most willing and actively helpful, feeding the children at meals and generally helping Aung Hla pass things. I found her the other night ironing the children's clothes in their room with about 25 watts of light. (The iron, by the way, cost us more than a month's wages for Salina. Salina: K80; iron: K85.)

When I had a little bout of dysentery or something a couple of weeks ago, she came to me where I was moaning and agonizing on my bed and began to knead my stomach with her strong little hands. After the first shock, it was amazingly relaxing. Then Ohm Ghi flipped me over and dug and soothed my muscles and whatnots from the shoulders to the heels. This is such a good medicine; it is good for the people who administer it, too. It costs nothing and permits them to give tangible expression to their concern and desire to help.

Salina came from Rangoon with no possessions or clothes, poor thing, having left under rather strained circumstances, the complexities of which didn't unfold themselves until later, as I shall shortly relate. When I gave her her first half-month salary, Lewis took her to the bazaar; they came back and showed me the three or four toilet articles they bought and some pieces of cloth to make blouses. She has been wearing Lewis's wife's *longhis*. She would dearly love to wear her *sari*, but she saves it for church (Catholic). Lewis explained to me how grateful she was, and Auntie and Uncle were "like Mummie and Daddy to she's."

She would never dream of refusing a request, of course. Except once. The other day, as we sat at lunch, a great blue lizard (a chameleon, I suppose) showed himself quite close outside the house. We said, teasing, "Salina, go and bring in that lizard." She started back with a shudder and a shake of the head, but participated happily in the laughter following. She got her revenge the next day, however. She came running in and said eagerly, as if calling me to a great treat, "Oh, Auntie, come see!" — and beckoned me outside. There was Aung Hla holding up a dead lizard by the tail and advancing toward me with it. So it was my turn to shudder and back hastily away and theirs to lead the laughter.

When she gives you something, she doesn't hand it to you; she presents it on her palms-up two hands together. When she has to move or pass in front of you, she bends forward and down like a roadrunner bird crossing the street. At the USIS library the other day, Salina, sitting on a low library bench with Sally, was deep in a book when I started to round them up, with my stack of books two feet high for the children — two each: that's eight. (Without TV, they have begun to gobble books.) I asked Salina if she would like to bring a book home; she was so pleased, and we brought two. They were in Burmese, of course. The one she was reading was about Thomas Jefferson.

She reads in bed at night, in a very bad light. Judy says she has a picture of the Virgin Mary under her pillow.

So that was Salina — was, and I hope will be again. If my verb tenses are confused, it's because she has gone away to Rangoon, and we don't know if she will be back.

When Lewis brought Salina here, he said that she had left "Convent in Rangoon" and that he had undertaken to be responsible for her. She had been very unhappy in Rangoon. She had lived for a while "with Aunt," who had been unkind to her. And that was all we knew until, out of the blue, her mother showed up (with her little brother) and said she must come to Rangoon; her father wanted to see her. Everybody, including the servants, was devastated. It would take forever to elaborate all the details, but the gist of it seemed to be this: when the convent closed for two months during Lent, she went home to her parents, but they fought all the time and this made her sad, so she went to stay "with her Aunt. Her Aunt is bad womans, took Salina's earrings and her clothes, and pawned them." She was very cruel to Salina, and when Lewis saw her she was all swollen with tears and hadn't been eating. He told her she could follow him to Mandalay and he would be responsible for her and try to find her work. Now her father wanted her to come back and tell about the Aunt so they could get Salina's belongings back. She didn't want to go, but when father says come, you come, I guess.

So after an enormous confabulation during which Edwin emphasized that she must return in one week, Edwin wrote a letter to Salina's father, almost at Lewis's dictation, saying we would care for her like a daughter, etc., etc. The mother, a large betel-chewing type whom I didn't much care for, was favorably impressed by Salina's set-up here and promised to return her.

There followed a most touching scene in the kitchen, witnessed by the hordes who had forgathered, in which Salina kept saying, "I come back, Auntie. *Saik me kaung boo,* Auntie ("I am very sad"). I come back, Auntie." She then dropped to the floor in a little ball and kissed Edwin's feet. He said afterwards that though this is embarrassing to us, it is natural to them. But it was more than embarrassing to me, it was awful, and when she tried to kiss my feet I couldn't stand it and hauled her up by the shoulders muttering, "Now, now, none of that," and kissed her cheek and told her to come back soon. The other servants said they would all do her work for her while she was away.

What slayed me was Lewis saying, "I no worry about Salina, Madam. I worry about madam and master, all this trouble I am bringing." I said, "Never mind that. Let's worry about Salina." So off they went to sleep at the railway station on the platform that night, to be able to get on the train in the morning. (This is standard procedure for second-class passengers. They had a pass because her father is a diesel driver.)

Well, fine. So one morning a couple of days ago, when I was beginning to look for her return, up she came in a pony cart with another, a different, little boy, and a strange man. "Hooray," do I hear you say? So did we. But, no — the man was an "Uncle" who lives in Mandalay and who was brought along to explain in his superior English that they had not yet been to Rangoon. They had been to Maymyo (the delightful mountain resort near here).

Then came a cock and bull story about how they had to go to

Maymyo to get the pass signed before they could return to Rangoon; the Uncle who was to sign the pass was out of town, and therefore they had to spend five days in Maymyo. Salina had refused to eat, had done nothing but weep. Now they were going to Rangoon, and Salina would be back in three days for sure. I was so upset by all this I turned my back on them and left the room.

I have real confidence in Salina but was extremely annoyed by the others. Lewis was fed up and refused to take part in the new discussion. In this one, the Uncle said, "Please do not be offended, Madam. I will tell you the truth." I said, "Good. I like to hear the truth, and wish I heard it more often."

The Uncle went over the old story but added the part that the Aunt in Rangoon had been countering accusations against her with the tale that Salina had been involved with boys and had run away. If this lie was not stopped, the Uncle pointed out, her life would be ruined. So the father wanted to show her to everybody to demonstrate that she had not run away and that she was all right. You may speculate, as we do, about the unanswered questions (e.g., who are all the little brothers?) and the discrepancies.

During all this, Salina was overjoyed to see Sally. Sally, on the other hand, was not pleased to see Salina and turned into an immovable object, clinging to me, and all too convinced that plus Salina equals minus Mummie. However, I bribed Sally to go to the playground with Salina, permit her to wash Sally's hands, and generally fuss over her.

After a couple of hours of this, during which I sat Salina down and gave her some lunch and she reiterated that she would come back and that she was very sad and that Auntie was her mother and Sally her sister (a new English word for Salina), I packed the lot of them off to the station to wait for the evening train.

Edwin missed this round, having been at the university at the time. He had not been optimistic about the chances of her returning, naturally. But I was and still am — and tomorrow, I suppose, will tell. If she comes back, I have promised a party, and Lewis will play his guitar and Ohm Ghi and Aung Hla and Salina will sing and dance, and we'll all beat on drums, and there will be treats for the children.

I write all this not as a unique situation but as one variant of a very common one. And what, tell me, is the poor sap of a Westerner to do?

This letter is all out of balance, and I can try to right it only by making it All About People.

You ask about the Burmese character — no, you don't, you ask about the Art — but I'll tell you one or two things anyway, sort of initial modifications of the generalization we heard before coming: namely, that the Burmese are lazy, indolent, indifferent. These have not been borne out in our so far limited experience. I would say rather that they are mentally alert and physically energetic.

This applies not only to the servants but to the university students and teachers and to the people we've met socially as well. And they are not indifferent, but emotionally quite alive, judging particularly from the tales one reads in the newspapers of murders and mayhem stemming from passion. Emotionally, they may be repressed, but not very. I think the characteristic which leads to the former impression is that they are perhaps not ambitious, or rather that their ambition is very short-range. Ambition, which is so closely linked to aggression, is of necessity damped down here (personal inner necessity, I mean, stemming from social necessity) because there is no healthy expression for it; otherwise one would go quite, quite mad.

I think it is true, as people say, that if the Burmese wanted to they could solve their problems (e.g., the chaos of the government, of the educational system), but it's a vicious circle, I would say. How can they dare let themselves want to, when the disillusionments and failures and difficulties are to date so overwhelming?

I know I should be describing the national dress and the municipal sanitation system or lack of it and the hospitals and doctors and the role of Buddhism and stuff. But I would so much rather tell you one or two incidents about Aung Hla.

I'm uncertain about whether Aung Hla understands much English outside his own sphere of operation. Here's how it goes:

Me: Aung Hla, how do you feel this morning? Better?

A.H.: Better. (Nodding, all attention.)

Me: Did the aspirin help?

A.H: Aspirin.

Yes; did it help?

Help.

Did the aspirin help?

Aspirin. Help.

Did it make you feel better?

Better. (Nodding.)

And round and round.

Every day, there is a great commotion in the front yard of shoutings and thumpings and great brown bodies galumphing, as Aung Hla requests the herd of cows (which insists on daily detouring through our yard) to leave. Today, Aung Hla became very fierce when a lone cow visited us and, yanking viciously on its halter (alternately grinning up at us in the window), detached it from one of his carefully tended plants. It came loose with a large leaf hanging from its pouting lips. Aung Hla growled a furious tirade at the old woman who came belatedly to look for it and pretended to tie it to the garage for keeps, while the old woman waved her cigar, and the cow relieved herself in the driveway.

The school schedules are unpredictable here. Not only the university, but the children's schools. St. Peter's English School for Boys and St. Joseph's Convent School, though Catholic, observe the Buddhist calendar. So, suddenly last week, David and Robert had five days off. Last Thursday was the beginning of Buddhist Lent, celebrating the Enlightenment.

We gave Aung Hla and Ohm Ghi "the day off" — which means they take off about three hours. An advantage in having a Buddhist bearer and a Catholic cook is that their days off don't coincide; however, Lewis, too, though we expect him to take off most of Sunday, shows up most of the time anyway. So they appeared in the morning all dolled up, Ohm Ghi looking lovely in a stunning *longhi,* rushed through their chores, and then went off to a pagoda to offer flowers and cakes and cooked rice and candles.

We, too, went to witness "*Waso,*" the day of enlightenment, at the Arakan Pagoda, one of the oldest. We were sidetracked by a parade of lepers begging. They are supposed to be in the Leper Asylum, but they get out, and the police make a show of rounding them up, but only a show, because they are afraid to.

There is here a WHO program of leper control; one of the doctors is an energetic Frenchman — a French bucket of charm. "Now, my girl, we want all of you to come and stay at our house in Maymyo, by George, it would be good to get out of this damned heat, but we share the house with my colleague Noussiton (?), a splendid chap, by George, first rate, damned fine doctor, but they are Bohemian like us, and we don't plan."

But back to the Arakan Pagoda. We walked the long, long gamut of little shops in the covered bazaar, bought a few lacquer pieces — one a tray on which David then carried all our shoes — and paused and paused to permit effusive expressions of admiration of Sally: "*Ah kaley hla*" ("Pretty child"), "*Chiseyeah, chiseyah*" ("Lovely"). Then we'd prod Sally to say "*Thwa ba chimeh*" (the Burmese version of "Goodbye" — literally "I'll be going now"). Of course, this would bring on a fresh outburst of enthusiasm. We let Sally give coins to the pink-robed Buddhist nuns who sat and begged, and when they said "*Cheh-soo-tin-bah-deh*" ("Thank you"), we told her, "Sally, say '*Kesa ma shee boo.*'" But Sally thought we said "Kiss them!" and did — offering her little face to those wrinkled, blinking ones.

The pagoda itself was crowded with people, some sleeping, some sitting on their heels praying, some women praying and smoking, scores of children, everybody in their best; several men crawled around on the main image of the Buddha, sticking on gold leaf (an offering). This seemed a redundancy to me, since he was already completely slathered. Most of the pagoda was badly deteriorated, parts crumbling away; there was one tin flower vase there to receive flowers. By late morning, this was more than filled and people simply stacked the flowers in an ever-mounting, pointless, sloppy heap. A couple of flower vases would have served more purpose than more gold leaf, I should have thought.

This is so characteristic: everywhere one sees old, crumbling pagodas and neglected Buddhas. People prefer to build new ones rather than maintain the old ones someone else built, because there is more "merit" in it, toward the achievement of *nirvana*. Yet this custom does not appear to obtain with the Arakan Pagoda.

On *Waso*, Buddhists do not eat after 12:00 noon, but Garlans do, and we had brought a picnic lunch to have at Sagaing, the village across the Irrawaddy where there, too, are many pagodas. This village was a power before the coming of the kings to Mandalay and is still a center for silver work and brass work.

We drove up and around Sagaing Hill and found a relatively attractive spot next to the river. It had a large shade tree, the shade mostly preempted by bullocks and by others who got there first. But we spread our straw mat and had our picnic and watched young men jumping into the river and monks setting off for somewhere in long, low boats.

It was uneventful until we had difficulty prying open a tin of cookies. This challenge, however, activated the incipient interest of the erstwhile modestly peeking villagers, who now collected in droves around us. One resourceful chap went off and came running back with a knife. Another undertook to pry the tin open, encouraged, urged, advised, and finally cheered by everybody. Edwin offered him a cookie, but the man refused it, pointing instead to Edwin's cigarette. Edwin offered him one, which he accepted, and was again cheered and laughed at for his boldness by his fellows. Some of the others accepted a cookie — obviously not Buddhists, or at least not good Buddhists. Then one young man posed backward on the edge of the riverbank and invited Edwin to "take picture" of him jumping in. Edwin did and caught, I hope, a back flip.

I must make an end to this and hope to write next time about all the things I hoped to write about this time, and also about the tapestry we bought and the dinner party the servants gave us and the further adventures of Salina . . .

Love, Patsy

P.S. Here is Edwin's description of *Waso*. Do we concern ourselves with different things, or what! You can see why we need each other.

Mandalay (Edwin's letter about *Waso*)
July 1961

This is the season of "Lent" in *Theravada* (Burmese) Buddhism. It begins with the new moon, the Moon of "*Waso*" (about the 27th of July) and continues through September. It is marked first by the absence of big parties or festivals, and since most of these are associated with either the "*shinbu*," the entrance of the young boy, around puberty, into his monastery life for a shorter or longer period, or the "ear piercing" for the girls — at about the same age, or marriage, or, finally, some religious event occurring outside of Lent, none of these activities takes place during this period! There is, I am told, a rush of marriages just before and an even greater rush just after the Lenten period.

The second mark of Lent is more positive, since it exacts of the Buddhist (I refer to the lay, not the monks, the *Phongyii*) visits to the pagoda, where, at the pagoda proper or at one of the smaller shrines, which are parts of the pagoda or in or on its grounds, he or she offers small prayers of short duration.

These visits may be daily for the pious, and especially the old, but the general run go on the "Sabbath," which, for some reason I have not yet fathomed, does not fall regularly on the same day but on different days of the different weeks. (This makes attendance at schools, where the Sabbath day is observed, a variable matter. During Lent, even the Catholic schools, where David, Judy, and Robert go, observe the amenities of the day.)

At present, this day has been falling on Friday. It is supposed to correspond to the four quarters of the moon, which one would suppose would have a certain regularity, despite the association of fickleness with this particular goddess. The Burmese Buddhists, by the way, have eight days to a week; they get another day in by dividing Wednesday, such that from sundown Wednesday evening until sunrise Thursday morning, there is a "short" day. It has its own name and symbol. The symbol is, I believe, a tuskless elephant, Wednesday proper's symbol being a tusked elephant.

These visits to the pagodas are as much social affairs as they are acts of piety. For here, friends meet friends; there is much strolling about, and the small bazaars set up at all pagodas do a fair business, mostly with gewgaws, trinkets, bowls, mementos, playthings. Thus our Aung Hla and his wife, Ohm Gyi, brought back for our kids a drum, a paper tiger, and a paper elephant, both of the latter having heads that shake up and down in a breeze.

Just what "Lent" is, the average Burman does not know. So far, I have not had a single authoritative answer from anyone. The variant explanations of its beginning are not far apart from one another, all having to do with the "enlightenment" of Gautama Buddha under the bo tree. Some have said it marks the enlightenment itself; others have said it marks his first sermon — setting the wheels of the law in motion at Benares to his 500 disciples after his enlightenment. But why the two-plus months? It is de facto connected with Buddha's retirement during the rainy season, but mythically or symbolically nothing else seems fixed. Buddha, like any sensible person, did not like to travel very much during the monsoon period and stayed within some grove close to a large city during this time. The period corresponds to the period of intensive paddy cultivation and terminates somewhere around, more or less, harvest time.

I fully expect to find at least four or probably more explanations before quitting this conversational gambit. The reason for my confidence is that so far, neither mythos nor logos seems to be firm in any. Much less so than with the average Christian, which is poor enough. Here, there is both little concern with these matters, or, what has proved so far to be more likely, one will find all kinds of schemata for any given symbol. For example, one commences as close to uniformity as possible in the interpretation of the various stances of the Buddha: lying, sitting, standing. But even here, when we consulted the "caretaker" of the large reclining Buddha (34 feet of him) as to its meaning, we were given a long story, the gist of which was that the Buddha was expecting an evil *nat* spirit to visit him and so, for reasons that didn't get clear, he lay down with his head to the south and his feet to the north.

This variability is all the more surprising because Burmese Buddhism does not admit of the wide variety of sects as does the Mahayana forms, as, for example, those of Japan, where the variety of sects is bewildering. Here, there are recognized two orders of monks, distinguished outwardly by the different shades of orange (saffron) gowns worn. One is a stricter order than the other, but the doctrine is otherwise (somewhat) the same — as far as I have found out.

But all this is on major doctrinal elements. For the rest, there is difference personified, most of which is related to the extent to which either "Dewas" (like the Indian Devis, higher spiritual beings) in various orders, or *nats*, the indigenous animist beings of forest, stream, and home, or both, enter into the broad framework of austere Buddhism and become, in some ways and for some purposes, the living center of their religious concern. Add to this mixture heavy quantities of astrological beliefs, and you obtain a popular religion as complex and muddy as one could desire. The distance therefore between the scholar's Buddhism and the people's religion is at least as great as that between St. Thomas and the average Catholic.

But back to *Waso* and Lent. A few of the old and very pious Buddhists copy the monks and do not eat after 12:00 noon. But that is as far as it goes. Everything else goes on as before. What all this means is that our introduction to these various basic festivities, all connected with puppets, *pwes* (plays), and ballets, will have to come after September.

However, the Burman in Mandalay still has his favorite forms of entertainment, namely, sports and betting. The football field is only about six blocks from where we live. Here, almost daily, are the soccer games, played in heat and in rain. The place is always crowded with long lines waiting to buy their tickets. Our landlord, U Than Po, took us to one game recently. (Patsy discovered that she was the only woman present in the large mob.) I found the match quite engaging, and so did the Burmans, but they add to their enjoyment of the game the excitement of betting. The betting is a form of mutual, and most of them make bets. So also every Sunday there are horse races throughout the whole year, except for the very hot season of March, April, and May. The Burmans' love for betting finds its profitable expression in the national lotteries run by the government four times a year. I suspect that a lot of the costs of government are met in this way.

August 17 (a postscript): It turns out that I am wrong about no public entertainment during Lent. Sunday, we went to a dance-and-song *pwe* sponsored by some university students who belong to some Buddhist school alumni association. It only goes to show that anything here is, as Aristotle would say, "only for the most part." No one I have spoken to about this disagrees as to what is supposed to be the case, but the discrepancy is taken as normal, too.

The production was a short version of the usual entertainment, we were told. It consisted of dances and songs — classical and contemporary — with the chief performer, Hnee Hnee San (a beautiful, vivacious actress, the idol of all the college boys . . . and professors) supplemented by a second female singer and dancer and by a troupe of over-performing "clowns" — three of them. These latter are straightforward equivalents of our own burlesque. They quip and pun (very broad, indeed), poke, kick, hit one another, caricature the dancers and singers, make political comments, insult the audience, etc. The girls enter into some of this, changing from a serious to a comic mood without hesitation. It was all great fun, if only because of the warm audience response and participation. The performance is really a live transaction with the audience.

(*Pwes* take place on an improvised platform in a neighborhood field. We, in the audience, sit about in the field on blankets spread by our bearer, Aung Hla, who also spreads out the picnic from the basket he has brought. Intoxicating drinks are also the order of the day for the clusters of increasingly boisterous audience participants, and, of course, are not foreign to our lips.)

By tradition, all changes of costume, putting on new makeup, etc., is done on the platform — only somewhat protected by the orchestra instruments and players. The "stage" is in all about 15':15'. During the performance, the children tend to climb up on the stage, and occasionally one of the "clowns" goes after them and sweeps them off the stage — with much banter.

Patsy wants to get her long-held letter off, and so, without further ado,

All our love and affection, Edwin

So there you have it.

And, on a totally other theme, before I do get this letter off, my "teaching career" under Maryjane's tutelage is moving forward apace.

Her approach to teaching English is one that is being used with much enthusiasm and success these days. It is based on the English As Spoken notion. In the schools here, the kids get a more or less (mostly the latter) introduction to formal English but are practically tongue-tied.

However, for the teacher, this means throwing out grammar — that is, not presenting it at all. The emphasis is on the position of words in sentences rather than on the parts of speech as such. The three areas of interest — besides intonation, which is seen as crucial — are (1) structural words (this includes everything except verbs and nouns and adjectives, I think — i.e. articles, prepositions, conjunctions); (2) inflected words — that is, words changed by "–s," "–es," "–ly," "–ingly," etc.; and (3) word position in the sentence. These are learned by example, not precept, and repetition ad nauseam.

I will know more about the teaching methods shortly, because it looks as if I shall be pressed into service: the USIS has asked me to conduct a little course, in spite of my ignorance, and I have with great trepidation accepted. I've roped in another Fulbright wife, Mrs. Silverstein, whose husband is here from Wesleyan College, to do it, too. It goes very much against my rule-ridden grain to do some of the things Maryjane recommends, but it is very challenging and will be good for me, I think, if not for the students.

The course will be for university students, some of the older

St. Peter's boys, and a few doctors, businessmen, and what-have-you, all to be conducted in a huge lecture hall stuffed with 100 to 200 "students"! It is to be a course in Conversational English, and the one thing we really hope to be able to offer them is a chance to hear and practice with a native speaker.

Mandalay
November 9, 1961

We have been traipsing around — we being Edwin, Patsy, David, and Judy — first by plane into the Kachin State, near the border of China, and returning to Mandalay by boat down the Irrawaddy. Next we went to Kalaw and Taungyi in the Shan States. There was a Fulbright conference at Kalaw, followed by a raucous and ribald parody, "The Taungyi Conference," at the Coopers' (Fulbrighters) for Charles Powell (the other fourth-year Fulbrighter) and Maryjane and us'ns. The agenda prepared by the Coopers was very funny and kept us entertaining ourselves for two days, at which time, during the temporary absence of the conference chairman (me, socially irresponsible mother of four), it was suddenly and inexplicably terminated. I won't burden you with details of the hysterical parody conference, except to point out one feature: there were three or four speeches scheduled, as, for instance:

> 9:00 p.m. Dr. Edwin Garlan, "Reactions to Taungyi"
> 9:05 p.m. Suggestions & Discussions
> 11:00 p.m. Etc.

Where does the time go? (1) We sing & sing & sing. No TV, no radio, etc. I think we crave music, so we sing by the hour, *en famille*, with friends, etc. (2) I find myself lacking in energy and am very lazy. (3)

People are constantly dropping in, and we can lose whole afternoons and evenings with the steady comings and goings. (4) The Servant Problem takes hours. I won't broach the topic, even, in this note, but I suppose my next saga will dribble into it. I hate to get started on anything because I become long-winded, and this note must get off.

The Buddhist Lent is just over, and the season of weddings and *pwes* and all begins. We were taken to a fancy Burmese wedding the other day. U Nu was supposed to tie the knot but sent a general instead. The couple has been living together for three months, because it is improper to marry during Lent. The wedding was very pretty; all the ladies sat at tables on one side, very colorful in silk *longyis* and all their jewels; the men on the other side in silk *longyis*, white jackets, and Burmese headdress. The old ladies smoked cigars, everybody ate cakes and ice cream, and "*le-peh-tho.*" *Le-peh-tho* is little piles of pickled green tea, toasted coconut, nuts, sesame seed, etc. You pick up a bit of tea with your fingers, dip it in the other things as desired, and pop it in your mouth. Everyone was very friendly and welcoming; almost everyone seemed to be related to the bride and groom. The bridal party sat on the stage (the wedding was at a municipal auditorium); the bride was very sad and cried because her parents were dead and therefore could not be present on the happy day.

Here is a letter written by me in December to Joan Corcoran and transcribed and circulated to family by the ever-faithful Mamba. As mentioned in my introduction to these letters, Joan, a world-traveler living in Rome with her family, is the person who paved the way for us in Japan, Hong Kong, Burma, Greece, and Spain. Her husband is a leading executive of Sterling Pharmaceutical International. But if you ask her what he does, she will say, "He peddles pills."

In the following letter, you will note that Salina did come back, but that return is part of the Salina saga to be recounted later.

My dearest cousin,
This morning I am sitting in the park, watching Salina cut bamboo stalks into interesting shapes for Sally and Robert. I had some early-morning mixed doubles with two hard-hitting Burmese boys, followed by a hot bath (alone), and I am at peace with the world (if not with myself — never that). The weather these days is perfect — the Mandalay winter. Spring days in Santa Barbara couldn't be lovelier.

We are beginning to plot our movements from March, middle of, to August. I want to consult with you about various things, particularly when you are going to be in Rome and when we can hope to see you. We want to spend about two months in Greece, quietly on an island somewhere. We anticipate going for two weeks or so first to India — Madras, I think, possibly New Delhi — but we are very uncertain how to pursue the rest of it. Can you advise? As usual, we have a financial problem, so must do what we can to find inexpensive places to be. Do you know any nice Garlany islands in Greece? Do you know any likely hotels in Cairo? Where else should we stop? Assuming we take about one month from Rangoon to Greece, how to divide it? After Greece, we thought south of Europe, then a quick peek at friends in England and Scotland, and then home to the U.S. What factors are we not thinking about? Please advise.

I am too lazy to launch into anything about our life here. There is so much! These days the great stir in the family is over my new *sari,* which Salina decided I should have at least one of, and she went to the bazaar and bought some red shiny stuff for a blouse — tight, tight sleeves, high collar, low bodice, and tummy showing — and white georgette for the *sari* — all with her own money. And she and Judy and even me sometimes are busily sewing sequins on it: red, gold, and black, and pretty. And stunning, don't you think? And I have remembered 50 times in the last two days the time in Santa Barbara when you were in a sequin phase, and you made me a gray scarf with blue and magenta sequins, that I still have and dearly love because you made it.

Do you find that living abroad, your kids get very odd language habits? What corrupts us is the servants' attempt at English, that becomes so tempting and fun to use they all do it. This morning, for instance, Judy was digging around in her bureau, muttering: "Where go rubber band? . . . I *ma thee boo* . . . I think I do it this side, but *ma shee boo* . . . Where go?" Which, I think, if I still remember my English, means: "Where did my rubber band go? I don't know. I thought I put it over here, but it's not here. Where could it be?"

My passion for rice and curry — specially Indian curry — grows daily, as does my stomach. Lunchtime is feast-time for me, and the curry gets hotter daily. Evening time, because of the children, we have Western dinners — except when Salina has a creative urge and cooks for us *parata* or *pouri* or *chapatti*. Yum, yum. On these occasions, the cook gets a half-day off, which compensates for his disapproval about too much money going, because Salina is anything but economical in the kitchen.

What do you know of the train trip from Damascus into Greece?

Your doting cousin, Patsy

Mandalay, Burma
March 6, 1962

With Christmas safely behind us, and so many cards and letters from the types with long memories and people-with-Christmas-card-lists to jog my laze, it seems a good time to attempt a Christmas letter. Everybody complains more or less loudly about our address, so I shall begin by elucidating: "near DSP's House" means "near U

Than Pe, District Superintendent of Police's house." As a matter of fact, our compound is almost entirely surrounded by the Police Training School, which makes our *durwan* (guard) superfluous, one would think (unless one knew the Mandalay Police Force), which is just as well, as our *durwan* is a slow-witted, easy-going 18-year-old who sleeps soundly all night in the teeth of dog packs who invade our compound, visitors who open the gate and come unescorted and unchallenged into our very bedroom, and amorous cats that rouse (in the sense of "awaken") everyone but him.

Our house belongs to U Than Pe, or, rather, to his wife, who is built like a barge and is the property-owning hunk of the family — a quite typical arrangement among the Burmese. They are good landlords and are very willing to take care of little things that go wrong with the house, rushing to correct uncertainties in the plumbing by replacing the old "bell" with an older one, lending five unskilled carpenters to turn small cracks in the plaster walls into filled gashes, and, in an excess of untutored exuberance, resettling the wooden floor when it lifts and crests like ocean waves because it was not built with proper ventilation below.

Our house is built in a nice old section of Mandalay, with gardenia and magnolia trees, big old wooden houses, and rather more open fields and pastures than were here before the war and the Japanese bombing. We are not really aware of the police force, except at 10 minutes to 9:00 in the evening, when hearty male voices belt out "Bamma Pyay" (Burma Country), the national anthem, and then I think all of Mandalay is awake.

I've never been clear about whether the rest of our address reads "Old Civil Lines" or "New Civil Lines," but in any case it has something to do with the former, or current, as the case may be, borders of the city. We are a few blocks from one end of the old castle walls. The castle was leveled by bombs in the war, but the walls stand and extend two miles in each direction. The walls are surrounded by the moat, which turns very beautiful colors at sunset, due, I suppose, to the impurities in the water, and which provides drinking water for the unfortunate many. We have our own artesian well, but even so we boil the water, and even so there is usually someone with diarrhea, because of the water or something.

Two of our friends here are Dr. Nagaswami — known as "Naga" — and his wife, Ranjini, who is also a doctor (gynecologist) and quite beautiful. She grew up in Madras and London. She practices in a *sari*, and I don't think I've seen her wear the same one twice, though we are in their house/office/hospital nearly every day for the usual mixture of chitchat (they have almost a "salon") and medicine. Ranjini teaches me how to wear the *sari* and lends me joolry from her vast store. She and Naga love kids — having none of their own — and ours rendezvous there after school as a rule. Ranjini would steal Sally, I think, with a little prompting.

Yesterday, Ranjini let me help deliver a baby — the fourth offspring of Aung Hla and Ohm Gyi. We had it in the quarters here, and it was wonderful and not too terrifying, except that Ranjini popped back down to the office for the half-hour that turned out to be the one preceding by 10 minutes the birth of the baby. This left me holding the bag, as it were. She never told me what to do in case, and we expected the baby with each contraction.

Fortunately, Ranjini got back in time, as when the head appeared the cord was around the neck, and I somehow feel I would not have known exactly what to do. During the hard labor period, we all sat cross-legged on the board that was actually her bed. Ohm Gyi's mummie, who had come from her village, said 20 Buddhist prayers, Salina said two Catholic ones, and I just sat about and gripped her hand hard when she wanted it and held her knee as directed. No anesthetic, of course.

At first I didn't think I would be able to be there, because Ohm Gyi sent a message by Salina for me please to stay away till afterwards; she would not be clean; I was Madam and she was servant, she was shy, etc. I sent a message back by Salina, "*Kesa ma shee ba boo*. Never mind, you are a *mayma*; I, too, am a *mayma*; you have four children; I too. Baby-come-time, I am not Madam and you servant. When my babies were born, I, too, was unclean. I should like to help."

Then everyone was all smiles. Aung Hla said, "Thank you, thank you, Madam, first Ohm Gyi *anadeh* and you now. Ohm Gyi would so like you to come; our other madam, when Jan-daung was born, said 'Ugh.' You very good Madam," etc.

Now I would like to try to explain "*anadeh*." But it is a very difficult phenomenon to grasp, much less to explain. In fact, if I could understand this one thing in Burma, I would feel I'd really gotten at something. It is related to face-saving, I think, psychologically. And it relates somehow to "power" or "to have power." One uses the word indirectly in conversation. For instance, if there is some specially nice food around, and I ask Aung Hla, "Please taste it," Aung Hla will say, "No, thank you, Madam," or maybe, "I no like; thank you." I could beg and plead. He would still say "No." BUT, if I say, "*A ma na ba deh*" (that is, "Don't feel *anadeh*"), he will either laugh and take some and say, "Thank you very much," or he will say "*A ma na ba boo*," which means, "This is not a case of *anadeh*; I really don't like it."

What is so difficult to understand for me is just whose "power" is at stake. Everyone shows such tact about not depriving you of power, of not embarrassing you or putting you on the spot or requiring anything of you. And, contrarily, if one takes food or favors from someone who is not a friend, one loses self-respect; one loses a bit of one's own innate independence; and yet it involves not a feeling of pride, but of humility and diffidence.

It is not restricted to certain classes, and in Burma people of the "lowest class" (if there is such a thing here, which is also problematical) have a delicacy of feeling and a perception of human sensitivities that make me blush for us gross Americans. They will willingly serve, they will do anything for you, they will kiss your feet, without any loss of dignity or self. On the contrary, this adds to it. But they reserve the right to refuse what they do not wish to take. The Westerner finds himself always in debt, and it is the distaste for this feeling, I think, that leads to an understanding of "*anadeh*." The subtle combination of humility and dignity and pervasive generosity can only be met by the development of this quality in oneself.

I think one would find that "*anadeh*" is related, too, to the easy flaring of tempers here, which permits a man to stab his best friend or throttle someone in the street he met 10 minutes before. It is present, too, in transactions in the bazaar, when you know damn well you are being grossly overcharged, and you work to narrow the discrepancy without loss of "*anadeh*" for anyone.

Now, reversing Robert's Rules, we come to Old Business. For those who are following, as a friend puts it, "the cereal," here is an account of Salina's Return, and the Departure of Lewis. It would take a book to record the complexities of these events, but, fortunately, a feeble memory has buried a lot of them.

Salina, as you will have gathered, did come back, and we did have a party and everyone sang and danced Burmese songs and dances, and Aung Hla appeared in costume and did some splendid clowning, and Salina did some Indian dances and had brought presents for the children and was altogether so excited and filled with joy that she sang a couple of songs from her Catholic hymnal which had a haunting resemblance to hymns.

We then settled down to a period of stress and turmoil that practically brought the house down about our ears.

It turned out that the major reason Salina was lugged off home to Rangoon was for her father to demonstrate to all the friends and relations that she had not run away with Lewis, as many had been unkind enough to suggest. She returned with strict orders to stay clear of him, and the carrying out of these orders caused Lewis increasing misery, because, as we later discovered, Lewis's interest in her was neither brotherly nor cousinly, and he had a real intention of making her his "second wife" — of which he has several.

There finally came a flare-up; Salina spoke to us at dinner to the effect that she didn't want to take her meals at his house any more, she was afraid of him, and his wife wouldn't give her good curry. Then Lewis came barreling in and said Salina no longer showed him any respect or gratitude. Then there was a heated exchange in Burmese and Indian.

Aung Hla sat cross-legged on the floor with his back discreetly half turned, and when we asked him what was going on, he smiled and tactfully, but not too accurately, said he didn't know.

Everything got more and more heated, Lewis putting his case to us in English (Salina knew very little English at the time, but you should hear her now!) and Salina finally going around the corner and repeatedly banging her head against the wall out of sheer frustration and distress. On this and the many subsequent occasions, Edwin and I said, "Now, now, we know it's very difficult at times, but we really must all try to get along; we cannot try to judge between you — you, Lewis, are a good cook, you, Salina, a good nanny — please try to settle your differences and, come on fellas, let's settle down and have a little peace and quiet."

It wasn't till much later that we put together enough of the story to know of Lewis's designs and, even later, to be convinced of Salina's innocence (at least, at the worst, an unintentional provocativeness). At the time, we were simply quite shocked at the spirited and, on the whole, rather rude rejoinders to her "cousin's" complaints about her lack of respect.

I think it was that evening that the Nagaswamis dropped in and began to get the story clear for us. Salina gratefully unburdened herself to them, and it turned out Lewis was absolutely no relation of hers. She has been in a desperate situation at her Auntie's house — her Auntie kept trying to foist off various men on her — to which she had fled because her parents were fighting. She jumped at Lewis's offer to be a brother to her and take her with his family to Mandalay. We were also unaware of how extreme some of Lewis's language in Tamil was; our ears would have burned right off if we had known — as we broke in with our "Please, now, everyone . . . "

Lewis's passion turned to jealousy and pique; he more and more lost control of himself — not helped, I am sure, by Salina's spirited laughing and dancing and playing with our kids. One day, Edwin told him once and for all he must pull himself together, because we could not allow this situation to continue. The next morning he threw his wife out (without the four children, one of whom is nursing), and that afternoon we sacked him.

It later turned out that he had been helping himself copiously from the till and from the refrigerator — considerably more than is, well, customary. I tore my hair over my stupidity at not having discovered this sooner, though I had dutifully scanned his careful accounts every day. But not even our family uses 24 limes and three pounds of rice a day!

Now we have Sceral, a funny, frightened old chap whose wife died, or left him, or something, who drinks up his earnings and who is as terrified by a compliment to his cooking as by a reprimand. He can cook well, and sometimes does. And if we send a message to the kitchen — "Very good!" — he will gasp and say, "Ohh! What did I do? How did I make it?" and gaze helplessly around the kitchen, seeking answers in the pots. This will be reported to us by a mirthful Aung Hla or Salina. He still has hopes for acquiring a new spouse and every day reports that someone is in love with him. So far, he has considered the potato woman and the onion woman and the bean woman and I don't know who-all.

Far too many words have been consumed by our domestics,

in these letters — and there is all of Burma to write about . . .

(I am interrupted by the cook coming in a whirlwind to say that someone ate one of the four pieces of chicken he was reserving for *paratta* for today's lunch. "See, Madam, and put the chicken bone on the plate!" David? "No." Judy? "No." Robert? "No, Mummie." Sally? "No, Mummie." Salina? "No, Auntie." Thon Shive? "No, Madam." Ohm Gyi? "No, Madam." Aung Hla? "No, Madam."

Okay. "*Kesa ma shee boo*. (Never mind, it is a matter of no consequence.)" "Big *dulka shee-deh*. (Suffering, of the kind that all life is, exists). One piece of chicken small *dulka*. *Kesa ma shee boo*."

I follow Sceral into the kitchen, where, meanwhile, the kerosene stove has gotten outside of itself, and through the soot showering on my white blouse, I ask him to calm himself and simply tell me if this happens again.)

As I was saying, there is all of Burma to write about . . .

(I am interrupted by Salina, who wants 25 *kyats* to buy peanuts for everybody from the peanut woman. Salina buys peanuts and shells them for me. They have been boiled in salted water and have the sallow complexion of an Oregonian after a typical winter. They are, however, delicious.)

I think I'm too lazy right now to write about out trip to North Burma, the Kachin Hills, the Shan Hills, and our wider life in Mandalay. I suppose I have an excuse: "I been sick." (Remember? Why the ant said he could not defeat the elephant?) Amoebic dysentery felled me finally, a couple of weeks ago, just in time to knock out Bangkok and Angkor Wat, for me. Edwin staunchly set off by himself, determined to have a good time anyway, because, as he said, we would be so disappointed if he hadn't. We're expecting him home today or tomorrow, when he will be required to relive it for an eager audience of five.

Everybody will probably have expected me to "go native," and Edwin to have remained his pipe-smoking self. Actually, he has taken to the *longyi* (the ankle-length, wrap-around cloth worn by both sexes) more readily than I. In fact, after one or two trials, I gave it up, partly because I can't keep the cussed thing on and partly because of the disappointed look I got from everybody. You're supposed to have a cute, little, but pronounced bottom to look right in a *longyi,* and I just don't qualify a posteriori. As a long-tapering neck is to the Japanese, so the above-mentioned item is, to the Burmese, the mark of beauty.

I have, however, hopefully adopted some of the beautifiers. I haven't brought myself to plastering my face with *thanaka,* though I should, because it really is wonderful for the complexion. But I scrub my teeth with forefinger and charcoal daily, probably ruining the enamel but producing, I think, a dazzling effect — not to say startling.

I also use Burmese hair "shampoo," which takes a strong stomach. Salina brings to my shower a pan of dark brown liquid, with pieces of scented, torn-up bark floating in it, and brown, old prunes or something and God knows what-all. But Salina thinks my hair is improving; I think she hopes it will lose its gray and assures me, "This do it your hair very long and coming." I will say, "No, I really don't want to use coconut oil, because my hair wouldn't look right all long and sleek and shining like yours." Or, more exactly, what I say is, "Oh, Salina, I thinking my hair very nice and coming, *theh kaun-doh and chischeah* (very good and pretty). Now why me coconut oil and doing? I *ma chi boo* (I don't like it)."

Salina tells me that people in the bazaar stare at me, because they have never seen gray hair on a young person. I am an oddity. This is why I should use her various beautifiers. I tell her it is what we call salt-and-pepper, and at home people admire it. And, yes, it is short and curly, not long and shiny like hers, but, well, that's because I am I and you are you.

Today there is a slight breeze. The hot daytime is coming. But we will be gone before the worst of it. In about two weeks, on March 10th, we leave Mandalay, and on the 20th Burma. There are going to be parties — a dinner at the Golf Club, at which Edwin will have the honor of presenting a Cup (and the expense). Suckling pig and a bonfire at the "Brewery" Estate, thrown by the Nagaswamis; a Chinese dinner featuring some rare and probably aphrodisiacal (as every Chinese vegetable seems to be) moss, yet, from the uppermost reaches of China. There will also be a feeble "do" by us for 70 assorted Burmese, Indians, British, Persians and Americans. Thank Heaven for commissary Scotch.

As usual, we are a little bit behind in our social obligations. It's a simple life, but we like it.

(PATSY'S LETTERS AND THE KIDS' SAY-SO)

On March 30, Mamba wrote to her correspondence circle of friends and family:

Dear People:
There has been quite a little burst of mail, so I thought I'd send you some bits and pieces — from David, Patsy, and Judy.

March 10, 1962
David's Bit

In every letter you ask me the news. Things are pretty dull. But, in case you don't know, there has been a revolution going on. The army has taken over the government. They have arrested most of the people who were in charge before. Some of our good friends are out of a job. I only hope we can get out of the country.

We are planning to leave Mandalay today, so we are sort of in a hustle bustle. I am rather sad to leave Burma. Burma has become a second home for me. I will miss it all.

Love, David

March 25, 1962
Madras, India
Patsy's Letter

We left Burma around 2:30 in the afternoon. I can't bear to describe the departure, with its separation from the weeping Aung Hla and the wholly desolated Salina. We had attempted to ease the pain of leaving with thoughts of a return in two or three years, but this solace was grabbed away from us during the last week, when the new government "suspended" the Fulbright program and the others, like Ford and the Asia Foundation. We had brought Aung Hla and Salina to Rangoon with us for our 10 days there (which is about what it takes to wiggle your way out of Burma). All my nicely laid plans about Salina's future are now uncertain.

U Thun Myaing, U Hla Bu, etc., saw us off at the airport. And Maryjane, but we are to reunite shortly in Greece.

Leaving Mandalay was even harder for the kids. We left by evening train, and all their friends — American, Burmese, and Indian — saw them off. Fully three-quarters of the American "colony" was there (Fulbrighters, Ford people, USIS and Embassy, missionary friends, U Than Pe and his wife, other Burmese friends, all Edwin's students, and the Nagaswamis). U Sein Tu was on the same train, going to Rangoon to bring off a long-plotted reunion with his estranged wife — by sleeping with her!

That's all I'm up to about Burma at this time. You ask about the beef; I can't think why. Everybody is delighted; it will bring prices down, and the people need it desperately to supplement their rice diet. I don't think anyone but U Nu has the least scruple about it, and U Nu is incommunicado. (I suppose you mean because, as Buddhists, they don't eat meat? Pish, tush. There's no carry-over at all.)

The keynotes of the Revolutionary Government seem to be a sort of austerity program — doing away with the superfluities like dancing schools and WHO's malarial control program — and a stepped-up "Burma for the Burmese" attitude, which means that Americans, with their various programs, may be less than welcome and also that the large Indian population may be kicked downstairs further. Somehow, there still seems to be room for the Israelis, the Chinese, and the Japanese helpmates.

Madras is a perfectly beautiful city, a bit like Santa Barbara, with its flowering trees and deep blue sea. The men wear white and the women brilliantly colored cotton *saris*. It is a treat to be in a city that is clean, and one so unified and integrated after the polyglot of Mandalay and even greater mish-mash of Rangoon.

We are very lucky in having been taken in tow by Naga and Ranjini's parents and brothers and sisters. In Bangalore, too, there is a brother, and in Bombay we are to stay with a brother who is at the moment here in Madras. We have found that there is simply no comparison between the kind of experience you have if you know someone and what happens if you just go into a city cold.

Tomorrow, we're off to Bangalore. And on the 7th of April we bestow ourselves on Athens, Greece.

Love, P

March 1962
Madras, India
Judy's Letter

We are in Madras now. It is just like Santa Barbara. It has a beach, and all the buildings look like missions.

The other day we were in Calcutta. There was a holiday, and

everyone was squirting colored water at everyone else. We were riding in a bus on the way to the airport, and one of its windows was open. A little Indian boy squirted at the bus, and since we just happened to be by that window, Mummie got squirted in the face. Robert calls that day "Squirt day."

With love, Judy

P.S. Yesterday I got some silver things for my ponytails or braids and two *saris*.

More bits and pieces from Mamba:

May 16, 1962
Postcard from Patsy

In Greece, at last! All set up on arrival by Maryjane, who preceded us, and the Czarnowskis (Joan's friends). On Poros, right by the sea in a little bay, all quiet and loverly, with pine trees and a lemon grove. I sent you an envelope and letter from Bombay, but an idiot — or I should say economical — clerk in our friend's office sent it by sea mail! It was full of clippings and pictures from the Burmese papers.

Edwin is working on Buddhism; the kids do schoolwork in the morning. Though it's chilly enough for the hardiest, they attempt swimming and generally enjoy themselves.

May 1962
Letter from David

We are now staying on an island called Poros. It is almost a perfect island. A rowboat, an old Turkish fort, a ruined monastery, and huge hills to explore are all included free of charge.

The other day, all except Mummie went to look for Poseidon's temple. After three hours climbing up a hill, we found it. It was shaped like a circle, about 40" in diameter, with thin flagstone rocks on edge around and flat ones laid out in such a way that they all fitted together in a flat smooth surface.

May 1962
Trisinia, Poros, Greece
Patsy's Latest Letter

I'm sitting on the shore. Sally is sitting beside me, singing. Robert is splashing in the water. And there are seven tall brown young men laughing nearby, about to take the plunge. One has just dashed in; there is wild applause and Greek calls from the others. So if I seem a bit distracted . . .

The sea is calm today. Or I should say now, because it changes in minutes, the sky blue and the mountains opposite very peaceful, especially the Sleeping Lady. It is very like a large lake here in our part of the island. We are in a large cove, and the mainland opposite completes the impression of a lake. The town of Poros is around a bend, about 10 minutes away by boat, with all its little white houses clustered like a crowd on steps up the hillside, their big black eyes gazing out to sea. It is 11:30 — almost *retsina* time! Presently I shall pull Edwin off his Buddhist tome, and we'll begin guzzling this pine-sappy wine. After that, we shall have artichoke stew. You eat the whole artichoke and soak up the olive-oily gravy with your chunks of bread. Then you sleep it off.

Burma has pretty well closed its doors to American personnel. Fulbright is suspended and Asia and Ford have been asked to pull their people out. But most Americans in Burma are not resentful and prefer not to rush to the conclusion that this is expressive of anti-American and anti-Western sentiments. Let's give General Ne Win a chance, seems to be the attitude; he is someone for whom people have a great deal of respect.

But don't confuse yourself with comparisons with the caretaker government. The people are mostly the same, but this time it's a revolutionary coup. There is no talk of stepping down, and their whole approach is different — more leisurely, more long-range, and probably much more far-reaching. Primarily, the need for the coup was an internal one, involving, for one thing, the rapidly worsening relations with the Shan States and the do-nothing, or worse, approach of U Nu.

Did you hear about U Nu's proposed solution to the problem of the dogs in Burma? The poor, sick, yapping little beasts that can find nothing to do with themselves but propagate and howl and get maimed by army trucks — and threaten to overrun the country? He proposed to build two large kennels, or preserves, one for the gentlemen and one for the ladies, with periodic intervisitation privileges. Do you wonder how he proposed to feed them and keep them from going out of their skinny little minds and stuff? So did we all. And anyway! But, then, when you're not the head of state, it's easy to nag.

Later: One day we crossed to the other side and went by bus to the village of Troizen and then by foot up the mountains and across a gorgeous gorge to the ruins of Theseus's Troizen. Broken columns and walls and a stone floor plan remain of what must have been a quite extensive village. It was certainly a beautifully situated one, with its back to the mountains and looking out over cypress-studded fields to the distant sea and the hills beyond.

But we made no sacrifices and saw no gods. We came upon a group of nomads, who probably travel from Macedonia and all over the place. Their straw shelters were covered with huge goatskin blankets. All their possessions were handmade, including tools, the saddles on their donkeys and horses, and ropes, woven of wool or something. They were a bit standoffish. One woman, who did not have a knife between her teeth, probably because she didn't need it to make an impression, asked us what we wanted and refused to be photographed. We returned to modern Troizen to a lunch of *retsina*; bread and tart, white goat cheese; omelettes; and green olives.

Financial constrictions threaten to preclude much jogging about in Italy and Switzerland. So it will probably be Spain for us most of the time and the cheapest corner we can find. But you never know, maybe Scotland in August.

Now, in the little cleared area where our cottages sit among the pine trees, I soak up the sun on the front porch, listening to the slow wind in the pines, breathing the sweet scent of the lemon groves, and eyeing the now-glassy sea, all squared in segments to my view by the bare pine trunks.

Love, Patsy

(INDEPENDENCE DAY: A CHILDREN'S STORY FOR GROWN-UPS)

Far away across the sea, in a land where the bamboo grasses grow tall as houses, and the trees hang heavy with bananas, and the sky smells like perfume, and the sunshine lies hot and yellow on the air, and the buffaloes stand in the rice paddies, and the children play in the wild fields . . .

There lived a little girl named Sally. Her real home was America, but she and her family were living in Burma for a while.

She was too young for school. She was even too young for nursery school. She was Not Quite Three. And, in the mornings, when her brothers and sister went off to school, Sally had nothing to do.

One day, Sally's mother said, "Sally, here is a new friend for you. She is 'Nanny.' She will play with you and take care of you. Now run along with Nanny and find *something to do*. I am very busy."

Sally said, "How-do-you-do." But she did not want her mother to be very busy. And she was not *sure* about Nanny, who was so new.

Sally's mother had already begun to be very busy. Her eyes looked right through Sally and Nanny at some grown-up thought of her own. She didn't even see them when Sally jumped up and down, trying to make eye contact. So, when Nanny said, "Come on, Sally; we go to Park," and kneeled down and gathered her up with a long, thin arm firmly under her legs, she allowed herself to be taken away.

Nanny was a funny person. She was so thin and small that when she was carrying her, Sally was taller than Nanny. Sally peered down into Nanny's smooth, brown face. She was very much younger than Sally's mother, not really grown up. She had a little black "!" right between her eyebrows. She looked up at Sally and smiled, showing a lot of white, white teeth. Her hair was pulled tight on her head and ran down her back like a long, black rope. Sally lifted up the shiny rope that was Nanny's hair. And there, at the top, it had a pink flower in it. She wore a purple shirt, and Sally, bending over, saw that on her feet she wore — nothing!

When Nanny talked, her words were funny, too. She probably had not talked in English very long. On that first day, Nanny pushed Sally's swing in the Park. When they came home, Nanny said to Sally's mother, "Sally good girls today. Sally very high and swinging." That was the funny way Nanny talked. Nanny said, "We seeing big snake. Green snake. Very bad. We home and coming."

Next day, and all the days after that, when Sally's brothers David and Robert and her sister Judy were at school, Nanny took care of Sally. She liked to do everything for her. She helped her dress in the morning. She stood behind her chair at the dining table and helped her eat. She showed her how to pick up her curry-rice with just the tips of three fingers. She peeled her oranges and peeled off the little tough bits inside. She carried Sally everywhere.

Now, Sally liked to tie her own shoelaces. She liked to comb her own hair. She liked to walk all by herself. She liked to do things her own way.

So Nanny took Sally to the market, called the Bazaar, and bought some sandals for her. No more shoelaces! And she made a tiny little rope out of Sally's hair and coiled it up on top — and put a pink flower in it. She dressed her in a long skirt, tucked in tight at her tiny waist. She dabbed white chalk on her cheeks. This was the way for Burmese girls. And she took her by the hand, all fancy, into the living room, where the grown-ups were having cocktails.

Sometimes, Sally and her sister Judy and Nanny sat cross-legged on the bedroom floor and brushed and brushed their hair, and Nanny wove flowers in their hair, and took her paint, and right between Sally's eyebrows she made a "!" She wrapped the girls in small silk robes called *saris*. That was the Indian way.

One day, Nanny was washing Sally's clothes, squatting at the well and laying them on the grass to dry. Sally sat in the soft, slippery grass, looking for little bugs to play with. Nanny said, "Nanny going in house. Quickly back and coming. Sally staying. Yes? Wait for Nanny."

But when Nanny came back, Sally was gone!

Sally had gone to the Park. She wanted to ride on the swings. But sliding through the tall grass came a long, green snake, silently following Sally. When she saw the snake, she became enthralled and came close to the snake and saw how beautiful it was. She didn't touch the snake, but played hide and seek for a while, until the snake hid so well that she could not find it.

Then she heard Nanny calling and calling. She waved goodbye to the snake, wherever it might be, and ran home to Nanny. Nanny hugged her tight and stroked her face and scolded her sharply and hugged her some more.

At dinner that evening, with Sally's brothers and sister and mother and father, Nanny did not mention the Park. Standing behind Sally's chair to help her with her supper, Nanny said, "Sally good girls today. Nanny call and Sally quickly coming."

‡ ‡ ‡

Capturing China

In Eight Little Poems

APRIL 1981

BEIJING — all bustle
and bulk.

The powers of heaven
and earth

Have long conspired here —

Old men whispering
In a curve of the
Great Wall.

:: :: ::

Near XIAN, the terraced hills
Shutter the tombs of
emperors

Like an old house sheltering
its own

Hostile
To the prying eye, the
prizing hand

The stranger.

:: :: ::

Yin-yang in LOUYANG
Machine clang,
Buddha gong;

The way true,
The journey long.

:: :: ::

In NANJING, politics crackle
in the city streets,

March in procession through
the thirteen gates,

Trade and traffic like
junks

On the Yangtze River.

:: :: ::

Beautiful watery
ancient HANGZHOU

Heaven's above, it's
below.

And if heaven's as
crowded with
"Foreign Guests,"

I'm not sure I want
to go.

:: :: ::

At the Lingering Garden
of SUCHOW

You go through a small
wooden door — like Alice —

Into a space where no
space was,

Into a wrinkle in time.

You must be quick
To catch the rustle of silk,
The flash of a cherry-colored
sleeve

Behind the locust swarm
of foreign guests.

:: :: ::

SHANGHAI is an anthill
of comings and goings.

Every day from the outlying
fields
Farmers in rows speed fare
to the workers.

Nine million souls sustain
themselves here.

And disaster must be but
a footstep away.

:: :: ::

GUANGZHOU, an overstated
Chinatown, U.S.A.

With its tussle, hustle
and ticky-tacky

Is a return to the China
we thought we knew.

But the real China glistens
in the eyes
Of Sun Bing, our guide,

As he braves through the bars
of the railway gate

Our heavy departure.

‡ ‡ ‡

The Great Getaway

OF 2001

A Grown-Ups' Holiday at the Florida Keys

WHO'S WHO?

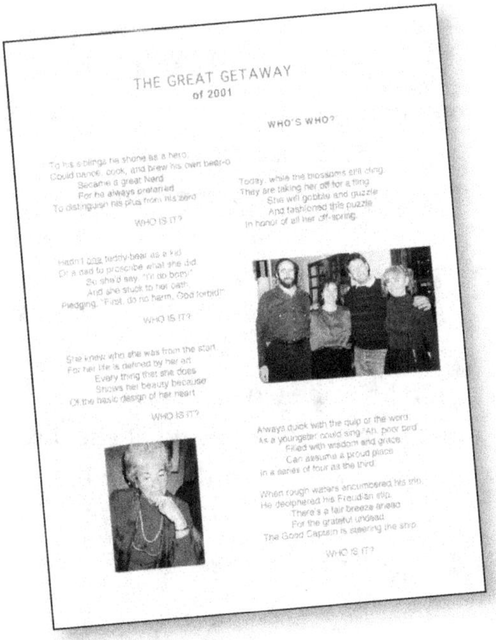

THE GREAT GETAWAY
of 2001

WHO'S WHO?

To his siblings he shone as a hero,
Could dance, cook, and brew his own beer-o
Became a great Nerd
For he always preferred
To distinguish his plus from his zero

WHO IS IT?

Hadn't one teddy-bear as a kid
Or a dad to proscribe what she did
So she'd say, "I'll do both!"
And she stuck to her oath,
Pledging, "First, do no harm, God forbid!"

WHO IS IT?

She knew who she was from the start
For her life is defined by her art
Every thing that she does
Shows her beauty because
Of the basic design of her heart

WHO IS IT?

Today, while the blossoms still cling
They are taking her off for a fling
She will gobble and guzzle
And fashioned this puzzle
In honor of all her off-spring.

Always quick with the quip or the word
As a youngster could sing "Ah, poor bird"
Filled with wisdom and grace
Can assume a proud place
In a series of four as the third

When rough waters encumbered his trip,
He deciphered his Freudian slip.
There's a fair breeze ahead
For the grateful undead
The Good Captain is steering the ship.

WHO IS IT?

Today, while the blossoms still cling,
They are taking her off for a fling.
She will gobble and guzzle
And fashioned this puzzle
In honor of all her offspring.

WHO IS IT?

To his siblings he shone as a hero;
Could dance, cook, and brew his own beer-o;
Became a great Nerd
For he always preferred
To distinguish his plus from his zero.

WHO IS IT?

Hadn't one teddy bear as a kid
Or a dad to proscribe what she did.
So she'd say, "I'll do both!"
And she stuck to her oath,
Pledging, "First do no harm, God forbid!"

WHO IS IT?

She knew who she was from the start.
For her life is defined by her art.
Everything that she does
Shows her beauty because
Of the basic design of her heart.

WHO IS IT?

Always quick with the quip or the word;
As a youngster could sing "Ah, poor bird";
Filled with wisdom and grace,
Can assume a proud place
In a series of four as the third.

When rough waters encumbered his trip,
He deciphered his Freudian slip.
There's a fair breeze ahead
For the grateful undead.
The Good Captain is steering the ship.

WHO IS IT?

‡ ‡ ‡

About the Author

Patsy Garlan has published poetry, stories, personal essays, syllabuses for drama students, and, with coauthor Maryjane Dunstan, two college texts published by Prentice Hall, about the future, and two children's books published by Viking Press, set in Burma, where she lived for a year with her husband and their four children.

She also wrote the book and lyrics for a new musical, *Wings of Fire,* adapted from Bernard Shaw's *Saint Joan,* with the help of the Society of Authors in London and the Shaw Estate and in collaboration with New York composer Nick Scarim. And in 2012, she published *Sea Change: The Uncertain Realm of the Married,* her first novel.

Born in Santa Barbara, California, she attended Reed College in Portland, Oregon, where, upon her graduation, she remained for many years as a faculty wife and whence she traveled extensively abroad with her husband and children.

Later, in San Francisco, her professional career included 22 years as a development director for KQED public television and 10 as an editor for Dr. Paul Ekman in his Laboratory for the Study of Human Interaction and Conflict at the University of California.

As a writer and project director at a repertory theater in Northern California, she developed a program to expose high school students to live theater. She has also served as a consultant to the California State Department of Education, where she assisted in the development of the Drama Curriculum Framework for the California public schools.

Today, she lives and writes in San Rafael, California, where she plays giggle tennis and golf and relishes the fact that her four far-flung children and their seven offspring occasionally come to visit.

‡ ‡ ‡

. . . And that's the Thing.